THE LAKE GUNS
of
SENECA AND CAYUGA
and
Eight Other
Plays of Upstate New York

Edited by A. M. Drummond and Robert E. Gard

# THE LAKE GUNS
## of
## SENECA AND CAYUGA
### and
### Eight Other
### Plays of Upstate New York

WITH AN INTRODUCTION BY HAROLD W. THOMPSON

IRA J. FRIEDMAN DIVISION
KENNIKAT PRESS
Port Washington, N. Y./London

## ALL RIGHTS RESERVED

CAUTION: The plays in this volume are fully protected by the copyright law. All rights, including professional, amateur, motion pictures, recitation, television, public reading, radio broadcasting, and the rights of translation into foreign languages are strictly reserved.

For amateur productions and for any form of non-amateur production (professional stage or commercial radio) permission must be obtained in writing from the publisher and royalty fees paid. Inquiries concerning royalties should be addressed to Kennikat Press, Port Washington, New York.

THE LAKE GUNS OF SENECA AND CAYUGA

Copyright, 1942, by Cornell University
Reissued in 1972 by Kennikat Press by arrangement
Library of Congress Catalog Card No.: 72-86786
ISBN 0-8046-8098-1

Manufactured by Taylor Publishing Company    Dallas, Texas

EMPIRE STATE HISTORICAL PUBLICATIONS SERIES NO. 98

In Recognition of

The More Than Four Hundred Cornell Students

Whose Work Made Possible the First Productions

of These and Some Forty Other Scripts

Written Under

*The Project for New York State Plays*

1938 – 1942

# PREFACE

These dramas and comedies of Upstate New York have been chosen from scripts collected by The Project for New York State Plays sponsored by the Cornell University Theatre and by the Rockefeller Foundation. The general purposes of the Project are to encourage the writing of plays of regional interest and of New York State flavor which will be suitable for little theatre production, and to make these plays available to the amateur groups of the rural and small-town communities of the State. The first stage presentation of most of the plays written under the Project have been by the Cornell University Theatre. The directors of the Project, A. M. Drummond and Robert E. Gard, have edited the plays selected for the volume and have added the brief prefatory notes. In completing the manuscript they have had the constant assistance of Maryo Kimball Gard.

# CONTENTS

|  | PAGE |
|---|---|
| PREFACE | vii |
| INTRODUCTION  *Harold W. Thompson* | 1 |
| THE LAKE GUNS OF SENECA AND CAYUGA  *A. M. Drummond* | 9 |
| A DRAMATIC LEGEND OF THE FINGER LAKES COUNTRY | |
| LET'S GET ON WITH THE MARRYIN'  *Robert Gard* | 77 |
| HERE COMES THE BRIDE TO A WILDERNESS WEDDING | |
| DONALDS O'ROURK  *Louise O'Connell* | 101 |
| A DRAMA OF SETTLERS AND IROQUOIS ON THE NEW FRONTIER | |
| A DAY IN THE VINEYARD  *E. Irene Baker and A. M. Drummond* | 125 |
| BALLAD AND FOLK-SAY AMONG THE GRAPE PICKERS | |
| CHENANGO CRONE  *Edward Kamarck* | 151 |
| A DRAMA OF THE HORSE-RUNNERS AND OUTLAWS | |
| RAISIN' THE DEVIL  *Robert Gard* | 179 |
| PARSON DOW SCORCHES A SCHOHARIE CONVERT | |
| FAMILY COOPERATIVE  *Ella L. Thurston* | 199 |
| NEIGHBORHOOD COMEDY SPICED WITH AGRICULTURAL ECONOMICS | |
| OVER FOURTEEN: AND SINGLE  *Lauren Williams* | 221 |
| COURTIN' BY DECREE BEYOND THE GENESEE | |
| MIXING UP THE RENT  *Robert Gard* | 251 |
| HUDSON VALLEY RENT WARS SUNNY SIDE UP | |

# THE LAKE GUNS
of
SENECA AND CAYUGA
and
Eight Other
Plays of Upstate New York

# INTRODUCTION

*by*

HAROLD W. THOMPSON

# INTRODUCTION

*by*

HAROLD W. THOMPSON

# INTRODUCTION

The publication of a volume of regional American plays without a single shotgun wedding is so remarkable that the incredulous reader will hardly wish to be detained by a prosy preface before discovering whether "these things can indeed be after these ways." However, the dignity of University tradition must be satisfied—and thereafter happily abandoned—while you are informed briefly what was intended in The Project for New York State Plays, how far the intention has been fulfilled, and what may fairly be expected in the future.

Not to be too owlish over the affair, it should be admitted that from the first years of our national life Yorkers have wished to make romantic interpretations of their region and its folk, and that our earliest writers were remarkably successful in this attempt. Washington Irving presented the Hudson in its noble scenery, dreamy legends, and folk-humor; James Fenimore Cooper placed within our charming and varied landscape no less than four heroic types: the intrepid frontiersman, the sometimes noble Red Man, the liberty-loving farmer, and the valiant warrior. More clearly than most critics have realized, both Irving and Cooper knew that their true romantic subject was the Empire State itself, in all its virile beauty. Later writers added enduring landscapes and portraits. Eben Holden is Bacheller's humble and loyal farm-hand, but he is also the magnanimous North Country; David Harum is Wescott's humorous hoss-trader, but he is also the friendly Finger Lakes. In three books Edmonds has taken the Erie Canal for his hero; in three others Carl Carmer has interpreted the "unstandardized Yorker" of all Upstate—his folklore, his humor, and his pioneering strength. Here at Cornell we have always sought to develop what T. S. Eliot calls the Individual Talent, but we have been equally mindful of that other element mentioned in his famous essay, "Tradition and the Individual Talent." If, as Professor Carl Becker has so truly said, Cornell means Freedom with Responsibility, it is not difficult to find that tradition in the earliest legends of our region and its folk.

How to get the tradition into plays written by the people of New York State about themselves, in their own speech, for their own stages, has been the long study of Alexander M. Drummond, "boss" of the Cornell Theatre. The son of a respected fellow-townsman of Secretary William H. Seward of Auburn—the son of a man who was soldier, farmer, and lawyer, Drummond was further educated as a student at Hamilton College and as a teacher at Cornell. You can depend upon him to know what the Upstate tradition is. Years ago he founded at the Syracuse State Fair a project for the presentation of rural plays and managed to obtain a number of actable ones for publication. But it is only within the past three or four years that, with the assistance of the Rockefeller Foundation, he has conducted the new State Project, surveying the little theatres of the region in a study made by an assistant, Dr. Darkes Albright, and encouraging the writing of such plays as are contained in the present volume.

Within this brief period the Cornell University Theatre has produced more than two score of these new plays, written by himself, his students (including Robert Gard, who hails from Kansas but has mastered in a remarkable fashion our folklore and history), and many other enthusiasts from various walks and gallops of life. So far, none of his followers can match Paul Green of North Carolina, an earlier student at Cornell; he has not yet developed an interpreter of Upstate to compare with so accomplished a playwright of the Big City as his own pupil Sidney Kingsley; but he has obtained and produced plays about the Empire State that will arouse the emulation of some Green or Kingsley now wearing a freshman "dink," or some

# INTRODUCTION

other Yorker who may never cheer the Big Red Team but who will profit by the reading of this book. In one of the fairest regions of these States something is growing as native and as wholesome as the farms which owe their fertility to Cornell's College of Agriculture.

These plays are to be acted—and for at least three years they may be performed in any Grange Hall, school, or little theatre of the State without royalty; but they are also to be read—by historians, folklorists, farmers, students, or anyone else who loves laughter and "the brave old wisdom of sincerity." Especially they are to be read by those who would like to present on a public stage their own Idea of the place they know best. In geography the plays range from the manors of the Hudson to the vineyards of Chautauqua County, with stops at regions especially rich in lore: Schoharie, County of the Old Frontier; westward into Oneida and Madison Counties, homes of Hamilton and Colgate; on to the Finger Lakes and the Military Tract; and finally to the first Far West of Cattaraugus and Chautauqua Counties—to Lake Erie "with Norse-blue eyes." In chronology we advance from the frontier year of 1790 to 1941, lingering longest in the first half of the nineteenth century, era of the canawls, the hoss-thieves, the circuit-riders, the rent wars, and the ballads, but reaching on to the era of the Dairyman's League and Welch's grape-juice.

The subjects, too, have variety. To be sure, and rightly, romantic love is far in the lead, but frontier folkways are a close second; and even such economic problems as quitrents and the price of milk find place. One play was suggested by an incident in the life of an Indian chief; another was suggested by the saga of a notorious band of horse-thieves. I emphasize the word *suggested*, because it rarely happens that a folk-tale can be taken over body, boots, and britches; it gives the hint to a writer of imagination. An exception, perhaps, is the play about Ren Dow, the Revivalist, which follows its source pretty closely.

As in all art, the treatment is what counts; here you find a chief justification for a volume which gives hints to future playwrights of the folk. Conventional types of plays are not lacking: *Chenango Crone* is an effective melodrama, and *Raisin' the Devil* is a good example of the well-planned farce. But other plays seem to have new forms growing out of the material. *A Day in the Vineyard* might be called a ballad-play; certainly it seems built around the old song of "Grandma'am's Advice," known from Long Island to Lake Erie. It might also be called an example of folk-say: the language is as proverbial as Sir Walter Scott's—you could cull enough proverbs for an article in the *Journal of American Folklore*. There is not much plot, but there is enchanting atmosphere, and characterization of a kindly folk who sing at their work. Yet the sentiment is not false; having worked in the vineyards of Westfield, I know that the authors are telling the truth.

No less than four of the plays create atmosphere through the use of ballads. Another is a conspicuous example of the effectiveness of a richly poetical speech: Chief Cornplanter's white father may have been a Dutchman, but Miss O'Connell has art on her side as well as racial predilection when she accepts another tradition that he is Irish; this permits her to see how far in *Donalds O'Rourk* language of strong rhythm and deep emotion can carry dramatic incident.

What variety of treatment is possible is further illustrated in *Mixing Up the Rent*. The anti-rent wars were fundamentally grim affairs, but Robert Gard took from the words of a satirical ballad and the grotesque Indian masquerading of tenant rioters hints for burlesque. To at least one audience the play was a hilarious romp and damn the plot, but there are subtler elements in the writing—even bookish ones: there is satire upon Cooper's heroines and upon certain stock characters and situations in our early American drama. Again, our milk strikes are serious in economic implications, but Ella Thurston chose to mellow this theme into the laughable if pointed domestic comedy of *Family Cooperative*.

The one long play deserves special comment, because it shows how it is possible to present dramatically the atmosphere of a region. When *The Lake Guns of Seneca and Cayuga* was presented at the annual convention of the New York State Historical Association at Geneva in 1941, the enthusiastic audience generally agreed that the "show" had done more to vivify history than all the admirable papers which had been read plus an historical tour of the countryside. The inspiration for the playwright lay in several legends which have attempted to explain the booming heard in Lakes Cayuga and Seneca, but lay also in the haunted beauty of an eerie region. A secondary theme is the eternal conflict between brash science and enduring romance. As a member of the audience saw it—and the author himself will later give his own purposes in a preface— the play opens in the present and gradually works up an atmosphere of mysterious suspense, notable in the Old Man of the Hill's rhapsodies upon the glory of our State's geography— speeches daringly long but justified by their poetry. In the second act we are transported to "down under," where all the contrivances of balladry, folk-tale, topical allusion, and legendary characters lead from farce to a melodramatic close. The third act returns to this our world, to the temporary solution of conflicts, to the atmosphere of mysterious beauty, and to a curtain which, as in all the best plays of this sort, leaves the audience suspended in the mood of a region's romance.

Many other interesting plays developed from the hundred and fifty scripts already submitted to the Project could have been printed; for example, Drummond's and Gard's plays have included a full-length "show," *The Cardiff Giant*, and a serious three-act play about our abandoned farms, *Wild Hills*. The files are fairly full of stage-worthy one-act plays—the chief goal of the Project—being revised for print. Just enough has been included here to introduce you to the men and ways of a land where the folk still believe, with Thoreau, that "there is more day to dawn."

# THE LAKE GUNS
## of
# SENECA AND CAYUGA

## A Dramatic Legend
## of the Finger Lakes Country

*by*

## A. M. DRUMMOND

# THE LAKE GUNS
## of
## SENECA AND CAYUGA

THE INDIAN knew that our Finger Lakes Country was more than a land of fertile beauty. The friendly God was never far away and wrought good magic from its skies and across its hills. In the shadows of its forests men dreamed dreams that became masters of their lives for good or evil. From soil and springs rose mysterious vapors which moved men to strange visions and strange powers. Boding voices called from a vast underworld where giants and malicious spirits moved darkly in lake bottoms, endless caverns, and streams under-earth.

The settlers who inherited the Lake Country did not escape this magic. That the white man was as sensitive as the Indian to the subtle influence of the "land where God put down his hand," the prosiest history of his first century in Central New York makes clear. You need not be a Mormon, nor a Spiritist, nor a Jemimakin, to feel that the region nurtures preternatural experiences and spiritual exaltations. If you were born and bred among the Finger Lakes, you know that this is so. If you come as a stranger to probe the deposited wisdom and the folklore of our people, you will be convinced. Native New Yorkers have a special feeling about the Lake Country. It is a feeling they do not discuss glibly; but if they will speak what they truly believe, they will tell you: "It calls to something in the blood; and when it calls you have to answer."

The characteristic voice of the Finger Lakes is the phenomenon known as the Lake Guns, or Lake Drums. These mysterious sounds are like the crescendo of distant cannon booming from the lakes' depths and dying in receding echoes along the cliff-bound flatness of the water; or like great drum-rhythms shaking down across the lakes from the high hills and fading as the drummer marches on over the distant ridge. The Guns are heard best on Seneca and Cayuga Lakes after the first hot still days come, or perhaps under the gray clouds of an early snowfall; some hold they roll loudest when the Northern Lights play.

These baffling thunders seem to have increased with the coming of the white man, and are more intimately interwoven with his life and folklore than with the Indian's. Old-timers have many contradictory explanations for the Guns. Scientists have always been at least as vague as legend; a brash few predicted that borings for gas would end the Guns, but keen-eared lakers declare the lake boomings echo on undiminished.

Similar guns or drums are occasionally heard on the smaller lakes and ponds of the region; they are heard on Canadian lakes; they are reported in Portugal. Indeed the scientific term for the phenomenon, "Barisal Guns," comes from far-off India. For centuries, at the mouth of the Ganges, the town of Barisal has heard "strange and puzzling thunders as of distant cannonading coming from the direction of the sea." And this fact casts such dubious light over materialistic explanations of the Finger Lake Guns that sensible people may well prefer "folk-say"; it offers satisfying choices for almost every taste.

As a stage piece, for perhaps it is not a play, *The Lake Guns of Seneca and Cayuga* essays to cast the Region as a dramatic character, to place it against a background painted in the romantic colors of the Region's scenic and historical places, and to suggest the richnesses of fantasy and sentiment that underlie the familiar landmarks of the Finger Lakes. If it must have a moral, it might be this: "to curb a little the empirically-minded destruction of our myths and symbols by calling, unabashed, upon feeling and imagination to assist us to a truer appreciation of our native environments."

TIME: *The present.*
PLACE: ACT ONE—*The crest of Butcher Hill looking north over Seneca and Cayuga Lakes and the wide sweep of old Indian country beyond.*
ACT TWO—*The mythical "down under": perhaps in caverns between the Lakes; more likely in the bottom of Cayuga; or where you will, so long as we end up in deep water off Taghanic.*
ACT THREE—*Taghanic Point.*

## THE CHARACTERS OF THE PLAY

THE OLD MAN OF THE HILLS.
THE GEOLOGIST.
BLONDE MARY.
HASKEL.
MINNA.
JOHN.
JOHN'S WIFE.
A FARMER.
THE FIRST GUARD.
THE SECOND GUARD.
A PATIENT FROM THE ASYLUM.
AN INDIAN.
A SQUAW.
THE OLD MAN OF THE LAKES.
OLD BILL SULLIVAN.
TAUGGY, *the Dwarf Stone "Giant."*
WANETA.
TESS OF THE STORM COUNTRY.
SPINKSTER JOHN SMITH.

The Scientist.
The Great Serpent of Bare Hill; *or Part of Him!*
A Girl.
A Boy.
A Man.
The Drums, Cannon, and Lights of the Lake.

# THE LAKE GUNS
## of
## SENECA AND CAYUGA

### ACT ONE

### ON BUTCHER HILL

THE SCENE *is the crest of Butcher Hill where it drops off toward the north and overlooks Seneca and Cayuga Lakes and the wide sweep of country beyond. There are perhaps two or three trees, a bit of tumble-down fence, a weathered sign reading in rustic lettering "Butcher Hill—Elevation 1600 Ft. Two lakes, seven counties, one city, may be seen"; and a few logs, rocks, or whatnot to sit on.*

*The clear evening darkens to clouded moonlight during the Act.*

[*At the left sitting perfectly still facing north, that is toward the audience, is the little* OLD MAN OF THE HILLS.]

[*The* GEOLOGIST, *a studious young man with conspicuous glasses and near-sighted manner enters from right, cracking a rock in his hand with his hammer. He sits down at the right, pulls a map out of his pocket, spreads it out on the ground, and with a brief glance out over the audience toward the landscape, studies the map near-sightedly and keeps pounding on his rock.*]

[*A group is heard coming on from right, chattering and singing: the student* BLONDE MARY; HASKEL, *an athletic young physician, one-sixty-fourth Indian;* MINNA, *a stylish young woman, one-eighth Indian;* JOHN; *and his* WIFE. *All wear informal but colorful tramping clothes. They exclaim over the view.*]

HASKEL. Well, here we are! Here's Butcher Hill! And how's that for a view?!

MINNA. Oh! It is marvelous, isn't it!

BLONDE MARY. What two big lakes are those stretching off in whatever direction that is?

HASKEL. That's to the north. On your left, Seneca Lake. On your right, Cayuga. You're seeing twenty miles of both lakes from here. Right below you is Ovid; and beyond it the big Kendaia ammunition dumps and airports stretch pretty near from lake to lake. Those buildings down on the lake with all the lights beginning to come on, looks like a college, is Willard Insane Asylum. Way off at the end of Seneca Lake where you see columns of smoke and a light or two twinkling, that's Geneva . . . and swinging right you may see, come dusk, a glimmer that's Waterloo, and farther right another glimmer that's Seneca Falls. . . . Then you're back to Cayuga Lake, way up at Cayuga Village.

MINNA. I never knew there was such a view anywhere around!

BLONDE MARY [*exclaiming*]. Look right here in front of us . . . berry bushes . . . flowers . . . what a mass of tiger lilies! It's an old flower garden! There must have been a house up here in the old days! My! they looked over all creation, didn't they?

[*From the left the* FARMER *strolls in. He is tall, amiable, shrewd—a kindly person. He stops alongside the group taking in the view.*]

MINNA. I suppose this must be old Indian country we're looking over. Haskel, your sixty-fourth Indian blood came from there somewhere.

HASKEL. I suppose it did. Though I don't know whether the

Onondagas lived here, or maybe farther east. And maybe, Minna, your Indian great, great, great grandmother lived out in there somewhere, too.

MINNA. Maybe so! Though from what I've heard I guess I'm descended from some gentle, captive tribe you fierce Iroquois warriors kept out in the Caroline Hills, or Pony Hollow.

WIFE [*laughing*]. They seem to have been nice people, anyway, Minna!

MINNA. Nice enough so the whites married most of them up. . . . We're all middle-class now, if not in the best families! Only Haskel's lordly Iroquois got trapped on the reservations, or followed British fire-water into Canada, or went visiting poor relations by the century out West!

HASKEL. Easy now, on Lo the Poor Reservation Indian! Just because we once conquered you folks down in Ca'lina, don't you-all try no Gone-with-the-Wind triumph over us redskin Romans o' the Yankee No'th!

JOHN [*laughing*]. Just how much Indian are you supposed to be anyway, Minna?

MINNA. Just eight times Haskel's ridiculous one-sixty-fourth! . . . one-eighth red man!

JOHN. Oh, why not call yourself squaw, and be done with it!

[MINNA *laughs back, and sticks her tongue out at him.*]

HASKEL. Not so ridiculous either now! It supported my family without WPA labor; it put me through Haskell Institute; it let me become an absurdly well-paid football coach and professional athlete, with plenty of time for medical school . . . paid for by me, thank you, not by the Great White Father in Washington! Brain-work by me too, thank you again! . . . And what's maybe more, if I have the itch, it gives me, *in perpetuum*, right to fish and hunt over yon fair, wide landscape, without let of license or of season, whatever quarry of field or stream God and civilization permit, and the Conservation Commission of the Excelsior State lavishly bestows!

JOHN [*applauding ironically; the others joining in*]. Hear, hear! Yessa! Yessa!

WIFE. Who is there to mourn for Logan!

MINNA. Well, dear, I'd be the mighty Nimrod this year! When the Cayugas all move back to the Finger Lakes, with equal privileges, and less fagged by brain-work, they'll leave small pickings for you citified hunters, whether pure-white or half-breed.

WIFE. You'd better marry him for his bedside manner, Minna, not for his fishing rights!

MINNA. I'm marrying him for his money!

[*At the remarks about Indians the* FARMER *and the* OLD MAN *commence to betray interest.*]

FARMER. Quite a view we've got here, isn't it?

BLONDE MARY. Marvelous! How far can you see from here on a clear day?

FARMER. Well, ma'am, on a clear day, if you've got the eyes, there's nothing in the way of seeing clear to Lake Ontario. The land falls away here everywhere to the north. [*Pointing at a 45 degree angle to the right.*] Off to the right you've got a great sweep over Aurora . . . over the Great Gully where the big Indian villages used to be . . . over Frontenac Island . . . over that Algonquin Indian village they dug up . . . and beyond lies Auburn and Skaneateles. . . .

[*During this speech the* OLD MAN *has been getting more and more excited; he jumps up and stands in front of the* FARMER *pointing excitedly in the same direction; he has a high, nervous, half-wild voice and a wild eye.*]

OLD MAN. Yes, sir! If you squint your eyes that way . . . taking a beeline . . . you're seeing direct over Skaneateles on to the salt flats at Onondaga Lake . . . on to Fort Brewerton, Oneida Lake, an' Frenchman's Island . . . on to Florence Hill, where that school for blacks used to be 'way before the Civil War . . . and up back of Florence Hill is Constableville. Ever been to Constableville? By Gad, I wuz there in

1840! Had the goldarnedest, cutest little cabinet-work bar, all cut out o' black-and-white wood doweled together in stripes; never seen a bar a drink tasted off so good in my life; you go there some day and try. . . . Way up beyond Constableville there's Castorland where the Frenchies settled . . . . and then you're bang right against the North Woods, 'n Nat Foster, 'n the Beaver Country, 'n Paul Bunyan . . . not a thing in the way . . . if you got eyes to see . . . and them's *wants* t' see *can* see! [*He turns to the left on a 45 degree angle.*] And over here to the northwest you are looking over . . . not a thing in your way . . . You want to tell 'em, Mister Farmer?

FARMER. No, I guess you know better 'n I do. I know you're looking toward Penn Yan and Bare Hill.

OLD MAN. Yessir, you're looking right down over Seneca Lake . . . right where she ain't got no bottom . . . and you're looking into New Jerusalem . . . where the Lady Universal Friend went to walk on the water . . . only she didn't have to 'cause they all believed she could, so why should she wet her sacred feet? . . . And you're looking over Penn Yan to the valley of the Brook Kedron as it flows into Keuka Lake, where the Friend built her palace . . . and where she lies buried agin the Resurrection, nobody knows where, 'ceptin' two men, going down through the generations, and they won't tell 'cause of eternal hell-fire if they do. . . . And beyond the Brook Kedron you're looking toward Bare Hill, towering over Canandaigua Lake . . . the sacred hill where the Seneca Indians was born . . . where the Great Serpent coiled round the hill with its tail in its two mouths except when it took the tail out to swallow the Seneca tribe it had penned on the hilltop. . . . And there he lay and swallowed them all except two. . . . And then the great Manitou sent down a message to the man that was left, and he shot his arrow into the heart of the Great Serpent, and that finished him. But in his death struggles he swept all the forests off the hill and he spewed up living all the good Indians he'd swallowed and they became the Senecas and being as they'd been in the Serpent they was wise and crafty . . . everybody knows a snake is a wise bird . . . and then he fell in the Lake and there he lies . . . unless as some say he wriggled underground into Seneca Lake and lays there yet, a-breathing and rumbling and making the water rise and fall like tides. . . . 'Course they're *lots* o' strange things in Seneca Lake what ain't got no bottom but runs right out somewhere deep to the big ocean, just as it runs deep under us here through a cave into Cayuga . . . and where else all, I don't know . . . 'cause if it's a strange world on top it's a stranger world down below! I don't guess the Serpent'll ever die, a snake don't die till the sun goes down, and that snake's so big Death can't get over him till it's sunrise again. . . . And he just lies there shudderin' and dyin', or tryin' t' crawl underground to Cayuga . . . maybe he gets weaker, I don't know! . . . You can go over to Bare Hill yerself and see how he swept the mountain-top smooth, and you can see all the heads he coughed up, them that wasn't fit to be good Senecas, turned to round rocks . . . an' they ain't finished yet rolling down from the top of Bare Hill an' bouncing on the shore an' jouncing down into Canandaigua Lake. And right beyont Bare Hill cross the lake . . . 'r' you all looking? . . . [*To the* FARMER.] Ain't what I'm telling 'em true?

FARMER. Well, I've heard it all said.

MINNA. Go on! Go on! What's beyond Bare Hill?

OLD MAN. Beyont the lake you're looking across the Bristol Hills where th' burnin' springs be. . . . Many's the olden time I seen 'em light th' springs till th' burnin' made all th' night yellow . . . 'n folks come from far 'nd near 'n foreign countries t' light th' springs with their own hand 'n see th' wonder : . . 'nd in them hills wuz th' dangedest rattlesnakes. . . . Why, Bill Bristol, late ez 1823 when we wuz all civilized, Bill, just in one noonin', just when he wuz baitin' his ox-team, Bill killed 488 rattlers without even movin' off th' rock where he wuz havin' his bread 'n whiskey. . . . And one ball o' rattlesnakes rolled down out o' th' cliff top o' th' hill, thicker through 'n a tall man, seven-nine-foot ball o' solid rattlesnakes rolled down on Bill's ox-team 'n smashed his bull-tongue-plow all t' smithereens, 'n they rolled on into th' crick 'n dammed it up 'n made a flood so Bill had t' move out o' his log cabin for two weeks till th' spring warmed th' water 'n thawed th' rattlers t' move so th' crick c'd run!

FARMER. Been over there ez a boy myself when th' only sport . . . 'fore tame pheasant shootin' come in . . . wuz goin' out in th' hills 'n pickin' rattlers up by th' tails an' snappin' 'em . . . snap their heads off like a sling-shot!

OLD MAN. Past th' Bristol Hills there's Big Tree 'n Canawaugus on th' Genesee 'n Fort Hill on Allen Creek, 'n where Spring 'n Bigelow's Creeks 'n Black Creek all run t'gether ya come t' Punkin Hill . . . 'n Punkin Hill's some place 'n if I had time I'd tell ya 'bout that. . . . An' past Punkin Hill is Medina, 'n th' terraced locks steppin' down through Lockport, 'n through a hunderd miles o' heavy-laden orchards, th' Ridge Road runnin' on t' Fort Niagara, over agin all Canada. . . . But now look straight ahead of you toward the north and I'll tell you somethin'! . . .

[*Two husky fellows enter from the right, the* FIRST *and* SECOND GUARDS *from* Willard State Hospital; *their entrance holds up the conversation for a moment.*]

FIRST GUARD. Evenin', folks. Enjoying the view? Quite some sweep of country you get here from Butcher Hill.

SECOND GUARD. It's purty!

FARMER. Yes, these folks was just tryin' t' take in the view and I stopped by t' help 'em out! The Old Man here was pointing out points of interest.

FIRST GUARD. Well, don't know as there's much unusual 'cept th' view . . . but then, I was brought up down here on

Lake Seneca so maybe it's all old stuff to me. But it's sure one of the swellest pros-pects you c'n find anywheres round here.

MINNA. This man says the lake over here hasn't got any bottom. That can't really be so, can it?

FIRST GUARD. Why, sure it's so, ma'am. . . . [*Pointing.*] They tried I don't know how many times ten miles up 'n down there off Dresden to find bottom and they ain't none. Everybody on Seneca Lake knows that. . . . And you know these two lakes is connected underground, everybody knows that, too. . . . [*He turns to the* FARMER.] Say, we're from the Hospital down here and looking for a patient didn't turn up when the gates closed. You ain't seen a fellow around here, have you?

FARMER. No, I don't think we've seen anybody. . . . You folks didn't see anybody looked like a patient from the Asylum down here before I come, did you?

[*There are various "no's" and shakes of the head, with doubtful glances toward the* OLD MAN.]

HASKEL [*in an undertone*]. Not unless this old bird has escaped from somewhere!

OLD MAN [*in a high voice*]. Ain't nobody crazy around here, except them won't believe what their eyes see and their ears tell 'em! *Now*, I want to tell you folks somep'n! Them Bristol Hills rattlesnakes and that Bare Hill Serpent, they ain't really *nothing!* . . . You see here . . . north . . . the way the land falls away smooth and worn-like and flat, clear off there for twenty mile till you get to them Wayne County sugar-loaf hills? . . . 'N I'm telling you that trough goes pretty flat 'n reg'lar clear from Niagara to Albany . . . and I'll tell you what made it . . . that is if you want t' know!

WIFE. I certainly want to know!

OLD MAN. Well, ma'am, back in the old days when even the Injuns was new they was a real big snake here, more like a giant blood-sucker, and he stretched three hundred mile clear across York State. . . . And with his mouth he'd a holt onto Goat Island in Niagara Falls, and his tail he'd twined tight round where the falls goes down to the Hudson at Cohoes . . . and here he was stretching through all the country the Iroquois Injuns come to occupy. . . . And he stretched and pulled and wore the hills down and flattened out this big trough clear from Niagara to the Hudson. . . . And his body was stretching all across these here lakes . . . and the Injuns couldn't get by him from the north or from the south, neither by land 'r by water. . . . And then the great Manitou, to help the Indians out, he sent down a magic knife, so sharp it would cut even that broad sucker-snake . . . and a Injun chief took it and he sliced him right out here somewhere between these lakes. . . . *An'* when the blood-sucker snake felt the sharp knife a-cuttin' him he knew he was done, and he let go with his mouth at Niagara Falls, an' he let go with his tail that was lapped around at Cohoes, and he was stretched so hard he just sprung together kawhang right here in the middle. . . . And the half of him to the west fell into Seneca Lake and the half of him to the east fell into Cayuga Lake . . . but the head half of him in Seneca Lake makes more trouble than the tail half of him in Cayuga Lake, him being blood-sucker-like. . . . It 'ud be th' other way round if he'd been a snake.

[*The group all look toward the* GUARDS *as though this tale might be sufficient indication that here was a crazy man; but find the* GUARDS *nodding their heads wisely with approval.*]

FIRST GUARD. Yessir, that's right! All the old folks who ever knew any of the old Injuns through here can tell you that something like that is *so.*

[*During these disturbances the* GEOLOGIST *at right has been registering repeated incredulity and impatience, now and again laughing with scorn as he continues to study the map and pound his rock; but at this point he jumps up and interrupts.*]

GEOLOGIST. See here, you folks, a sensible man can stand just so much of this ignorant balderdash . . . and I'm a sensible man! *Now!* There's nothing to these yarns these old fellows are telling you. . . . They're myths, phony legends, or plain lies . . . and ought to be stamped out. And it's my business to expose them!

FIRST GUARD. What d'ya mean . . . lies? You mean what I said . . . ?

GEOLOGIST. Yes, about that lake having no bottom, and . . .

FIRST GUARD. Why, everybody *knows* that's so! And plenty o' people seen in it, what I didn't tell about—the Wandering Jew! Ain't that so, Pete?

SECOND GUARD. Sure, that stump-like thing that moves around sticking outa th' lake, like one o' them there peryscope gadgets, now with the storm, now agin it, making rumblin' noises. . . . That's the old Injun chief that the stump was before the lightnin' blasted him an' the tree he lent against into the lake. . . . An' the noises is the ghost of the Old Chief callin' his braves to battle!

FIRST GUARD. Plenty's seen an' heard it fur a hundred years! An' as for callin' lies, mister . . .

GEOLOGIST. All right . . . all right . . . pretty soon you'll be telling me about the Lake Drums. . . .

FIRST GUARD. Of course they's the Lake *Guns.* . . .

FARMER. Pretty hard to convince people around here, mister, there ain't no Lake Guns . . . as they generally calls 'em . . . too many's heard 'em!

SECOND GUARD. Heard 'em! Why, not so long ago over between Watkins Glen 'n Geneva, they knocked a freight train right off th' track! My Uncle Bill told me about it th' mornin' after the Guns 'ud rattled th' house so they shook me outa bed, 'n woke me up hittin' th' floor.

First Guard. Sure, a sensible guy believes what he and his folks before him have seen an' heard.
Geologist. Now, see here, I'm a geologist . . . and if you look at my map here I'll show you! There is no tunnel between the lakes; there are no serpents. . . . This is the only remarkable thing . . . in front of you . . . and this is science . . . probably you can see it out there, but you can see it plainer on the map . . . at least *I* can, because I'm a bit near-sighted. . . .

[*Some gather about to look at his map.*]

Wife. I'm all ears and eyes!
Geologist. Now, here! . . . In prehistoric times, before the glacier covered this country thousands of feet in ice, the Seneca Lake outlet into Cayuga Lake was right across here in front of us, in this west-east hollow . . . instead of ten miles north where the modern outlet carries the Barge Canal. . . . You can trace it on the map plain as your nose.
First Guard [*with an ugly and disgusted laugh*]. And he called me a liar!
Second Guard. Sam, don't he look like our man?
Geologist. Now, I can show you in this rock I've broken open . . .
First Guard. Why sure, sure . . . uh *course!* Gosh, I got so interested . . . [*Changing his temper entirely.*] Now, see here, mister, it's about time you came back in. . . . It's long past closin' time, so suppose you 'n me an' Pete just mosey along back to the Hospital . . .

[*The two* Guards *close in on the* Geologist.]

Geologist. What do you mean? Hospital! . . .
Second Guard. Right there on yer map, mister! Willard State Hospital.
Geologist [*panic stricken but standing his ground*]. Why, I'm out here studying geology. . . .
First Guard. Grab 'im! [*They both grab him.*]
Second Guard [*as the* Geologist *struggles*]. Now take it easy!

Everything's goin' to be all right! Take it easy!
GEOLOGIST [*fairly shrieking*]. I can identify myself!
FIRST GUARD. Well, what you got? Got your driver's license?
GEOLOGIST. No, I keep that home so I won't lose it.
SECOND GUARD [*laughing*]. Got anything in your pockets?
GEOLOGIST. No, I changed my clothes, and . . .
FIRST GUARD [*into his pockets already*]. Nothin' but pockets full o' rocks!
SECOND GUARD. Oh, he's nuts all right. Put a twist on him an' come on!
FIRST GUARD. Sorry to seem a little unpleasant, folks, but if they won't go peaceable we have to take 'em.
BLONDE MARY. Wait a minute, officers! I know who he is! He doesn't belong with you.
FIRST GUARD. What d'ya mean, miss?
BLONDE MARY. I thought he looked familiar . . . and as soon as he began to talk . . . interested, you know . . . I was sure. Just give him to me, officer, and I'll take good care of him.
SECOND GUARD. Who do you think he is?
BLONDE MARY. I *know* who he is. He's my geology instructor at Cornell Summer School!
FIRST GUARD. Is that right?
GEOLOGIST [*first to* GUARD, *then to* MARY]. Yes, . . . but who are you?
BLONDE MARY. Do you remember any "M's" in your class, Professor?
GEOLOGIST. Y-e-s-s . . . "M" . . . a Miss Morgan . . . sat in the back so I never saw her . . . but she had a nice voice.
BLONDE MARY. That's me!
GEOLOGIST. She was a consistent "C."
BLONDE MARY. That's me, too, Professor.
GEOLOGIST. Come closer, so I can see you.
BLONDE MARY [*approaching*]. I've always liked *your* looks very much, Professor!

GEOLOGIST [*peering at her with dawning delight*]. Gee, Miss Morgan, why didn't you sit down in front? You're at least a "B." . . .
BLONDE MARY [*to the* GUARDS]. Here, I'll give the stones back to the Professor. . . . [*Looking at them.*] Why, Professor, these are *fossils!!*
GEOLOGIST [*delighted at the results of his teaching*]. Miss Morgan, you don't know how *gratified* . . .
BLONDE MARY. How about "B plus" or "A," Professor?
GEOLOGIST. But I've sent the grades in, Miss Morgan!
BLONDE MARY. I don't care about the Registrar, it's what *you* think, Professor!
GEOLOGIST. If you stay where I can see you, Miss Morgan, it's "A" with me!
BLONDE MARY. Well, I don't know as I'll ever let me out of your sight again!
GEOLOGIST [*breaking down*]. M—Miss M—Morgan . . . I never wished so much that I could see better . . .
BLONDE MARY. Here, let me wipe your glasses, Professor.
[*The* GUARDS *have stepped back, shrugging and dusting their hands as though to assert that, "He's a 'nut' all right, but not our business."*]
OLD MAN [*beginning on an intenser key*]. Now folks, havin' glanced t' th' north-east 'n t' th' north-west, let's look at what's between . . . rollin' away from ya t' th' north . . . over th' Seneca River . . . over th' Montezuma Marshes that spreads out like a inland sea . . . over th' old Clinton Ditch, over th' Er-i-e Canawl, over th' Genesee Turnpike t' th' Western Country . . . over whatever's come after them linking th' East an' th' West together. . . . Over them queer shoveled-up hills in Wayne County, beyont where th' land keeps flattenin' away fer sixty mile t' Lake Ontario, an' Sodus Bay harbor where th' British landed in 1812, an' from where th' Canawl was to run t' connect Ithicy an' Watkins with Canady an' across the ocean . . . an' where along the inlets

them natural iris gardens makes one o' th' beauty wonders o' th' world! . . .

Now, right out here in front o' us, along an' beyond th' falls o' th' Seneca is the mysterious country where from th' beginnings o' time th' Injuns worshiped dreams, an' th' dream they worshiped was a god who spoke to them in their sleep an' commanded them t' obey their dreams, an' their dreams was master o' their lives, an' through th' dream they had they knew th' will o' God, an' what they had t' do for their lives. . . . An' the Injuns knew that the soul leaves th' body when th' body sleeps, or maybe when it dozes, an' goes off, the soul does, questing objects, during th' dreams, an' returns t' th' body when th' dream is done!

[*Gradually increasing in apocalyptic intensity.*] But plenty went a-dreamin' out in that country besides th' Injuns . . . ! Maybe the old giant gods shook all them Wayne County hills outa their giant sifters, screening fer gold, I dunno . . . but white men had dug over ever' foot o' them hills followin' their dream o' buried Spanish gold, an' found no gold, none 'cept Joseph Smith, him as the dream commanded t' dig in th' highest pointed hill, the Hill Cumorah, where th' lost tribes o' Israel met after wanderin' over th' whole globe an' destroyed each other in a great battle, an' left nothin' but th' golden plates o' the sacred book that Smith dug up where th' angel Moroni in a vision told 'im the great shafts o' light would shine out o' th' north on 'em . . . an' they did with sounds as of a great thunderin' organ, an' of a great church bell, an' of a great bugle echoin' celestial across th' hills. . . . An' lots o' people followed his dream with 'im, out West some'eres th' place people used t' go following their dreams . . . !

An' I remember th' day th' story on them gold plates was published in a book, March th' 26, it was, 1830—a day that seemed like th' beginning of th' crack o' doom, an' th' grey rain ran thick outa th' sky, an' th' clouds hung black an' solid on th' hills, an' awful thunder shook th' windows of houses, an' quivered the earth, an' th' people in Palmyra an' Manchester 'n thereabouts, shut themselves in their houses an' closed th' blinds. . . .

But I remember better seein' with my own eyes the Prophet Joseph Smith a-standin' in th' bright shudderin' light out of th' North Star, and him a-standin' over six feet o' mighty brawn, like a handsome young giant, with th' light gleamin' on his golden upstandin' curly hair an' in his blue eyes lookin' far away. . . .

An' of a decent night you can see that light shining still, now an' again, offen Cumorah Hill! . . . An' I bet if you went over there to-night you might see the Angel Moroni looking out over the hills o' th' Injuns' dream god. . . . But young Smith, he went West an' I lost track of 'im.

Over in them low hills, too, is where th' Fox Sisters started th' "Hydesville Rappin's" at Hydesville, that they tell me spread all over th' civilized world, like a religion, an' into th' stars, I guess, 'cause th' dead talk to th' livin', if there is any dead, an' th' livin' t' th' dead. . . . Maybe they're walkin' in the old dream. . . . An' they tell me more people right nowadays is dreamin' this dream . . . an' with every war there's more rappin's! . . . Smith went West . . . but—
[*With a humorous touch.*]—the Fox Sisters went t' Rochester an' they had to call 'em "Rochester Rappin's," 'cause the Rochester folks was tony even them early days. But Rochester'll never catch up with Geneva that was a tony place when Rochester was just some hick shacks set in th' mud. . . . [*He says a good word for Rochester.*] But they got religion to Rochester, 'cause with my own eyes I seen Cobb Hill there crowded white with believers waitin' through th' night all robed by thousands for the pearly gates, when the Millerites dreamed t' end th' world in 1832.

[*He concludes in mysterious solemnity.*] Oh, there's strange things been laid out in that land before us, an' strange

sounds echoin' back into th' high hills o' these here lakes.
. . . An' some thinks these Drums, er Guns, we was a-speakin' of comes down from Injuns' dreamin' with that old Injun dream-god; an' some thinks they comes from white men's dreamin', with the god himself lyin' unbeknownst t' them out in that mysterious soil an' all its under-earth streams an' caverns, workin' there forever!

For these sounds men hear come now from here, 'n now from there . . . from where you dunno! An' sometimes th' drummin' lies along th' flat ripples o' th' lakes, sometimes it rises from th' deep depths as though from cannons 'r thunder in th' bottomless water . . . an' sometimes it comes down from th' topping hills, fillin' th' valleys an' echoin' across th' waters between th' cliffs! Ain't any o' you heard it . . . ?

SECOND GUARD. Sure, we hear them Lake Guns every summer 'n every fall . . . hear 'em good round Lodi Landing 'n cross at Dresden.

FARMER. Ain't a fisher or cottager long either lake ain't heard 'em.

FIRST GUARD. I heard th' drumming from th' hills, too.

OLD MAN. Ever heard what makes that hill drummin'?

FARMER. 'Course, there's been any number of good drummers along the Finger Lakes. There's De Gory Prowt whose body's buried somewhere round Sheldrake, who drummed right through from Fort Stanwix t' th' surrender o' Cornwallis . . . an' some says he's drummin' yet . . .

An' there was little Charlie Barrett that was only fifteen when he went with the Dundee Brass Band to fight in Virginia for Abe Lincoln, an' died at Norfolk . . . an' has his monument in Dundee Cemetery, a broken column with the flag of this Union, an' his fav'rite tenor drum carved on it out o' stone . . . that they say, when th' moon's right, th' fella off th' hills comes down an' drums on, shakin' across the lake . . .

An' over t' Flint Creek Hollow beyond Jerusalem was Uncle Arch Armstrong . . .

SECOND GUARD. Hell, everybody down Watkins way knows who drums over th' hills! Heard it from my grandfather when I was a shaver. . . . It's th' hare drummer, Mad Willie . . . climbing th' highest hills and runnin' across th' ridges beatin' his bass-drum where th' sound'll spread out all ways, 'n maybe rid him o' th' crazy banging in his poor half-wit head!

FARMER. Yeah, that's so, too! Some says crazy Willie was captured from Sullivan's army 'n tortured crazy; some says he just got lost in the hills 'n that made him batty; some says he's a crazy Dutch boy come with Williamson from Pennsylvany . . . th' Dutch is apt t' be half-witted. Some dunno. But they all call th' kids in. No dog 'as ever been willin' to trail 'im. Nobody'd follow th' dog if he did! Everybody's been kinda sorry for poor Willie though fer over a hundred years. . . . 'Tain't so good to be crazy . . . er even be half-wit!

GEOLOGIST. It ain't Willie that's crazy, it's the folks who believe in him!

BLONDE MARY. Now don't start an argument, Professor!

FIRST GUARD. Don't forget *your* little pipe-dream, young feller!

MINNA [*laughing, but nervously*]. When you think what Haskel's drop of Indian blood did for him, it all sounds quite reasonable!

OLD MAN. If they calls to somethin' in yer blood ya hafta answer!

HASKEL [*laughing uncomfortably*]. I certainly begin to have a very strange feeling that I have been here before . . . and that something had happened to me was going to happen again . . . like a nightmare . . .

MINNA. I'll be imagining I hear those Drums! . . . or do I?

HASKEL. . . . like a nightmare that happens to you over and over again . . . !

FARMER. This is th' kind of night t' hear 'em!

OLD MAN [*with mystic insinuation*]. An' somethin's a-tellin' me someone here has a story o' th' Drums he c'd tell!

FARMER. There's other explanations, of course.

OLD MAN. Let him tell his story!

WIFE. John, this all reminds me of something in your family . . . something you told me. . . .

OLD MAN [*in a high singsong*]. If they calls t' somethin' in yer blood . . .

JOHN [*laughing self-consciously and nervously*]. Well, maybe you'll think I've been holding back on you . . . but there *is* a story come down in our family that matches one of the local legends about these Drums.

OLD MAN [*in singsong, and beating time with a finger*]. . . . somethin' in yer blood you'll hafta answer. . . .

HASKEL. You aren't going to claim relations with Minna and me?

OLD MAN. . . . 'll hafta answer. . . .

JOHN [*laughing, but speaking seriously*]. Nothing so probably regal as that! No . . . but there's a story come down in our family that we,—well, say I, to be specific—am the descendant of a British army officer who deserted to woo and wed my which ever-great grandmother it would be, she being the daughter of a staunch Continental soldier; that the British captured him, executed him for desertion; . . . and that the drums beating his death-march are the mysterious legendary Drums of these lakes. I'm not at all sure that some of my forebears were not quite capable of making up that yarn! But I understand some such explanation of the Drums has long been current through the Southern Tier.

FARMER. Lots think that's the explanation.

JOHN. And I must say it gives me a peculiar feeling. . . .

OLD MAN [*chanting*]. If they calls t' somethin' in yer blood . . .

JOHN [*cutting in*]. As our friend says, "you have to answer"! And it's a damned spooky feeling, thinking that with your own ears you *might* hear, or even *fancy* you heard, drumbeats that marched your ancestor to execution a hundred and sixty-five years ago!

WIFE. Why, John, I never thought you took it seriously!

JOHN. I don't take it . . . as he says, it takes me. . . .

OLD MAN [*chanting and beating time*]. If they calls t' somethin' in yer blood you'll hafta answer!

GEOLOGIST. It's all a fancy story, not a scientific . . .

JOHN. To hell with your science! I know how I *feel* . . . and I wish the subject hadn't come up . . . and I wish I hadn't come . . . and, come on, dear, let's be for home . . . [*He laughs, but shakily.*] . . . before I think I hear the damn Drums!

WIFE [*getting up to go*]. I'm awfully sorry, dear. . . .

[*In time with the* OLD MAN's *rhythmic finger, a faint drumming is heard back on the hill; it might be "Wild Willie" rather than the regular beat of death-march drums. All stand arrested and startled, listening, turning upstage. A crazily pleased smile shines on the* OLD MAN's *face as he beats time with the drum.*]

[*From upstage comes a gurgling, frantic cry, as of someone running; it is repeated over and over with cries of "Help, help" mingled in and "Oh, guards! Where are the guards! Come save me!"*]

[*The* PATIENT FROM THE ASYLUM *bursts into the group, wild with terror, and sobbing with relief. Trembling with fear he sees the* FIRST GUARD, *goes to him, kneels, grabs his hand.*]

PATIENT [*pointing back upstage*]. I seen 'im! Wild Willie with his drum a-beating . . . comin' down against me from the high hill. . . . Don't let him get me! Take me back safe! Don't let me hear him! [*Puts hands over ears.*] I'll never run away again!

SECOND GUARD. This is our guy, Sam.

FIRST GUARD. Yeah, *he'll* heel you down without no leash, Pete.
SECOND GUARD. I'll take you down, fella, an' nothin'll hurt you. [*To the group.*] An' lemme tell you I ain't sorry t' go. You folks c'n have all th' spook knockin's an' welcome!
GEOLOGIST. I'm going to get down out of this, too!
BLONDE MARY [*grabbing him firmly*]. Not without me you don't, Professor!
FARMER. How about us all goin' down on Taghanic Point an' listenin' for th' Guns there . . . It's a fine night . . .
FIRST GUARD. Yeah, let's!
FARMER. Th' Northern Lights is goin' to show . . . an' that's apt t' bring th' Guns on th' lake.
OLD MAN [*with prophetic fervor*]. Let them as wants t' go down on Taghanic go down! Let them as feels th' call t' go down t' th' caverns under th' high hills, an' betwixt th' lakes, an' below th' waters . . . let them folla me. . . .

[*An* INDIAN *and a* SQUAW, *in full Indian dress, and with hypnotic eyes, have silently entered center; they stand with folded arms waiting.*]

[MINNA *and* HASKEL *move together as though irresistibly drawn.*]

OLD MAN. The path down below is as short in time as yourn by th' roads on top. . . .
MINNA [*to* HASKEL]. Shall we go?
OLD MAN. We'll meet you on Taghanic Point when them Northern Lights blaze good . . . in half an hour. . . .
HASKEL. We shall go!
OLD MAN [*moving upstage*]. If they calls t' somethin' in yer blood you'll hafta answer. . . . Follow th' Injuns up th' path. [*He runs off with a high-pitched laugh.*]

[*The* INDIANS *move and hold out hands ready to lead* MINNA *and* HASKEL, *who move slowly to them.*]

[JOHN *stands rigid as though drawn to follow, but resisting; his* WIFE *grasps his arm to hold him from going.*]

GEOLOGIST [*bursting out*]. You damn fools! . . . Haven't you ever heard that if you try to solve the mystery of the Guns, you'll never live to tell it?!

HASKEL. We don't go to solve the mystery. . . .

MINNA. We're a part of the mystery. . . . You'll have to solve that, Professor.

FARMER. See you on the Point.

WIFE. John, you're not going?!

JOHN. No. . . . No . . . of course not!

[*The drum is heard upstage; the* INDIANS, MINNA *and* HASKEL *move off to its beat; the others shrink back, leaving* JOHN *alone and conspicuous.*]

[JOHN, *shaken by the drum and irresistibly drawn, decides to go. He turns and thrusts his* WIFE *into the* FARMER'S *arms.*]

JOHN. Take care of her! [*He strides off, following the others.*]

FARMER [*calling after him*]. Okay! Meet you on the Point in half an hour! [*To the* WIFE.] There, there, lady, it's all right. . . . It's all in th' way of Nature! [*The* WIFE *is crying; the* FARMER *pats her on the back.*]

FARMER [*to* FIRST GUARD]. Let's get goin'!

[*The scene darkens, as though a heavy cloud were passing over.*]

FIRST GUARD. My God, that's a spook black cloud roofin' down on us!

SECOND GUARD. Looks though th' Serpent mighta blown off Bare Hill!

FARMER. Le's get goin'! You fellas got flashlights? [*The two* GUARDS *show flashlights.*] Ladies, c'n you drive yer car?

WIFE [*tremulous and weeping*]. Yes, but . . .

FARMER. Le's have Sam drive it. . . . He's a good driver. An' I'll go with th' Professor.

GEOLOGIST. There's only room for two. . . .

BLONDE MARY. Then you can't go with us, Mister!

FARMER. All right! I'll ride with Sam and th' lady. An' you follow our tail-lights close, Professor.

GEOLOGIST. Don't know as I can see.
BLONDE MARY. Yes, we'll follow your lights, Mister.
FIRST GUARD. If anything's wrong, honk yer horn.
BLONDE MARY. I will. Come on, Professor. Put a bit of light in our path, will you?
SECOND GUARD. I'll light 'em to th' car, 'n then go down.
FIRST GUARD. 'Ll you be following down t' th' Point, Pete?
SECOND GUARD. I will *not!* I'm gettin' inside 'n lockin' th' gates! An' I ain't wishin' anybody any more bad luck 'n they're fixin' fer!
FIRST GUARD. Well, so long!
SECOND GUARD. G'night, everybody . . . 'n pleasant dreams! . . . Get goin', buddy . . . down where th' docs c'n take care o' both of us!
WIFE [*to the* FARMER]. Do you think he'll be all right?!
FARMER. Sure, missus! Sure! You city folks don't understand; but up here in the Lake Country we've lived with this business a *long* time . . . 'n while it's cert'nly mysteerious, it's a leetle somethin' t' make life interestin'! [*And they are out of sight.*]

[*The drums keep faintly beating.*]

[*The cloud passes and the sky and scene brighten a little with moonlight.*]

[*The drums rise to a faint crescendo, and die slowly to silence*]

After the CURTAIN

## ACT TWO

## IN THE "DOWN UNDER"

THE SCENE *is "down under," perhaps in the caves between Seneca and Cayuga Lakes, more likely in the bottom of Cayuga; it may move from place to place; at times it is light; at times dark; effects of shimmering green water appear intermittently, and now and then a strong greenish-yellow light as of rays of the sun into deep water.*

*In the center and across the back is a structure of stratified rocks. Through a crevice in the rocks the* GREAT SERPENT'S *head protrudes. A spring is piped out through a faucet on the face of a rock; on another rock is a large reel for taking up line.*

*There is a large heavy box down center. A beer keg; fish baskets or creels; two or three small brass cannon of 1600 design; a few timbers, boxes, and rocks to sit on; and an engine wheel from the* Frontenac *are variously distributed and worked into the setting.*

[*The opening curtain discloses standing on stage: the* OLD MAN OF THE LAKES, *in a generally nautical outfit;* OLD BILL, *who came with Sullivan and dug in; the Taughannock Indian "Giant,"* TAUGGY, *who paces gloomily;* WANETA, *the pretty Indian Maid;* TESS OF THE STORM COUNTRY; *tall* SPINKSTER JOHN SMITH, *of Bare Hill on Canandaigua Lake; the* SCIENTIST; *and the* SERPENT HIMSELF.]

[*On the opening of the curtain* BILL *rings a dinner-bell till ready.*]

BILL [*seeing the audience is settled and ready to listen*]. All right, we can go ahead with Act Two!

[*The characters sit; except the* OLD MAN OF THE LAKES, *who addresses the audience.*]

MAN OF THE LAKES. Well, folks, this Act Two scene is "down under" . . . right mysterious in its way, too . . . these caverns under th' high hills, an' runnin' betwixt th' lakes, an' below th' waters . . . an' mebbe into th' very bottom o' Seneca or Cayuga, deep down five-six hundred feet, below sea-bottom so the Scientist over there says . . . right mysterious . . . believe it or not.

An' as nobody's been able to settle just where "down under" is, but as everybody knows it tunnels around for miles in th' limestone an' salt-rock caves, this scene here has t' be kinda flexible. . . . You've gotta prepare to think it's movin' around almost anywhere. . . . Sometimes it's light an' gay with shimmerin' bright light; sometimes dark as deep dungeon caverns; sometimes they's a ghostish green light like a powerful sun dippin' into deep blue water, er mebbe colored Northern Lights waverin' phosphorescent-like among the fish . . . [*He laughs and blows smoke from his pipe.*] . . . Yes, sir, it's pretty shifty "down under," an' you'll have to take 'er as she comes an' goes . . . just so long as we end up in deep water off Goodwin's Point, that is, what used to be Goodwin's . . . Taughannock to you folks!

Now don't anybody get worried about us that's livin' down under in this limbo, kinda; 'cause we're all eyemaginary characters that wouldn't have no life at all if it weren't for all these legends about th' Lake Guns an' such! As a matter o' fact, we've been kept pretty spry, some of us fer over a hundred years, some of us fer less, tryin' t' keep up with th' folks up above . . . an' once in a while playin' a little joke on 'em all on our own!

Now . . . this here that rung th' bell is Ole Bill fer short. Bill Sullivan. . . .

BILL. That's me, folks . . . old Bill Sullivan . . . an' howdy, an' glad ta meetcha!

## THE LAKE GUNS

MAN OF THE LAKES. Bill come in here with Sullivan's expedition in 1779 an' dug in t' stay; that's why he's Sullivan. An' what Ole Bill don't know 'r make out t' know, 'r make up, an' what deviltry he ain't been up to . . .

[*A shiny red anchor is lowered from above.*]

BILL. Lookit what ta hell we got here! Fresh out o' th' hardware store! [*Goes to the anchor as it comes down and inspects it sourly.*]

MAN OF THE LAKES. Whose'll that be, Bill?

BILL. Well, I'd say this wuz some furriner. Prob'bly a hightoned cruiser fella from N'York. . . . They's always spewlin' oil over ev'rythin', put-puttin' around th' lake. . . . S'pose she'll be droppin' a line fer fish . . . after she's scared 'em all!

[*A shiny-looking hook, sinker, and silver spinner come down from above.*]

SPINKSTER JOHN. Yeah, there comes a bait an' sinker, like a lady's new hat!

MAN OF THE LAKES. Give him a carp. . . . He'll never know the diff!

BILL. How about givin' 'im them dopey dogfish slid down from shoal water!

MAN OF THE LAKES. Good enough fer *him!*

[BILL *puts on a dogfish and it goes up to the cruiser. Another simple line with a worm on it comes down.*]

MAN OF THE LAKES. Who's th' t'other? With a worm on his hook!

BILL. Looks like that might be Lou Smith from Ithaca . . . an' I bet *he rowed* out here like a *gent!*

MAN OF THE LAKES. Lou's a good guy, an' give him th' best ya got! An' hold on t' that anchor . . . that city-sailor'll think he's struck somethin' an' we c'n fill his ice-box with castoff dogfish 'n carp!

[*A flat stone on a rope for an anchor comes down.*]

BILL. Yep, that anchor's Lou Smith's all right . . . an' what

I call a sportsman's anchor. I'll see Lou gits a good catch! [*He hooks on a creel or basket of fish and it is drawn up.*]

MAN OF THE LAKES. Folks, ya see it's no idle life down here! . . . And that's, as I said, Ole Bill Sullivan! An' before they send down any more fish-lines fer us t' bite on, here's Waneta, th' Injun Maid from Waneta Lake way as has a mighty purty story t' tell you 'bout herself . . . [WANETA *bows.*] . . . deeciphered from a ole picture deerskin found where th' ole Catskill Turnpike runs between Lakes Lamoka an' Waneta, headin' from Tyrone t' Bath.

WANETA. I was a chieftain's daughter, betrothed to wed a warrior of my clan. But secretly I loved a youth of neighboring and bitter enemies. Night after night I paddled the black lake to lovers' trysts. One night as my canoe just touched the shore, a twig dropped for a warning . . . and in the stillness my love, Keuka, whispered to meet him at the lake's end, where the great pine tree made a tower in the sky. Slipping my canoe swiftly toward the pine, I heard, behind, the warwhoops of my tribe, and in a bright burst of the moon, I saw Keuka surrounded and wounded, but breaking through to rush along the shore to meet me at the pine. When his enemies, of my family and tribe, caught him beneath the pine and raised their tomahawks to kill . . . they saw Keuka stand, gaze fixed upon a little string of beads lying in shallow water off the shore, where I had stepped in quicksand and was swallowed in its depths . . . leaving my only trace in "the above" the circle of my sparkling beads, my name, and story.

Waneta's streams run south to join the mighty Susquehanna . . . but some of its bright waters sink in the underground to sparkle up at Crystal Springs . . . and by these hidden paths my spirit joins the streams that flow down to the depths of Seneca and Lake Cayuga.

MAN OF THE LAKES. Ain't no purtier story in all th' Finger Lakes than yourn, Waneta.

## · THE LAKE GUNS

[*A shiny line from the cruiser comes down again.*]
BILL. I'll let him dangle awhile . . . an' then hook 'im this sycamore root!
[*Another line with a worm comes down from* LOU SMITH.]
BILL. But I got a good catch o' fish here fer Lou Smith. [*And he hooks on another basket of fish, which goes up, as he calls.*] All right, Lou, there ya be. . . . Haul 'er in!
SCIENTIST. That friend of yours from Ithaca is making a good catch!
MAN OF THE LAKES. He'll have fish t' give away!
BILL. Lou's a friend o' ours an' he gits fish . . . an' if you're a friend o' Lou's *you* git fish. . . . He has 'em t' give away!
MAN OF THE LAKES. I bet they wonder in Ithicy how he does it!
BILL. Good fishermen never forgets their friends. . . . That's one way allays t' bring home a catch! [*A bottle of whiskey comes down on a line.*] An' this here bottle o' red-eye'll come in handy agin a damp day! [*They greet the bottle;* BILL *rings the bell, and* SPINKSTER JOHN *blows a great blast on his horn as it comes down.*]
[LOU SMITH'S *stone anchor starts to go up.*]
BILL and MAN OF THE LAKES. Much obleeged, Lou. . . . Come agin . . . any time . . . in season 'r out! So long! [*The anchor lifts out of sight.*]
BILL. I'll just aggervate this city-slicker a bit! [*He yanks the line to simulate a bite; the line yanks up and drops back.*]
MAN OF THE LAKES. An' now I want t' make ye acquainted with Spinkster John, wuz King o' Bare Hill over on Canandaigy Lake back more'n a hunnerd year ago. . . .
[SPINKSTER JOHN *rises slowly and advances slightly to be introduced.*]
MAN OF THE LAKES. This here's Spinkster John Smith, him of the long trumpethorn who become King o' Bare Hill after th' Great Serpent wuz druv down into th' lake 'n all these caverns. [JOHN *salutes.*] Tell 'em a bit about yerself, John.
SPINKSTER JOHN. I come into this country 'bout 1798, an' set-

tled on Bare Hill over on Canandaigy as he says. Somethin' sacred t' th' Injuns 'bout that hill an' there still is. . . . Settlers all looked toward it when somethin' wuz t' happen.

When I built th' big brush-heap fire a-blazin' t' th' sky, an' blew my long bellerin' boat-horn, th' boys gathered by th' hundreds t' march agin th' British when they landed at Sodus in 1812; they got in their boats 'n rowed off when they seen our squirrel rifles comin' . . . an' t' march agin th' British at Niagara; some tough fightin' there. . . . The War of 1812 wuz a big war in these parts, an' practically ever'body who could shoulder a rifle marched agin th' Redcoats sometime 'r other.

An' I built my fires on Bare Hill, an' blew my horn t' muster th' rollickin' rowdy boys fer the Anti-renter wars, an' agin th' Whigs, an' agin th' Masons that wuz after Morgan . . . an' fer no end o' noisy weddin' hornin's. . . . Th' boys liked *them* . . . an' such like.

An' I blew t' rally th' big wolf-hunt in 1811—an' I want t' tell ya 'bout that!—that started in Jerusalem, an' had a line o' twelve hundred hunters five rod apart stretchin' from Penn Yan eighteen mile into Steuben County on th' Cohocton River at Pine Hill . . . an' we druv th' wolves, swept 'em clean, climbin' right over Gannet Hill an' Stid Hill, an' anythin' that wuz in th' way, clear up t' Lake Ontario, sixty long mile! . . . An' they ain't been a wolf howl since, ez I've heard of! Though I can't say s'much fer rattlesnakes, so you folks be keerful if you come over our way!

An' along with my signal fires an' long bellerin' horn wuz sometimes Uncle Arch Armstrong from Flint Creek Hollow over in Middlesex beyond Seneca. . . . Uncle Arch wuz th' thunderinest drummer this country ever had. . . . They say he wuz th' greatest drummer-boy right through th' Revolution, an' General Washington said so. . . . An' they made 'im a big, deep drum headed with a hostyle Injun hide, skinned an' tanned . . . an' in 1825 Arch went clear to Can-

# THE LAKE GUNS

andaigy to drum fer Layfayette when he come through, an' ever'body made celebrations they ain't forgot yet! An' th' old Frenchie, when he heard that drummin', he knew nobody could drum like that 'cept Arch Armstrong that he remembered from the wars nigh fifty years before . . . an' th' General he got him down out o' his gilded carry-all in his shinin' leather boots an' he walked over t' th' tree an' called Arch by name, shook him by th' hand, an' kissed Arch frog-fashion on th' cheek, which shamed Arch no end seein' Arch wuz only used t' kissin' women . . . an' ever'body cheered, fer Uncle Arch wuz th' best drummer in th' world an' the home folks knew it, an' wuz glad Layfayette who'd heard all them furrin drum-beaters o' Europe thought so too!

MAN OF THE LAKES. An' Arch never drummed after that 'cept on th' Fourth o' July when he'd drum all day long, an' drink a long gallon o' whiskey, in recollection of when he wuz starvin' an' fightin' fer liberty in th' wars with General Washington.

BILL [*on a patriotic note*]. An' when Arch'd stand on Bare Hill an' drum, I bet that thunder'd go clear t' Niag'ra an' Newtown an' Stanwix an' Kingston before it really bounded back . . . on a clear carryin' day! An' if ya ask me what Injun drum's makin' these Lake Gun boomin's, I'd say *mebbe, mebbe* I'd say, 'twas Uncle Arch's, th' best drummer o' th' Finger Lakes an' of th' Revolution.

SPINKSTER JOHN. Arch wuz sure th' loudest drummer ever in this neck o' th' woods!

MAN OF THE LAKES. An' John here wuz th' loudest bellerin' boat-horn blower of th' inland waterways! Blow 'em a blow on yer horn, Spinkster, so they'll feel what it's like!

SPINKSTER JOHN. I blew when we got that bottle o' Caroline moonshine, an' th' echo oughta be bouncin' back about now from th' Bristol Hills or Hayvana er som'eres! Listen!

[*They listen, hand to ear; and a zooming toot-toot-toot echoes from backstage: it echoes again, louder; it echoes a third time, loud enough to blow the audience out of their seats.*]

SPINKSTER JOHN [*nodding approvingly*]. Like all these here lake echoes! Louder'n nature!

MAN OF THE LAKES. Spinkster John here c'n twang th' guitar, too, an' sing right loud when he's stirred t' it. . . . An' here's Tess of the Storm Country . . . [TESS *curtsies.*] . . . but you've mebbe read a whole book about her, 'r kin if ya want to. . . . An' here's the Scientist who's got ever'thin' figgered out, though sometimes it don't seem much use t' us ordinary folks! [*The* SCIENTIST *shakes his head gloomily.*] . . . An' here's the Sarpint o' Bare Hill himself, 'r what's left o' him. . . . His t'other head some says got stuck in th' caverns between th' lakes an' makes them Lake Guns, an' this feller gives some evidence that's so! [*He pats the* SERPENT *on the head and tickles him; the* SERPENT *opens his mouth and emits a great drumming sound; his mouth closes with a bang; and his great electric eyes blink. The* OLD MAN OF THE LAKES *scratches and pats the* SERPENT'S *head, and winks at the audience.*]

[*The* SERPENT'S *mouth opens again; with louder drummings and more violent blinkings.*]

MAN OF THE LAKES. Welll! I guess that means that somebody's on their way down from above! [*The* SERPENT *blinks rapidly.*] We're always gettin' interrupted! But before they git here I'd like t' give ya a sketch o' how we look at thin's, an' if Mr. Scientist here will tell ya what he knows about th' Lake Guns . . .

[*The* SCIENTIST *advances center from right; the Taughannock Indian,* TAUGGY, *advances center from left.*]

MAN OF THE LAKES. An' I suppose mebbe you're a bit curious 'bout this box I been sittin' on, an' these ole French cannon, an' th' windin' reel, an' other contraptions round here. . . .

[TAUGGY *advances to the* OLD MAN OF THE LAKES, *holding out a sheaf of newspaper clippings, tapping his chest,*

## THE LAKE GUNS

*and gesturing toward audience as though he wanted to be introduced too.*]

MAN OF THE LAKES. Now, wait a minute, Tauggy! Here, Tess, you c'n read. . . . Come read these ole newspapers over to 'im agin. [*To audience.*] We hafta keep readin' 'em over 'n over t' 'im. . . . It's a damned nuisance.

TESS [*towing the Indian away*]. Come, Tauggy, I'll read them to you again.

SCIENTIST [*advancing to address the audience*]. Ladies and Gentlemen: One legendary explanation of the Lake Guns is that the sounds are made by the ancient stone Indians who wander through the under-ground and fall off the subterranean cliffs, or plunge off precipices in the caverns. Tauggy is one of that tribe. An over-sized brother of his was dug up in 1879 above Taughannock Falls, the Taughannock Giant, and received a lot of attention and got in the newspapers. Tauggy has been very envious of his brother's success; but all he can do about it is to try to let people know he's a brother of that well-known giant, and shine in reflected glory. But the stony old fellow can't read or speak, so . . . well, imagine yourself in his melancholy place! . . . And every time he hears those newspaper clippings read, he feels worse!

TESS. He feels better now, don't you, Tauggy?

[TAUGGY *shakes his head in lugubrious dissent, with a gesture toward the audience.*]

BILL. He wants 'em read out t' all th' people, Tess . . . go ahead, you've been introduced!

[TESS *takes the papers from* TAUGGY *and addresses the audience, while* TAUGGY *stands by in simple caveman delight.*]

TESS. Tauggy's brother, the so-called Taughannock Giant, was discovered above Taughannock Falls on July 2, 1879, . . . ten years after the famous giant had been unearthed at Cardiff south of Syracuse. News of the discovery of the petrified prehistoric monster spread like wild-fire, and on the Fourth of July, Trumansburg and Jacksonville were crowded, and all the roads leading to Taughannock were blocked with carriages from miles around. Scientists from Cornell, Hobart, and Syracuse, and other nearby colleges, declared the wonder authentic. They found especially conclusive scientific evidence in the fact that the petrification contained all the chemical elements of the human body. The Taughannock giant was six feet seven inches tall, eighteen inches through the chest and weighed nearly eight hundred pounds . . . Tauggy is only a dwarf member of the tribe, and this adds to his sorrow.

These clippings of Tauggy's give but a hint of the vast publicity. Proprietor Thompson of the Taughannock Falls Hotel had by some lucky chance just laid in his summer's supplies and was able at high prices to keep the throngs from going too hungry! And I know Tauggy particularly wants you to hear the ode—it's a rather rustic ode—about his giant brother, which was read at a celebration for everybody who made money out of him, held at the old Taughannock Falls Hotel in late August, 1879—about a month after the great event. The manuscript of these verses was turned up only recently among some secret archives in the town of Trumansburg. Waneta has learned it by heart and can recite it for you very prettily. [TESS *bows* WANETA *toward the audience.*]

WANETA. Let our hearts be glad and merry
          With the porter and the sherry!
          And for deeper springs of gladness
          Count your shillings, without sadness—
          Folks were glad to pay to see
          Out of curiositee!

          Where Taghanic's Gi'nt presided
          O'er these chasms lofty-sided—
          Lift the glass and drink together!
          Do not pause to ponder whether

## THE LAKE GUNS

Truth is better than good gold
Paid to hear old wives' tales told.

Did he really live, fools wonder,
On these cliffs, or wander under?
Could we not dig up another
Sister giant, or a brother?
Count your coin before you go
And vote an ill-considered "no"!

Glasses high and drink to Tauggy
As he lies there rather groggy—
Not perhaps as good as Cardiff,
Still 'twould be a little hard if
We should not present him thanks
For the money in our banks!

Toast! Our stone man's had his glory!
Only whispered be his story.
Let our ledgers' profit pages
All be buried with the ages.
Folks may never wiser be
If we keep the mystery.

[TAUGGY *gestures violent assent; he,* WANETA, *and* TESS *bow to the audience;* TAUGGY *takes his clippings from* TESS *and bounces jauntily.*]

TESS. How can we keep the mystery when Tauggy insists on everybody hearing all about the Taghanic Giant? Well, I hope someday they'll give our Tauggy a party, and drink his health in circling bumpers!

WANETA. Let's give Tauggy a drink from our healing springs! [*She takes the tin cup off the pipe, turns the faucet, and draws* TAUGGY *a drink. As she does so they chant the Chant of the Country of Marvelous Springs.*]

ALL [*chant*]. Oh-h-h-h! This-is-a-country-of-marvelous-springs!
BILL [*chanting*]. When-we-come-with-Sullivan-we-found-wonnerful-springs . . . bubblin'-fair-cold-water . . . sulfur-springs,-burnin'-springs,-oily-springs, . . . [*Conversationally.*] but we never found th' secret Injun salt springs!
SCIENTIST [*conversationally*]. They found salt springs up at Montezuma!
ALL [*chanting as* TAUGGY *drinks and beats time to the chant*].

    Oh-oh-oh! This-is-a-country-of-wonderful-springs!

        Saline Springs!
        Sulfur Springs!
        Burning Springs!
        Curative Springs!

        Glen Springs!
        Bristol Springs!
        Clifton Springs!
        Wethersfield Springs!

        Dryden Springs!
        Spencer Springs!
        Sheldrake Springs!
        Livonia Springs!

        Grove Springs!
        Union Springs!
        Silver Springs!
        Slaterville Springs!

    Tonic—Sedative—Laxative—Springs!—Natural Springs! Oh! This-is-the—country—of—Wonderful Springs!

[TAUGGY *finishes drinking with a gasp for breath.*]
SPINKSTER JOHN [*still chanting*]. And - the - best - was - the - Crystal - Springs - to - Barrington - beyond - Jerusalem - that - cured - you - whatever - you - drank - the - water - *for!*

## THE LAKE GUNS

BILL [*displaying a case of bottled water*]. An' they're bottlin' th' old waters at Slaterville agin, an' ya c'n git 'em any time ya feel th' need of 'em!

[SPINKSTER JOHN *and* BILL *have a drink while the* SCIENTIST *continues, and* TAUGGY *acts out in dumb-show an obligato of interest and wonder.*]

SCIENTIST. There are, ladies and gentlemen, . . . as I was saying when interrupted! . . . various scientific explanations of the Seneca and Cayuga Lake Guns. Some say it is great bubbles of marsh gas breaking at the surface of the water.

WANETA. Some say it is the funeral drums of the Senecas mourning their lost lands!

SCIENTIST. Some say it is the explosion of gas accumulated in the fissures of the rocks expanded by hot sultry days.

TESS. Or echoes of Champlain's war-drums scared the Iroquois so they never forgot them in their dreams!

SCIENTIST. Some say it's great rock-slides off the underwater cliffs, some of which are hundreds of feet high.

[*From above a sounding line descends.*]

BILL. Hey, another damned fool's tryin' t' see how deep th' lake is! An' tryin' ta do it with a two-pound lead! . . . Why the undertow'll flatten that line out like it wuz a trollin' line from a speed boat!

MAN OF THE LAKES. Well, just do the usual, 'n hook it on th' reel 'n keep windin'! When they run out o' line, then as us'al, they gotta declare they ain't no bottom!

[TAUGGY *hooks the line on the reel and winds it down; they perhaps take turns at the cranking.*]

SCIENTIST. Some say it's salt mines collapsing and caving in under the lake, and driving up great bubbles of compressed air to burst on the surface.

SPINKSTER JOHN. Some say it's them cannon fired from Buffalo t' Staten Island for openin' th' Clinton ditch . . . thousands of 'em . . . still echoin' from th' hills!

SCIENTIST. Some say the lakes purify themselves by "turning

over" with violent gaseous explosions, and dead fish floating up.

MAN OF THE LAKES. Some say it's somebody dynamitin' fish!

WANETA. The Cayugas say when fishermen tell too big a whopper, the fish rise to the surface and laugh like thunder!

SCIENTIST. Some say the gas, before they drove gas wells, burst up through the bottom strata of the lakes.

SPINKSTER JOHN. Some say th' Bare Hill Serpent's caught in th' caves between th' lakes, an's blowin' t' git out!

[*The* SERPENT *opens his mouth and guns and blinks.*]

SCIENTIST. Some say . . . the gas drillers over beyond Watkins say . . . that now all the gas is drilled, the guns are silenced forever.

BILL, TESS and the OLD MAN OF THE LAKES. Why! plenty of people been hearin' 'em all this summer!

[*The* SERPENT *opens his mouth and guns and blinks again.*]

WANETA. Some say it's the echoes of Indian ghosts drumming their old rituals in the gorges along the lake shores!

TESS. Some say it's Catskill Dutchmen Washington Irving brought up to build his house at Cayuga . . . so he wouldn't get lonesome . . . playing bowls in the hills!

SCIENTIST. We tell you what science has said. *I* shall seek no farther to find out. And I advise others not to. Scientists laughed at the old-timers along Seneca who said he who sought the secret of the Guns would die . . . but that so-called superstition *I* found was all too true.

MAN OF THE LAKES. That's a fact! Poor young feller'd just decided t' make a repitation solvin' them Lake Guns, when th' Big Flood come an' swashed him an' his '35 Ford inta deep water where ya never come up . . . som'eres off Glenora!!

BILL. Yessir . . . there's mighty strange things hereabouts! Now . . . take it right over to Union Springs, Springport that wuz, them great springs there that boils up like a river, where do they come from? Nobody knows. . . . Mebbe from Owasco Lake, mebbe from Skaneateles Lake clear under ground under Owasco, 'r mebbe from Keuka divin' under *both* Seneca and Cayuga!

Yessir! Why, where we went through Springport with Sullivan in 1779, t' burn th' Injuns out o' Great Gully, they wuz a big limestone crick runnin' right across th' rocks an' fallin' roarin' into th' cove . . . an' when surveyors come t' chain it fer th' Military Tract they wan't hair nor hide o' that there river! . . . Gone, kerflooey! Underground! Yessir!

An' that there kag he's settin' on! Where'd that come from? I'll tell ye! It come from th' Cold Spring Brewery over to Auburn! I wuz feelin' a bit warm one day back in th' '90's . . . hot like a bit o' lager'd taste good . . . an' I just dove down an' followed th' current 'n come out o' Cold Spring at th' Brewery an' grabbed that kag an' swum back with it agin th' current! Good fifteen mile underground! An' damned good lager that they don't make round here so good since Prohibition! You c'n prove it fer yourself. . . . You c'n *see* that big Cold Spring boilin' up there right alongside York Street just a block 'r so off Route 5-20 on th' edge o' Auburn! [*The anchor starts to pull up, having caught on it a bit of shaft from the old* Frontenac.] Hey, this city-cruiser feller's gettin' under weigh!

MAN OF THE LAKES. Pull 'im back an' git that there souvenir of th' old Steamboat *Frontenac* off his flukes! One rusty wheel offen th' old *Frontenac's* worth a lakeful o' stinkin' gasoline noise-makers!

[TAUGGY *and* BILL *rescue the wheel and let the anchor go up.*]

BILL [*cupping his hands and yelling up*]. Go up into th' Barge Canal an' *stay* there!

[*The* OLD MAN OF THE LAKES *takes the wheel and eyes it sentimentally, moving down to address the audience.*]

MAN OF THE LAKES [*doing it poetic-like*]. I tell ya, folks, th' good ole days on these lakes wuz done when th' *Frontenac* burnt

. . . white-sailed cargo-boats puttin' off fer Oswego, 'n Albany, 'n New York . . . plaster 'n grain-boats comin' down to Ithicy 'n Watkins loaded fer Owego an' Elmira, th' Susquehanna an' Baltimore . . . 'r transship over th' mountains through Pittsburg t' th' Mississippi an' New Orleans . . . fer in them days these parts wuz th' breadbasket o' th' North! . . . Ferries a criss-crossin' o' th' lakes . . . long canal-boat tows from th' Erie Canal . . . packets linkin' th' Catskill Turnpike t' Geneva an' Cayuga Bridge fer Ohio, Indiana, Nebraska an' th' Far West . . . gleamin' side-wheelers crowded with travellers, picnickers, an' sightseers. . . . It wuz boats an' water made this country, an' you can't even *see* some of it 'cept from a boat! . . . An' the ole *Frontenac*—[*This cue gives* SPINKSTER JOHN *an idea and he warms up his guitar*]—she wuz th' best of 'em! An' when she passed we turned t' hard roads an' sixty mile an hour an' see what ya can if yer hat don't blow off! No wonder th' folks up north on Cayuga Lake made up a ballad 'bout th' burnin' o' th' *Frontenac!* How 'bout singin' that one fer th' folks, Spinkster?

[SPINKSTER JOHN *nods assent, twangs his guitar, and sings the ballad, to a free approximation of the tune of "My Bonnie Lies over the Ocean"; the last line is repeated as a chorus. The others in rotation intone firmly the passages between the verses, and join in the chorus.*]

    The story my song has to tell you
    Is the saddest these lakes ever learnt—
    'Tis how in a gale on Cayuga
    Th' side-wheeler *Frontenac* burnt.

WANETA. She - was - the - finest - and - fastest - of - all - the - fleet - sailing - between - Cayuga - on - the - New - York - Central - and - Ithaca - Landing.

    The *Frontenac* she was a beauty
    A hundred and thirty foot long—

# THE LAKE GUNS

Slender 'n white, with plenty of power
For speed, when they gave her the gong.

MAN OF THE LAKES. She - carried - four - hundred - passengers - and - set - a - darn - good - table - at - a - decent - price - and - her - tall - smokestack - with - 'er - plume - o' - smoke - and - 'er - red - walkin' - beam - a-rockin' - up - an' - down - wuz - fer - thirty-seven - year - one - o' - th' - sights - o' - th' - Finger - Lakes - country.

'Twas a Sattiday 'long in th' summer
July 29, 1907
They beached her ablaze up at Farley's
An' th' lives lost wuz ten er eleven.

SCIENTIST. She'd - left - Sheldrake - on - her - noon - trip - north - bucking - a - northwest - gale - when - off - Dill's - Cove - a - kid - saw - smoke - coming - through - the - hurricane - deck - abaft - the - gallows - frame - stairs.

It wuz blowin' a fifty mile wester
With th' waves rollin' harder and higher—
Life-boats was no good nor preservers
They jumped in the surf from the fire.

BILL [*dramatically*]. She - come - into - shore - silent; - they - didn't - whistle - for - they - wuz - usin' - ever' - pound - of - steam - fer - speed - but - Ferris - at - Farley's - seen - her - comin' - in - fast - 'nd - soundless - in - a - cloud - o' - smoke - with - flames - burstin' - afore - th' - sta'board - wheel - box; - And - he - yelled - 'nd - run - 'nd - all - along - th' - shore - campers - run - like - mad - where - she - wuz - headin' - into - shore, - along - th' - rocky - shore - knee - deep - in - bogs - an' - ooze, - seein' - th' - women - and - children - in - holiday - attire - droppin' - helpless - in - th' - soft - ooze - bar - off - Great - Gully - brook, - where - th' - rollin' - surf - battered - 'em - under - while - th' - roarin' - flames - licked - out - t' - git - 'em!

> Oh, Melvin P. Brown wuz th' Captain
> An' he wuz a hero that day—
> He drug folks ashore by the dozen
> Th' men wuz no help—so they say.

TESS [*with satiric force*]. One - passenger - safe - on - the - beach - yells - to - Jim - Murphy - of - Ithaca - who - was - doing - a - hero's - work - by - rescuing - eight: "Five - hundred - dollars - to - the - man - who - saves - my - wife!" - And - Jim - yells - back: "Save - her - yourself - you - big - fat - slob!" - (If - you - think - that's - what - he - said!) - The - woman - was - a - better - man - than - her - husband - and - swam - herself - ashore; - but - whether - he - paid - HER - the - five - hundred - nobody - ever - knew; - nobody - could - find - him - afterwards - to - find - out. - Probably - *not!*

> She wuz gone before you'd a thought it!
> Et up by th' blisterin' blaze.
> She sank a charr'd hulk to th' bottom
> Whilst th' rescuers fought in th' waves.

MAN OF THE LAKES. An' - what's - left - o' - her - lies - in - th' - mud - off - Great - Gully; - her - stern - swung - round - toward - shore - by - th' - gale; - her - bow - a-pointin' - out - into - th' - lake - along - th' - course - she - steered - on - 'er - last - run.

> The *Frontenac* she wuz a beauty!
> She's gone an' she'll never come back
> To sail o'er th' lake in her shinin' white paint—
> She's gone—an' she'll never come back!

[*They all sing in harmony a slow, sentimentalized repeat of the last stanza.*]

> The *Frontenac* she wuz a beauty!
> She's gone—an' she'll never come back
> To sail o'er th' lake in her shinin' white paint—
> She's gone—an' she'll never come back!

[SPINKSTER JOHN *takes a bow at the end of the ballad.*]
[*The* SERPENT *opens his mouth, drums loud, and blinks longer and more rapidly than before.*]

[*The ballad scene is intended to form a transition from the minstrel-show hilarity of this first section of the Act to the tenser drama and suggested mystery of the section which follows, with the* OLD MAN OF THE HILLS *continuing in a vein of mad hilarity and complete satisfaction with events through to the close of the Act.*]

BILL. Whoever they be somebody's comin' down!
   [*The* SERPENT *gapes and drums again.*]
MAN OF THE LAKES. Guess they're right here.
   [*Enter the* OLD MAN OF THE HILLS *and the two* INDIANS *leading the party from Butcher Hill;* HASKEL, MINNA, *and* JOHN *are awed but curious;* JOHN *shows a tense premonition of some impending doom.*]
BILL. Welcome, strangers, come right in! Anybody's welcome who feels th' call t' come!
OLD MAN OF THE HILLS. Here's some hears th' call of down in under . . . feels it stirrin' in th' blood. . . . [*The* SERPENT *drums;* MINNA *and* HASKEL *retreat in alarm.*] That's just th' Bare Hill Sarpint we wuz talkin' about.
JOHN. We followed that sound, yes; but that Serpent means nothing to me. . . . It is something else!
MINNA [*grasping* WANETA]. What is it we Indians believe explains the Drums, . . . the Guns?
WANETA. We Indians? [*Looking at her intently.*] Yes, I see. . . . You are Indian too!
MINNA. Yes! I am an Indian too! What are the Guns?
WANETA. They speak of old Indian legends of the Guns . . . but I know no Indian legends of the Guns. Perhaps the drummings came with the white man . . . perhaps with the white man's cannon here!

SPINKSTER JOHN. Sure, there's a *good* story about them cannon, lady.
HASKEL. What could these cannon have to do with it?
BILL. Now, there's a very probable sitooation, mister! These here French cannon got in th' lake off Taghanic Point this way. . . . You tell it straighter'n me, Spinkster. . . . Tell 'im.
SPINKSTER JOHN. These cannon o' brass, mister, wuz left by th' French hopin', I s'pose, th' Injuns ud use 'em agin th' British. But they never got t' fire 'em till Sullivan's army come through, 'n then they didn't know how t' handle 'em . . . an' when they tried t' fire 'em agin Sullivan's attack on th' Point, th' cannon just kicked 'emselves right out into th' lake . . . an' here they been ever since! . . . caught in th' rocks! 'N sometimes when th' Northern Lights is right they begin bangin' away agen about sundown, an' on into th' night, fillin' th' water with streaks o' fire . . . an' boomin' an' echoin' along th' lake bottom an' breakin' out into th' high air . . . sometimes in big bubbles like cannon smoke rings, 'r spouts o' water like a big fish jumpin' high an' comin' down kersplash 'n bellyflop!
OLD MAN OF THE HILLS. Th' Northern Lights is goin' t' sing tonight!
JOHN. And I feel something singing and pounding in my veins! Something mysterious, and overpowering.
HASKEL. And this chest? . . . What's this chest with the cross got to do with it?

[*All the "down-under" people shy off and look reticent and mysterious.*]

MINNA [*quickly breaking the pause*]. What mystery's in the chest? Anything to do with us?
OLD MAN OF THE HILLS [*chuckling*]. Now don't push 'em *too* hard on that, lady!
HASKEL [*moving toward the chest*]. Let's open it and see!
ALL THE "DOWN-UNDER" MEN [*rushing to stop him*]. Easy with that there box!

HASKEL [*backing away*]. What's the mystery about it?
MAN OF THE LAKES. That's just it . . . mebbe a secret no man's suppose t' learn.
MINNA. The secret of the Guns?
SCIENTIST [*moving away*]. Not for me. . . . I want none of its secrets!
SPINKSTER JOHN. We don't plan even t' talk about it, my friend! Leave 'er lay!
TESS [*advancing to address the characters and audience, her right hand pointing at the chest*]. Perhaps that chest contains Indian lead from Great Gully, that lead no white man's ever found; except an Indian bullet found him in brain or heart, too dead to tell if he had known what laid him low. . . .

Or Spanish gold that all along these lakes is buried as all men know . . . gold men have sought with magic and black prayers, digging at midnight by the proper moon, in ritual silence to confound the spell, guns loaded with the magic silver ball to kill the lion-big monster guards the gold . . . always to drop their shovels at the last and flee, as the black beast, tail curved above its arching back and spitting fire, leaps at the throat of him who first strikes coin, and sucks his blood!

This may be Rulloff's chest in which he sank his wife and babe heavied with stones in deep Cayuga . . . though on the scaffold he denied 'twas so! That mystery we cannot break. . . . Stand back!

Or here may be the Universal Friend's, Jemima's, secret burial spot . . . not to be known of men . . . unless she rise again of her own will!

Into these caves from underneath the Hill Cumorah may be the golden book of Mormon sank for keeping . . . while invisible above, the mighty Angel stands, ready to sear with pillared flame all desecrating hands and eyes!
SPINKSTER JOHN. Mebbe it's th' Devil himself in there! For 'twas a box like that, see that cross on it? . . . When Johnny Race wrastled th' Devil he woke up an' found a-settin' on

his chest an' chokin' him . . . wrastled him all through Lent, all round Keuka Lake, 'n wrastlin' him out on Bluff Point on Easter mornin', Johnny an' him rolled down hill through a buryin' ground kerflunk into an empty coffin layin' there . . . Johnny on top! An' Johnny slapped on th' cover, an' quick as quick-silver marked a cross on't with his huntin' knife . . . an' th' Devil wuz caught! An' Johnny . . . he wuz th' strongest man in th' seven counties, Johnny . . . he heaved th' Devil, coffin an' all, durn near ez fur as I cud uv myself, from Bluff Point four mile out into th' lake . . . where he sank down out from Urbana where th' grape-wine comes from!

No sir! I shouldn't be a bit surprised! Keep that cover on! And keep that cross-mark always good an' clean! [*He marks the cross deeper with his hunting knife.*] 'Course th' way th' world is there must be a Devil loose *somewhere!* But I'm fer takin' no chances, an' bein' on th' safe side . . . with an extry spike 'r two! [*He hammers the nails tighter, and drives in an extra spike.*]

[*They all move back a little.*]

[*The* SERPENT *blinks and gapes, but no drumming issues from his mouth. Instead, deep drums sound from the rear, beating in slow funeral-march time.*]

[*They all stand listening and alarmed; the high-pitched gleeful laugh of the* OLD MAN OF THE HILLS *shrills out.*]

[*The scene darkens.*]

SCIENTIST. Listen! listen! Those are the death-march drums!

[*A distant bugle blows.*]

BILL. He's bein' marched agin to execution!

SPINKSTER JOHN. Yeah, but where is he?

JOHN [*advancing in center to the box*]. I know now what this box is for me. . . . [*He throws himself down on the chest, facing front with staring eyes and grasping the chest with wide-spread arms.* HASKEL *and* MINNA *shrink back and hold each other.*] My coffin! . . . with bandaged eyes, kneel on

my coffin . . . before my open grave . . . face the musket . . . hear the death drums roll . . . the command to fire. . . . [*He collapses half-fainting on the chest.*]
[*The drums roll louder.*]
[*The distant bugle sounds closer, louder, more threatening.*]
[*The* OLD MAN OF THE HILLS, OLD BILL, *and* SPINKSTER JOHN *advance toward* JOHN *pointing at him.*]
BILL. It's him . . . it's him . . . ez I see 'im in '79 . . . th' spittin' image! [*Calling like a trumpet.*] Death . . . fer desertin' in th' face o' the enemy! . . . Face th' firin' squad . . . !
[*A piercing cry of "John! John! John!" comes from the left wing.* JOHN *rises and staggers toward it, as his* WIFE *dressed in 18th century costume enters left; they embrace passionately.*]
[*The drums are louder. The bugle sounds closer, louder, more threatening.*]
HASKEL [*shouting*]. Man the guns . . . !
[MINNA, TAUGGY, WANETA *and the two* INDIANS *stand by the brass cannon, as crews to load and fire them.*]
JOHN [*to his* WIFE]. Goodbye, my dear . . . goodbye . . . goodbye. . . .
WIFE. Goodbye . . . !
[JOHN'S WIFE *slips from his arms in a faint.* TESS *catches her and lets her down easily to the ground, cradling the* WIFE'S *head in her lap.*]
HASKEL [*shouting commandingly*]. Ready at the guns! . . .
MINNA [*from the other cannon in a fierce voice.*] Ready!
[*Bits of costume they throw on give the* OLD MAN OF THE LAKES, OLD BILL, *and* SPINKSTER JOHN *a vague resemblance to British frontier soldiers.*]
[*In step with the beating drums,* JOHN *marches to the chest and kneels on it;* SPINKSTER JOHN *bandages his eyes.*]
[*The* OLD MAN OF THE HILLS, *who has been laughing,*

*dancing and clapping his hands in wild-eyed glee since the great drums began to beat, mounts high in the center with a bass drum and beats in time with the rhythm as a military drum breaks into a roll which continues to the end. The great drums and the bass drums suddenly stop. The roll continues. The* OLD MAN OF THE LAKES *and* OLD BILL *stand at attention right center.*]

[*The bugle blows piercingly, close at hand.*]

[JOHN *tears the bandage from his eyes and faces the muskets in the right wing.*]

MAN OF THE LAKES [*saluting*]. Ready . . . aim . . . fire. . . .

[*The cannon and muskets flash and boom. The bass drum strikes with them.*]

[*There is a pause, while the roll continues; and* BILL *intones loudly in the pause above the roll of the drum.*]

BILL. As long as the grass grows, an' th' waters run, an' th' story holds true, he's got to be dyin'! . . . got to be dyin'!

MAN OF THE LAKES. Ready . . . aim . . . fire! . . .

[*The cannon and muskets flash and the drums boom.*]

[*Another pause; while the roll continues.*]

BILL. Over an' over again, as long as th' drums beat, his blood'll have t' be dyin' . . . be dyin'!

MAN OF THE LAKES. Ready . . . aim . . . fire! . . .

[*The cannon and muskets flash and boom again.*]

[*Another pause; while the roll continues.*]

BILL. Over, an' over, an' over again . . . in their dreams they'll be dyin' . . . !

[*The cannon and muskets flash and boom softer. They flash and boom again, and die away. The roll continues diminuendo.*]

[*The lights fade, except for a spot on the* OLD MAN OF THE HILLS *and his bass drum high in center, and the great glowing eyes of the* SERPENT *which blink slowly. The* OLD MAN'S *bass drum keeps a slow beat, with the great drum behind diminuendo.*]

[*The* OLD MAN OF THE HILLS *laughs wildly.*]
[*The lights fade out to darkness except in the eyes of the* SERPENT *which blink three times, then stand in an unblinking stare.*]
[*In the distance, dying away, the bugle blows Taps.*]
[*In the darkness the drums sound faintly; and the* SERPENT'S *eyes stare.*]

## SLOW CURTAIN

[*The drums sound on for a moment.*]

## ACT THREE

## ON TAGHANIC POINT

THE SCENE *is on Taghanic Point, looking north. There are two or three trees and a hedge row in the background; a table and benches to the left; a fireplace with a low fire at the right. It is a "white night" with a blue sky of stars.*

[The Boy *and* The Girl *are playing a portable phonograph at the left end of the table.*]
[The Man *in shirtsleeves, dressed somewhat like a fisherman or a hunter, comes quietly in and sits at the right of the table, facing toward the lake at the right.*]

The Girl [*producing another record*]. This hot rhythm doesn't seem quite the thing on a night like this. How about trying this?
The Boy [*stopping the phonograph*]. That's a fact! Not under this sky and stars! What've you got? . . .
The Girl. Choice of the Stephen Foster, or the waltz. . . .
The Boy. I'll like either. Let's put 'er on.
The Girl. It's so lovely and mysterious, maybe we'd better play nothing.
The Boy [*laughing*]. Just look at the stars, and listen to the waves, and hold hands?
The Girl. Yes!
The Boy. Well, we'll try this *one*. You know I've got to be getting *you home!* [*He starts the old waltz record.*]
The Girl. I *know!* It's an ungodly hour!
The Boy. You'll just about meet the milkman.

# THE LAKE GUNS

THE GIRL. Oh! I like that! [*She hums to the music and turns in a waltz step.*]
THE MAN [*turning to the young couple and speaking very pleasantly*]. Excuse me, I don't mean to intrude, but . . .
THE BOY [*a little uncertainly*]. Not at all, mister . . . if we're disturbing you . . .
THE MAN. Oh, no, I like that tune. I grew up to it.
THE GIRL. It *is* nice, isn't it? . . . Old-fashioned but lovely!
THE MAN. Yes . . . I could see you folks liked it . . . and I thought maybe if you liked things like that, and a night like this, maybe you'd like to try to listen to the Lake Guns . . . if we could hear 'em. . . .
THE GIRL [*puzzled*]. Lake Guns?!
THE BOY. Well, I've heard about 'em! But I didn't suppose there was really anything to hear . . . just a story. . . .
THE MAN. I've heard them often. And this is one of the nights when . . .
THE GIRL. Turn it off, Bill. I want to hear.
 [*He turns off the phonograph.*]
THE MAN. Well, this is a fine night for them . . . maybe . . . after a hot day. . . . And looks like Northern Lights too . . . the Guns come with the Lights. Thought I could hear something from my cottage up the shore, and came down on the Point . . . this is a good place. 'Spect you'll see some other old-timers coming to listen here . . . maybe.
THE GIRL. Tell me about them. Guns, you say? What makes them?
THE MAN [*laughing*]. Well, there's different explanations . . . scientific and otherwise. . . . Some claim it's only fancy . . . or witching, or echoes! But maybe if you *want* to hear you can . . . lots of things *like* that, you know!
THE BOY. What do you think?
THE MAN. Well, I think the most reasonable explanation . . . that's why I came out on the Point . . . it was cannon the Indians had from the French, and when they was driven

out here on the point . . . maybe by Sullivan, I dunno . . . long ago, anyway . . . the Indians not knowing very well how to work the guns and snub 'em, they tried to hold 'em by hand. . . . They fired the battery—and guns, Indians and all, was kicked right out into the lake . . . right here off the Point . . . an' there they are now sometimes, down in the deep water, firing, firing . . . and when the Northern Lights is bright you can see the glow of the cannon fire in the water, 'n hear the boom of the sunken guns . . . ! Maybe it's all reflections, I dunno . . . but I like to think that. . . . Look, look! See the Northern Lights loom out! Listen!

THE GIRL. Listen!

[*The Guns are faintly heard.*]

THE MAN. Hear? Do you hear somethin'? . . . See that glow under the water when they sound?

THE BOY. I hear 'em! An' look at those pillars of light!

THE GIRL. Blue! Green! Purple! Dull red!

THE BOY. That's right! Hear that dull booming after the red shows in the lake! Like the sound takes time to reach you?

THE MAN. You're seein' something to remember!

THE GIRL. It's so weird and unearthly . . . and all so beautiful . . . it frightens me a little!

THE MAN. Yes, ma'am! Many that's seen it like you do, won't admit they've seen it.

THE BOY. They're dying down.

THE MAN. They come and go, sometimes, with the Lights. And sometimes I've been almost sure I saw the Phantom Canoe . . . white like a frosty roof in the moon . . . sliding fast as a squall over the smooth water . . . no paddlin' or nothing . . . just scudding along silent as a cloud cross the moon. . . . There's them as has seen it . . . sure!

THE GIRL. Do you suppose we could stay, Bill? It's awfully late!

THE BOY. Gosh, I'd like to . . . but you know your mother'll raise . . .

# THE LAKE GUNS

THE MAN. You might as well stay, young lady. I'll speak to your mother, know her well. I live just around the corner from you anyway ... though 'course you never noticed me. Knew you minute I saw you. Take after your mother, though bit taller and bigger-boned; and, if you don't mind my saying so, not quite so pretty as she was 't your age. [*Chuckling.*] She'll understand! Matter o' fact, twenty-five years ago, she an' I stayed darn near all night watchin' the Lights and listenin' for the Guns ... right here on this very beach ... 'course before they fixed it up as now. Your name's Margaret Sullivan, ain't it?

THE GIRL. Yes.

THE MAN. You see. You stay ... if you want to.

THE BOY. Here come the Lights again. Look at 'em climb right to the zenith!

THE MAN. I told you! Here come some people.

[*Into the scene come the* FARMER, BLONDE MARY *with the* GEOLOGIST, *the* GUARD *from* WILLARD, *and* JOHN'S WIFE. *She is on verge of tears and soon will weep bitterly.*]

THE MAN. Quiet if you don't mind, folks. We think maybe we're hearing the Lake Guns.

FARMER. Okay. That's what we're after hearin', too!

THE GUARD. My God, look at them Northern Lights roll again!

BLONDE MARY. Look, Prof! Whooo, look! Do you see 'em?

GEOLOGIST. I see something ... not very well ... you know my glasses....

THE MAN. Listen! Listen!

FARMER. I believe that's the Guns!

THE MAN. Ain't you Fred Sheppard from over beyond Butcher Hill?

FARMER. Yes.... Well, I'll be swigged, Tom Dean! Why, ain't seen you in ten year or near it. Say, Tom, ain't this some night ... an' you don't know the worst of it!

THE MAN. Whad'ya mean?

FARMER. The Old Man of the Hills is out ... an' half this

party's gone with him into the below. That's why she's scairt cryin'. . . . Her husband felt to go 'long with him.

THE MAN. Lord, Fred, the ole hare drummer ain't been seen that I heard of in fifty years! Not by nobody you'd believe!

FARMER. Well, you better believe it now! The Old Boy's out, sailin' high an' low, Indians an' all. . . . We're to meet 'em here when they come from under.

THE MAN. Maybe we'll see the Phantom Canoe. . . . What-d'ya think?

FARMER. *Anything* can happen on a hot, white night like this, with the lights rollin' and walkin' across the north 'n sheddin' a light to beat the full moon, 'n the water flat 'n polished like a black marble buryin' stone! An' the Old Boy himself rampagin' hill and deep water. . . .

THE GUARD. What's that white thing movin' under the cliffs across?

THE MAN. My God . . . the Ghost Canoe! No . . . no, there's a light on it, on a mast. . . .

THE GUARD. Yeah, that's right . . . must be a motorboat . . . big cruiser . . . yeah, hear 'er raddio. . . .

[*Across the water come strains of the "New World Symphony" from the cruiser.*]

THE GUARD. Big machine, too. This time o' night must be tuned into San Francisco!

BLONDE MARY. More likely a victrola . . . with that symphony.

WIFE [*in nervous tears*]. Thank God for anything real in this ghostly night. . . .

THE MAN. Ain't sure you could hear the Guns with that noise echoin' across from the cliffs. [*Aside to* FARMER.] Ain't I seen that big fellow before?

FARMER. Sure, 's a keeper from Willard got joined up with the party.

THE MAN [*laughing*]. Oh, we're all right then!

FARMER [*laughing back*]. I dunno. . . . You ain't heard his act yet! He might not get committed, but dang me if I think he could prove his way *out!*

THE MAN [*laughing concludingly*]. Le's knock on wood, Fred, that *we* ain't had to *try!*

BLONDE MARY [*to the weeping* WIFE]. Now, don't worry, dear, it'll all be all right. He'll be here any minute. Don't cry.

WIFE. Why did he go with those strange people? And where did he go? There's something mysterious and terrible about it all! [*She weeps again.*]

THE MAN. There, there, ma'am! This is a strange business. But all them as goes "down under" come right back . . . the Old Man sees to that . . . unless they was dead before they went. Ain't that right, Fred?

FARMER. That's right, ma'am. He should be here now . . . any minute. . . .

WIFE. But there was something drew *him* . . . as though he belonged to all this mystery . . . or insane hokum, whichever it is!

THE MAN. They'll prob'ly be coming with the next Guns . . . from somewhere. . . . [*Then excitedly to the* FARMER.] Fred, Fred, here! Look!

FARMER. What see?

THE MAN. Ain't that the Phantom Canoe coming in under the Northern Lights?

FARMER. Mebbe . . . looks like mebbe . . . ! If that damn cruiser would only bust that raddio 'r sink!

[*The cruiser's music is fading; the Northern Lights are rising; the little crowd stands tense looking off right where* THE MAN *points.*]

[*The* GEOLOGIST *and* BLONDE MARY *are in left front on the bench mindful only of each other.*]

GEOLOGIST. Miss Morgan, there's something plumb wrong with me . . . and I've got to change it!

BLONDE MARY. Now, Professor, you be calm. I'll take care of you.

GEOLOGIST. But, see, my hand's so used to that hammer, it keeps twitching and shaking without it!

BLONDE MARY. Now, Professor, just give *me* your hand! There, isn't that better!

GEOLOGIST. Oh, Miss Morgan, it's wonderful. . . . I feel *so* much better!

BLONDE MARY. Now, Professor, wouldn't you like to be kissed?

GEOLOGIST. Oh, Miss Morgan, I don't know what's come over me . . . but I *would,* honest to God I would!

BLONDE MARY. Well, here! [*Kissing him.*] How's that?

GEOLOGIST. It's wonderful . . . simply wonderful. . . . Miss Morgan, could I, do you s'pose, put my head down on your lap?

BLONDE MARY. Yes, Professor, stretch right out, and here's a lap!

GEOLOGIST. But don't let go my hand!

BLONDE MARY. No.

GEOLOGIST [*head in her lap*]. Oh, Miss Morgan, I'm going to be a different man. I'm going to change my glasses, instead of for all this close-looking, so I can see things afar off like other people . . . the moon, and the stars, and the Northern Lights . . . and you. . . . I don't care if it's crazy and not scientific. . . .

BLONDE MARY [*laughing*]. How about your hearing?

GEOLOGIST. Maybe my hearing isn't so bad. . . . I hear something thumping in my ears right now . . . like drums. . . . Maybe I hear the Lake Drums. . . . Do the others hear them?

BLONDE MARY. Not the same ones you do, dear!

GEOLOGIST. They sound awful loud to me!

BLONDE MARY. Then your hearing's good enough for me, dear!

GEOLOGIST. Hold my hand tight, Miss Morgan.

BLONDE MARY. Yes, indeed, Professor.

GEOLOGIST. You know, Miss Morgan, scientifically I don't see any reason why you should like me the way you seem to!

BLONDE MARY. Well, Professor, *scientifically*, I don't either!
GEOLOGIST. Maybe that's lucky!
BLONDE MARY. I think it is.
GEOLOGIST. Things are certainly lots different!
BLONDE MARY. And better?
GEOLOGIST. Oh, lots! To hell with it!
BLONDE MARY. You mean with Science?
GEOLOGIST. Yes, to hell with it! Anyway with too much of it!
BLONDE MARY. Certainly to hell with it!
GEOLOGIST. If you would like to kiss me again, Miss Morgan, I wish you would. . . .
BLONDE MARY. Here goes, get ready, Professor.
GEOLOGIST. But first, Miss Morgan, may I call you Mary?
BLONDE MARY. Yes.
GEOLOGIST. And you'll call me Harold?
BLONDE MARY. Yes, Harold!
GEOLOGIST. Everything's all right then. . . . Go ahead. [*She kisses him.*]
   [*The cruiser's music is silenced. The Northern Lights rise high and flicker. The listening group is thrown into sudden excitement.*]
THE MAN. Quiet! Now! Everybody! Look at them red flashes in the water! Listen. . . .
   [*The rumble of the guns is heard.*]
THE GUARD. Hear 'em! An' by God, looka the big white canoe sailin' like a streak for the beach!
THE MAN [*to the* FARMER]. We're seein' it, Fred! The Phantom Canoe!
FARMER. I never thought to see it!
THE GUARD. There's four of 'em in it—two of 'em's Injuns! Where's the other two?
WIFE. Is my husband there? [*She calls in anguish.*] John! Let me go down! [*And she starts to go.*]
FARMER [*holding her*]. No, ma'am, no . . . stay here. They'll be right up here. . . . She's beachin' now!

THE GUARD. Leave 'em get away from that spooky boat!

THE GIRL. They get out as though they were sleep-walking or doped!

THE BOY. Look . . . lookit! the canoe's backin' right off the beach by itself . . . slidin' back out into the lake!

THE GUARD. Look at the speed of it!

THE MAN. Shinin' like phosphorus . . . with a wake of flame! . . .

FARMER. An' steerin' right fer th' North Star!

THE GUARD. Open up here. . . . Give 'em room t' th' fire! [*Then excitedly.*] Here . . . only four of 'em! What become o' them civilized half-breeds?

THE GIRL [*to* THE BOY, *as they still watch the canoe*]. It's just a shining spot on the black lake now.

THE BOY. Do you think we really saw it . . . or is it some moon magic?

THE MAN. You've seen something to tell all your born days! Quiet. . . . They've been seein' somethin', too . . . by th' looks of 'em. . . .

[*They enter into the glow of the fireplace: the* OLD MAN OF THE HILLS, *groggy, weaving, madly pop-eyed;* HASKEL *and* MINNA, *now wrapped in Indian blankets and with simple headdresses so that until close up they look like Indians; and* JOHN, *coatless and with loosened collar and vest, looking a bit 18th century, on-his-way-to-the-gallows, who holds his elbows as though tied behind him, but carries the rope in his hand.*]

[HASKEL *and* MINNA *are in a half-coma;* JOHN *throws himself on the end of the bench in an attitude of tragic despair.*]

THE GUARD [*grabbing* HASKEL *by the shoulders*]. Good God, man, I thought you two was the Injun and his squaw. How'd you get rigged out like this?

[HASKEL *and* MINNA *look at their garb as though seeing it for the first time; they slowly slip off their blankets and their headdresses, staring at them in a daze.*]

MINNA. Why, I don't seem to remember quite how we got these. . . .

THE GUARD. Where's the two Injuns?

HASKEL [*looking around vacantly*]. Why . . . why . . . they've been right with us! Aren't they here? . . . [*He sits down heavily.*]

THE GUARD. No, they ain't! [*Turning fiercely on the* OLD MAN OF THE HILLS.] Where's them two Injuns?

OLD MAN [*in his high laughing cackle*]. Injuns? Who said they was any Injuns? We went didn't we . . . and here we be back. . . . [*He laughs crazily but knowingly.*]

[*The* WIFE *has been drawing up to* JOHN'S *figure.*]

THE GUARD [*to* JOHN]. Look here, mister! What's become o' them two Injuns? . . . You went with 'em. . . . You seen em!

JOHN. She didn't come back. . . . She wasn't in the canoe . . . my wife. . . . How did she get "down under"? . . . She didn't go with us. . . . [*He staggers up wildly and starts back toward the beach.*] I must find her.

[*The* OLD MAN OF THE HILLS *with a crazy laugh drags him back, turns him to face his* WIFE, *and points at her.*]

OLD MAN. Look there . . . there's her! [*His wild laughter rises in shrill crescendo.*]

WIFE. John! It's me. . . . I'm real! . . . Oh, John!

JOHN [*recognizing her with a sob of relief*]. Oh, my God! and I've been thinking . . . What a nightmare! [*He embraces her and holds her close.*]

THE GUARD [*to the* OLD MAN OF THE HILLS]. Say, you oughta be run in fer this. . . . If I was a State trooper . . .

THE MAN. Easy there, mister, leave the old fellow be . . . or maybe he'll witch *you!*

OLD MAN. Witch 'im? No, not me . . . but there's witchin' mebbe in th' moon, an' in th' rollin' lights out o' th' north . . . an' off th' high hills, when th' hare drummer's jumpin' from ridge t' toppin' ridge up t' th' highest where th' bangin' o' his flailin' drum spread out all ways! 'R when th' Wanderin' Jew's a-scuddin' agin th' north-west thunder-heads a-risin' across Lake Seneca! 'R when th' Injun Ghost Drums a-soundin' out o' th' hidden gorges o' th' lakes! 'R when th' dream-god that lies a-slumberin' under all this land o' ours wakes, an' sends a shudderin' shakin' through yer blood! . . . Fer when it calls t' somethin' in your blood, you got to answer! . . . You got to answer! [*He laughs crazily at* JOHN *and turns upstage.*]

JOHN [*releasing his* WIFE *and looking blindly right*]. Come on, let's get to our horses . . . and get on the trail home.

THE MAN [*to the* GUARD]. Leave the old boy be, if you know what's good for you!

THE GUARD [*pretty well scared*]. Mister, I wouldn't lay finger on that without it was in a strait jacket!

FARMER. Take it easy, mister, the cars is just a step over there.

JOHN. Cars?

WIFE [*shaking him*]. Yes . . . John . . . and the good old V-8! . . . That other is just a bad dream. . . .

JOHN [*rubbing his eyes and half laughing*]. Yes . . . yes . . . horses . . . cars . . . of course! [*Drawing his* WIFE *to him again.*] But it was a *bad dream.* . . . You'll never know . . . and what you don't know won't hurt you!

THE MAN [*pulling a flask out of his hip-pocket*]. Here, mister, take a leetle medicinal swallow and you'll feel better.

JOHN [*taking a pull*]. Thanks . . . thanks! That makes the world a bit more normal, I must say!

BLONDE MARY [*tipping the sleepy* GEOLOGIST *upright*]. Well, I'm glad *my* man isn't going to try to solve this Lake Guns mystery . . . and leave his bones in Davy Jones' locker!

GEOLOGIST [*half asleep*]. That's right, Miss Morgan, to hell with Science . . . and kiss me again, please. . . .

BLONDE MARY [*putting his hat on*]. When we get home, Harold.

# THE LAKE GUNS

HASKEL. And let's get home! Minna? . . . Oh, there you are. . . . Well, Minna, if our old Iroquois ancestors set this country up with magic like this forever . . . I say more power to them! But a sixty-fourth blood is enough for me. . . . I don't know but I'm scared to death of your one-eighth!

MINNA. I'm pretty scared of it myself, right now.

HASKEL. Maybe we'll forget it when we get back to civilization.

MINNA. But I'm not sure I want to get back.

HASKEL. By God, you'll stay without me! I'm even giving away my hunting privileges.

THE MAN. Gosh, I'd like *them*. . . . Wouldn't mind becomin' *half* Indian for them!

MINNA. I'm afraid you have to be born to it!

FARMER [*laughing*]. Tom Dean wouldn't've minded that a bit, miss!

MINNA. Well, if I'm going back to the white man's civilization, to rise with the alarm clock to study the romantic poets . . . let's get going!

WIFE. Yes, I want to get John home.

THE BOY. And I *got* to get you home, Peg!

THE GIRL. Get the machine and come on.

THE MAN [*in a tone of summing-up*]. Well, I guess you've seen an' heard it.

JOHN. I've seen and heard plenty!

BLONDE MARY. Come on, Harold, we're going. Step high in this meadow.

GEOLOGIST. You lead me along, and I'll follow.

FARMER. I know the path. . . . I'll take you to the cars.

THE GIRL. Can we give anybody a ride?

THE BOY. Room for two in our rumble.

HASKEL. We're all fixed, thanks.

THE GUARD. Say, it'll seem pretty tame after this back to Willard! But glad t've met you folks, an' any time any of you want to look over th' place, ask for Sam Jones . . . that's me, an' I'll give you an A-1 conducted tour . . . but it'll be nothin' like this!

JOHN. Thank heaven for that!

FARMER. Well, all set?

THE GUARD. Say, where's that crazy Old Man o' the Hills? . . . By God, he's gone, disappeared! . . . gone like them Injuns. . . .

HASKEL. He was here just a minute ago!

THE BOY. Why, he was standing right . . . Let's find the old nut!

THE MAN. He's gone an' you'll not find him, till he wants to appear to you . . . or to y'r grandchildren!

MINNA. Down into the lake?

THE MAN. Prob'ly bounded up the Taghanic Falls, up the cliffs . . . that's what they say . . . streakin' through the air like that canoe streaked out into the lake . . . you can see for yourselves what they say is true . . . maybe . . . boundin' up the cliffs up into the high hills. Here! Just once before you go, there's another pillar of the Northern Lights. . . . Listen again . . . an' maybe we'll hear the Guns from the lake . . . or maybe the crazy hare-drummer's drummin' out o' the hill-tops sinkin' down to the lakes . . . listen. . . .

[*They listen, and a rapid drumming is heard, not from the lake but high up in front . . . faint, and then fainter.*]

THE MAN [*pointing up*]. There he is skippin' and drummin' his bass drum across the high ridges. . . .

[*The drumming dies away.*]

FARMER. He's over the ridge and down, to send her boomin' down into Seneca Lake at Lodi Landin', an' off'n Dresden . . . if he don't come back.

JOHN. Well, we're off before he has a chance. Dying once a night is plenty.

[*They move off.*]

THE MAN. I'm staying awhile to enjoy the night.

## THE LAKE GUNS

ALL [*variously*]. Suit yourself. Good night. Good night.
HASKEL. See you some other crazy night!
   [*And they disappear in the darkness, following the flashlights.*]
THE GIRL [*running back to* THE MAN]. You'll explain to my mother?
THE MAN. Sure will . . . call 'er by breakfast time . . . hers, I mean!
THE GIRL. I think there's a couple of hot dogs and some rolls, if you want to stir up the fire.
THE MAN. Thanks, miss. . . . They'll taste first-rate after this wait!
   [THE GIRL *runs after the others.*]
   [THE MAN *stirs the fire up to cast a flickering glow over the scene; then moves up and sits looking at the lake and sky, listening, his back to the audience.*]
   [THE OLD MAN OF THE HILLS *steals in noiselessly, mounts the table, and in the light of the fire, pantomimes with silent laughter a slow beating of a bass drum, which sets the Lake Guns booming again to the rhythm of his drum-beat. Then he steals noiselessly out, shaking with silent wild laughter.*]
   [*The Guns beat on in the drum rhythm, as* THE MAN *silently watches. . . . They rise to a crescendo and then begin to fade as the* CURTAIN *slowly closes. . . . They continue fading for some seconds after the* CURTAIN *and then are silent.*]

### THE END

# LET'S GET ON WITH THE MARRYIN'

## Here Comes the Bride to a Wilderness Wedding

*by*

ROBERT GARD

## LET'S GET ON WITH THE MARRYIN'

When the author of *Let's Get On with the Marryin'* was scouring the countryside for ideas and plots for New York State plays, he came upon an historical marker which told of the Reverend Garrit Mandeville's coming to the town of Ithaca in 1805 as its first Presbyterian parson. Realizing the dramatic possibilities of early pastorates beset by the dangers, hardships, and crudities of the wilderness, the author looked for an incident or plot in which a frontier parson was the central figure. His search led him to a story in a copy of the Ithaca *Journal* for 1858 and ultimately to writing the comedy *Let's Get On with the Marryin'*.

The Reverend Morrison represents an educated preacher from the East taking up a charge in the woods not far from Ithaca on the Catskill Turnpike, about the year 1820. The story of the frontier "marryin' " woven around the Burkes' visit to the Parson's house is true to the time. Frontier folk often had to travel many miles to pay a call or to see a daughter married; and parsons had to perform their duties in makeshift ways which seem to us ludicrous and which must have been laughably trying even to men of infinite patience and good-will.

TIME: *1820, a morning in early fall.*
PLACE: *The* REVEREND MORRISON'S *cabin at Laketown, a Central New York village.*

## THE CHARACTERS OF THE PLAY

THE REVEREND MORRISON, *a frontier preacher.*
MRS. MORRISON.
MR. BURKE, *a backwoods farmer.*
MRS. BURKE.
SALLY BURKE, *a backwoods bride-to-be.*
TIM BURKE, *a boy.*
LEM LORD, *the bridegroom.*

# LET'S GET ON WITH THE MARRYIN'

THE SCENE *is the* MORRISON *cabin at Laketown, New York, a frontier settlement. Center stage is a table, right and left of which are chairs. Against the back wall is a crude fireplace, near which stands a fine armchair of simple American colonial design. In the back wall is a small window, and near the window hangs a rifle. A quilt stretched on a cord screens the upstage right corner of the room, setting aside a little space for dressing purposes.*

[*The* REVEREND MORRISON, *a backwoods preacher in his thirties, sits at the table fussing with an old clock. He inspects the works, lifts a part of the mechanism he has removed, tries to fit it back into place but fails, and with a puzzled shake of his head sets the clock upright on the table. He gives the pendulum a push, waits hopefully, then sighs in dejection as the pendulum stops swinging. His wife,* SUSAN MORRISON, *a hardy, good-looking woman, comes into the room from behind the quilt lifting it up to do so. She is dressed as though for an occasion in what is probably her best full-skirted, small-waisted dress.*]

MRS. MORRISON [*as she enters*]. Is the clock fixed, Jonathan?
MORRISON [*closing the case sadly*]. Yes, I've fixed it.
MRS. MORRISON [*going to the fireplace where she arranges some mugs on a wooden tray*]. Then we'll have clock time again.
MORRISON. I'm afraid not.
MRS. MORRISON. Oh Jonathan! You didn't break our only clock?

MORRISON. It was already broken. I just took out this doodad here, and . . .

MRS. MORRISON. Oh, now what are we going to do?

MORRISON. Learn to tell time by the sun. Like the Indians.

MRS. MORRISON [*returning to the fireplace to put a kettle on the coals*]. If people would only pay their pastor in cash instead of merchandise, maybe we could have some of the things we really need. How many weddings have you performed since we've been in Laketown, Jonathan?

MORRISON. Nineteen.

MRS. MORRISON. And how many bridegrooms have paid you in merchandise?

MORRISON. Eighteen. Johnny Moore didn't pay anything.

MRS. MORRISON [*shaking her head as she stirs the fire with the tongs*]. Nineteen weddings! [*Taking stock.*] We have pigs, bear meat, a barrel of sauerkraut, cabbages, potatoes, cornflour, venison, potash and fuel, a rifle, powder and shot, a dog, and a map showing where the Cayuga Indians buried a treasure; but we haven't *one penny* in cash!

MORRISON. There's very little cash in the country.

MRS. MORRISON [*putting water in the kettle*]. I wish they'd get New York civilized. Like Connecticut.

MORRISON. That'll come. Where's my Bible, Susan?

MRS. MORRISON. On the table. Right in front of you. [*She hands it to him.*] And this Lem Lord, who's coming here today to marry Sally Burke. . . . What do you think he'll bring you: a panther, or a litter of baby skunks?

MORRISON. Lem ought to bring something handsome. I've done enough for him. [*He opens his Bible.*]

MRS. MORRISON. He won't bring money. They never do.

MORRISON. Yes, sir, I've had a hard time winning that girl for Lem.

MRS. MORRISON [*turning to face him*]. Winning her?

MORRISON [*laughing*]. Oh, all I did was help persuade her. Sally Burke wanted something a little fancier than Lem Lord, but

## LET'S GET ON WITH THE MARRYIN'       83

Lem's a well-meaning young fellow, and they'll make a good enough match. [*Leafing through his Bible.*] Sally's got independence. Like to see that in a girl. [*Chuckling.*] Lem thought having a preacher marry 'em was a lot of nonsense; but Sally held out against him.

MRS. MORRISON. I thought there must be a reason why the Burkes'd drive twenty miles just to get a parson to marry their daughter. If the stories they tell about them are true, that Burke family's a wild lot.

MORRISON. Oh, the Burkes are all right. They belong to our church.

MRS. MORRISON. They've never been to the meeting.

MORRISON. Twenty miles is a long way to come, even for church meeting, Susan.

MRS. MORRISON. I suppose so. Is . . . is Sally Burke as pretty as I used to be?

MORRISON. No girl's that!

MRS. MORRISON. Well, I suppose she'll want to put on her wedding dress, same as the others. [*She goes to the quilt and straightens it along the cord.*] Old Aunt Lilly's top cover's done a good service for the brides and grooms of Laketown. What time did Mr. Burke say he'd arrive with his family?

MORRISON. Nine o'clock. [*Going to the window.*] Must be later than nine, now. Well, they probably got stuck in the mud. Catskill Turnpike's in quite a state since the rains. Time goes kind of slow. You'd think it was more than three years since we got on the stage at Catskill that morning to come West, leavin' the Hudson River and the East, just because Cousin Sim DeWitt wrote what a need there was for a preacher out here.

MRS. MORRISON. When I saw how rough things were, it took me quite a while to forgive Cousin Sim. [*Laughing.*] But I wouldn't go back now, Mr. Morrison, if I had the chance! [*There is a knock at the door.*] Here come the Burkes! [*She smooths her dress.*]

MORRISON. And I'm ready for the marryin'. [*He goes to open the door.*]

[*The* BURKE *family enters.* MR. BURKE *is a man of fifty, dressed in the backwoods fashion of the time. He wears ankle length trousers, tight at the bottom; a long coat, rusty with age and split at the tails; and a high-crowned, very narrow-brimmed hat underneath which his hair sticks out. He is a good, bluff pioneer.* MRS. BURKE *is a female counterpart of* BURKE *in speech and heartiness. She is dressed somewhat like* MRS. MORRISON *in a tight-bodiced, flowing dress with a shawl over the shoulders.* SALLY BURKE *is a girl of twenty-three, plainly attired in a home-spun dress like her mother's.* SALLY *carries a large bundle in her arms.* TIM BURKE *is a bright, curious lad of sixteen.*]

BURKE [*as* MORRISON *opens the door*]. Howdy, Parson!

MORRISON. Good morning, Mr. Burke. Good morning, ladies. Tim, how are you today, sir? [*To* SALLY.] Well, Sally! I'm glad you're safely here at last.

BURKE [*to* MRS. MORRISON]. This yer wife, Parson? Glad to meet ye, ma'am. This here's Lucy, my wife; my gal, Sal; and my boy, Tim. [*To* TIM.] Tim, yer in th' house. Take off yer hat. [*He suddenly remembers to remove his own.*]

MRS. MORRISON [*to the women*]. How-do-you-do, Mrs. Burke. Just put your shawl on the chair. [*She indicates the colonial chair. To* SALLY.] And this is the blushing bride-to-be! My, you're as pretty as my husband promised. Let me take your bundle?

SALLY [*clasping her bundle more closely*]. I kin handle it.

MRS. BURKE [*in a stage whisper to* MRS. MORRISON]. She's jealous of that bundle, Mis' Morrison. It's her weddin' dress.

MRS. MORRISON [*to* SALLY]. What a joyous day it must be for you.

SALLY. Got me a good dress, but ain't sure I want to wear it.

MORRISON [*who has been assisting* BURKE *to struggle out of his*

## LET'S GET ON WITH THE MARRYIN'  85

*coat*]. Oh, you're right to go through with the ceremony, Sally.

SALLY. I got plumb wore out denyin' Lem, Parson.

MORRISON [*laughing*]. Where is our bridegroom?

BURKE. Lem'll be along any minute. Said he'd be a bit late, account of havin' to ketch somethin' to pay th' Parson with.

MORRISON [*glancing at his wife*]. *Ketch* something, eh?

MRS. BURKE [*hesitating*]. Mis' Morrison, . . . Sal, she wouldn't wear her weddin' dress this mornin' what with th' mud'n all. We . . . thought ye might let her change it here.

MRS. MORRISON. I'd thought of that. [*To* SALLY.] You can step right behind the quilt, Sally. [*Apologetically, to* MRS. BURKE.] It's our only other room.

BURKE [*inspecting the quilt*]. That's a clever scheme. Guess we'll have to string up a quilt to home.

SALLY [*hesitating at the quilt*]. Right back here, Mis' Morrison?

MRS. MORRISON. Yes, that's right, Sally. I can hardly wait to see your dress. Can I help?

SALLY. Naw, I kin manage all right.

MRS. BURKE. Keerful ye don't rumple it, Sal.

SALLY [*going behind the quilt*]. I won't, Ma.

BURKE [*in pride*]. Sal's my little gal, and I sure hate ter part company with 'er. But ye know how it is. A young feller comes along and, blast me, th' next day ye ain't got no gal.

MRS. BURKE [*in a low voice so* SALLY *doesn't hear*]. We was so glad to get Sal here today, Parson. This mornin', early, she'd about made up her mind she wasn't comin', but we told her you thought it was best, and finally got her started. She sure has a power of likin' fer you!

BURKE [*also in a low voice*]. You know, Sal's put Lem off six seasons already, and it's beginnin' ter be a joke. Don't look just right, my gal denyin' Lem Lord, whose pa's got more fixin's on his land 'an anybody else hereabouts.

MORRISON. Well, it takes some folks longer to decide than others. Sally's made up her mind now, and that's the main thing.

MRS. BURKE. My Sal's more pertickler 'an some.

MRS. MORRISON. Have you folks had anything to eat? I've got something ready, in case you're hungry after your long trip.

MRS. BURKE. We had our breakfast before we come, and I put up a lunch fer on th' way home. So I guess we won't starve without botherin' you.

MRS. MORRISON. Well then, just take chairs till the bridegroom arrives to claim his bride.

MRS. BURKE [*elated at seeing the colonial chair*]. Mis' Morrison, if this don't seem like home! My ma gave me a chair like this one. Mine got lost acomin' up from Pennsylvany when we settled here. [*She sits.*] Yes sir, it *sets* like my old chair, too!

MORRISON [*to* BURKE]. Did you have a pleasant trip this morning?

BURKE. Right pleasant. Th' Pike is cut up bad from the rains and wagon travel on it, and my ol' hoss ain't none too spry, but we come right along. Th' trees is turnin' and it's pretty along on the hills. Say, Parson, this country sure has changed since I fust come out here with Sullivan in '79. Now we got th' Catskill Pike an' a stage coach, and I reckon Laketown's got all of forty cabins now, ain't it?

MORRISON. Just about.

BURKE. I recall comin' here with my wife ter settle. That was some trip. We come up from Pennsylvany like Lucy said, by way of Owego. There wasn't no trail but an Injun trail them days. We had to chop trees out of the way so the wagons could git through. Some folks packed their belongin's in on their backs, but I got a wagon in. [TIM *has slipped around to the back wall, has the rifle down, and is sighting it.*] Put up that rifle, Tim! [TIM *does so reluctantly. To* MORRISON.]

That boy don't want ter do a thing but shoot! [*As* TIM *swells pridefully.*] Just like me when I was his age. I could hit a squirrel in the eye every time I drawed a bead. I figure I was one of th' best shots in Sullivan's army.

MORRISON. You must have been just a youngster when you were here with Sullivan, Mr. Burke.

BURKE. Just eighteen. It was kind of hard t' watch th' things that was done in that campaign, but the Injuns deserved what they got. Gen'ral Washington would have it they was to get a lesson they'd never fergit.

SALLY [*calling from behind quilt*]. Ma! Come help me, Ma!

MRS. BURKE. There! She's havin' trouble with them stays. I knowed she would. [*She goes behind the quilt.*]

MRS. MORRISON [*to* BURKE]. There's not much light behind the quilt, but I think she can manage. It's been done before.

BURKE. Sal's had nothin' but firelight all her life. She kin see in th' dark good's a cat. She's sure made a fuss about marryin'. I'll feel more easy after the job's done good and proper. Her ma never had a weddin' dress, and there wasn't no foolishness when I married her, neither.

MORRISON. Were you married soon after you returned from the war?

BURKE. Sure was. Got back one day from whippin' th' Injuns, and the next day I went to Lucy's pa, and I said: "Jesse, kin I have your gal, Lucy, fer to marry?" Jesse, he chawed a spell and then he said he reckoned I could, seein' as how the season'd been poor, and there wasn't over-much in the house to eat. Lucy was alistenin' at a chink in the cabin. . . .

MRS. BURKE [*coming from behind the quilt and interrupting*]. Jest like I'm doin' now, John Burke. [*To the* MORRISONS.] It mostly ain't true. [*To* BURKE.] My ma and pa always had as much ter eat, er more'n yours did.

BURKE [*laughing*]. We was all hard up tergether.

MRS. BURKE. We sure was!

BURKE [*laughing*]. Before that day was out, Lucy an' me was tied up tergether. There wasn't no delayin', like Sal's done to Lem. I seen ter that.

MRS. BURKE. We lived in Pennsylvany ten year, till Burke found out he could get some land in the Military Tract. They give us six hunnert acres! Law, we thought we was rich! But we was land pore 'cause we ain't had nothin' since.

BURKE. Sal 'bout ready? Lem'll be comin' any time.

MRS. BURKE [*leaning forward*]. Say, Sal's goin' ter look real pretty!

MRS. MORRISON. There's nothing sweeter than a blushing bride!

MRS. BURKE. You was a right smart blushing bride yerself! You're prettier'n I ever was.

BURKE [*in robust humor*]. Did she hold back, Parson, er did ye convince 'er right off the start?

MORRISON [*laughing*]. She liked my preaching so well she married me to get it all the time.

MRS. MORRISON. Well, anyway, I didn't marry you because you were rich!

BURKE. Aw, ain't nobody rich hereabouts. Seems like ten year since I seen any real cash.

MORRISON. We . . . I broke our clock. [*He takes it from the table and puts it out of the way in a corner.*] But it hardly seems as if we'd ever get another one, unless times improve.

BURKE. That's too bad. Them wooden works are easy ter get outta order. Say, Lucy, Lem Lord's pa used ter be a clockmaker over in Connecticut. They must have six or seven clocks up to their place. It'd be kinda nice if Lem'd bring one of them clocks ter pay Parson fer th' marryin'. . . .

MRS. BURKE. Just wouldn't it, though!

BURKE. And I'll be thinkin' that's what Lem had in mind. He was sure actin' curious 'bout somethin'.

MORRISON [*enthusiastically*]. Won't that be fine, Susan?

MRS. MORRISON. I'll believe it when I see it. [*To the* BURKES.]

# LET'S GET ON WITH THE MARRYIN'

You folks must come to the meeting. There are few enough of the faithful, you know!

Mrs. Burke. Mis' Morrison, I'd like to, fust rate. But you know, I just don't dast go away fer that long a trip. I only come terday 'cause Sal wouldn't come 'less I did. Come year ago, Burke *almost* persuaded me to go with 'im ter visit a neighbor lives t'other side of th' holler . . . but someway I couldn't quite bring myself ter do it. I was sure glad I stayed at home, 'cause no sooner had Burke got outta sight 'an one of them big, brown wolves come right up ter th' door an' grabbed my pet sheep and like to killed it. Took me half an hour, fightin' hard with the fire-tongs, to chase that critter away! Since then I ain't thought o' goin' anywheres till terday, and th' good Lord only knows what mischief I'll find when I git home!

Burke [*taking up where she left off*]. Yes sir, seems like th' good Lord figured ter put a cuss onto us when he made all them wolves! It's gitten so's a feller don't dast go out at night without a dog er gun. Year er so ago, th' fellers over our county got tergether to drive the wolves out. . . . Made a line of men nigh eighteen miles long, an' we sure drove 'em! Trouble was, it made th' folks sa mad in th' county we drove 'em into, that they drove 'em all back again . . . so we've still got 'em!

Mrs. Burke [*calling*]. Sal! You 'bout ready? Lem'll be here most any time.

Sally. It ain't going ter hurt Lem Lord ter wait fer me a spell.

Burke [*to* Morrison]. He's been waitin' six year already!

Mrs. Burke. Lem's goin' to have a time quellin' that gal!

Burke. Aw, Sal'll be awright soon's she's married! She's just like a young colt 'at has ter play around a spell afore he settles down ter bein' a good, steady hoss.

  [Sally *slowly raises the quilt and comes into the room. She is dressed very fancily indeed in a full red dress with stays; her hair is done up and adorned with the yellow tail-feathers of a rooster; she wears a yellow neck-ribbon and cotton gloves.*]

MORRISON [*as they all exclaim*]. Why, Sally! You look just like the ladies in New York! Doesn't she, Susan?

MRS. MORRISON [*going to* SALLY]. You're a beautiful bride, Sally! [*She straightens* SALLY's *dress.*]

BURKE. Dog-gone, Sal, didn't know you was so pretty!

MRS. BURKE. And such a lot of trouble fer a weddin' you never seen! Why, she even pulled the tail outta my old yaller rooster to spark up her hair!

SALLY [*struck by all this admiration*]. 'Tis my marryin' dress! But there's just one thing, Pa. . . .

BURKE [*suddenly quiet*]. Yes, Sal?

SALLY. Someway I don't wanter marry Lem Lord today!

BURKE. Oh! oh! oh! now Sal! Wait a minute! [*Hastily.*] You done made up yer mind! Yer gonna get married! Ain't that what we come here fer?

SALLY. Yes, but . . .

MORRISON. We all get married some time. Why, matrimony's the perfect state! Eh, Mr. Burke?

BURKE. Give ye my word. Eh, Ma?

MRS. BURKE. 'Tain't half as bad as it seems.

SALLY. But Lem Lord's kinda *quare!*

MRS. BURKE. Why, Sal! There ain't a better young feller in our county.

SALLY. He's th' only young feller left in the county and I don't think . . . [*She begins to sob loudly.*]

MORRISON. Now, Sally, don't you cry. [*He puts his arms around her shoulders and draws her head onto his chest.*] We'll not let anything hurt you. Lem'll treat you all right. I'll see to that myself.

MRS. MORRISON. My goodness! I think it's time the bridegroom came to claim his bride.

BURKE. Lem's pa's got lots of nice things, Sal. All them clocks, that cleared land . . .

## LET'S GET ON WITH THE MARRYIN'

SALLY [*raising her head and speaking sharply*]. Pa, I ain't marryin' Lem Lord fer his money.
BURKE [*retreating rapidly*]. Why, whoever said you was, Sal? Never was no Burke yet married fer money!
SALLY. I heared what you said about it not lookin' right fer me ter keep denyin' Lem Lord. I couldn't help ahearin', and I just don't think . . .
  [*She is interrupted by a terrific booming at the door.* SALLY *bursts into louder sobs and buries her head against the* PARSON.]
LEM [*outside, shouting*]. Hi thar, folks! 'Tis me, Lem Lord, acomin' fer to marry me bride!
MRS. MORRISON. Well, we'll have to let him in, anyhow!
  [MRS. MORRISON *opens the door, and* LEM LORD *enters. He is dressed, like* MR. BURKE, *in frontier clothes. He carries a large bunch of stringy wildflowers. He has a rifle under one arm and a large, square package under the other.*]
LEM [*beaming*]. Wal, here I be! Howdy, Ma Burke. [*He bows to* MRS. MORRISON, *looking hard at her.*] Howdy, ma'am! Howdy, Paw Burke! [*As he turns to face* SALLY *and the* PARSON *he laughs long and loud.*] Wal, wal, wal! Parson's quite a feller with the gals! Hain't too late, be I? Wal, wal, wal! Sure a fine day fer marryin'! [*As* SALLY *wails loudly.*] Ain't it? [*He looks around at the others.*]
BURKE. Sure, Lem, sure.
LEM. Wal, let me stow away me bundle and me gun, and we'll git right ahead with th' ceremony! [*He places his package on a chair, puts his rifle in a corner.* TIM *watches the rifle, begins to move slowly toward it.*]
LEM. Git away from that rifle, Tim. Lem Lord's gun's primed to shoot! [*To* SALLY.] I done brung you some posies, Sal. Jerked 'em myself.
MRS. BURKE. Now ain't that skunk-cabbage pretty!
MRS. MORRISON. I'll get some water for the . . . flowers. No, Sally can hold 'em in her hand while she's being married.

BURKE. Lem's some feller! Ain't many men'd think o' bringin' posies to their weddin'! [LEM *swells with pride.*]
MORRISON. Now that the bridegroom is here we can proceed.
SALLY [*raising her head*]. We cannot! I ain't gonna marry no Lem Lord terday!
LEM [*startled*]. What's that? Say, Sal, you promised!
BURKE. Now Sal . . .
MRS. BURKE [*imploring*]. Sally, you got to!
MRS. MORRISON. Lem's a nice-looking young man, Sally.
LEM. That I be, Sal.
MORRISON. Sally, matrimony is a holy thing, not to be entered into lightly, but we all feel that you have duly considered it, and . . .
SALLY. 'Tain't any use, Parson. [*Beginning to sob.*] Hold me tighter. I just can't go on with it. [*To* LEM.] What'd you pull them posies fer, Lem? Wanter smell up everything?
BURKE [*plaintively*]. Sal, we come twenty mile!
MRS. BURKE. Now Sal, all this here's nonsense!
SALLY. I ain't listenin'. I know what I want! 'Tain't Lem Lord. Not terday, anyway. Nobody's gonna tell me what to do! [*She breaks away from* MORRISON *and runs behind the quilt.*]
LEM. Well, by swow! She's went and run behind that quilt!
BURKE. Fazzled agin! [*Sitting down.*] Twenty muddy mile fer nothin'!
MRS. BURKE [*appealing to* MORRISON]. Parson, can't you do something?
MRS. MORRISON. Yes, you talk with Sally, Mr. Morrison. She seems to like you.
LEM [*unwilling to compromise*]. I'll soon have her out! By swow, she ain't gonna foolish Lem Lord agin! Why, I'm th' best dog-busted feller in Tompkins County! [*He approaches the quilt, starts to lift it, but receives a severe kick on the hand.*]
LEM. Saay, you wildcat . . .
SALLY. Lem Lord, don't you dast lift this cover!

## LET'S GET ON WITH THE MARRYIN'

LEM. Aw, Sal! [*To the others.*] I shoulda listened ter ma! Ma said she'd do it! Made a fule outta agin! Wal, by crickity, 'tis th' last time. There's plenty o' gals that'd jump inter fire ter marry Lem Lord!

MRS. MORRISON [*pushing* LEM *to a chair*]. Now, Lem, you just sit down. The Parson'll talk with Sally, and maybe he'll persuade her.

BURKE [*hopefully*]. Sure, Lem. Gals needs lots of persuadin'. [*To* MORRISON.] Git on, Parson, bring her around!

LEM. 'Tain't any use, though. Sal's just stubborn. I swow, I'd sooner try ter 'suade a panther er a wolf as I would Sal! [BURKE *motions him to be silent.*]

MORRISON [*who has established himself by the quilt*]. Now Sally, are you going to keep this poor young man waiting longer? Out here is Lem Lord, a good man and a true! Think well, before you choose your final course!

LEM. I heard th' Parson preach one day. I swear, ye could hear 'im holler "Glory!" two mile away!

BURKE. Parson'll fetch her out!

SALLY. No use, Parson! Made up my mind. Lem kin go home! And I ain't comin' out till he does!

LEM [*stung and bounding up*]. Home, huh? Well, I'm gittin' tired of waitin', Sally Burke. And I *am* goin' home! Ye kin look fer 'nother feller to make yerself a fule out of. [*Snatching the flowers.*] Here's some posies fer *you*, Mis' Morrison. Reckon ye're twicet as pretty as Sal, anyway!

SALLY. She ain't neither!

LEM. She is! [*He stops and sees the point.*] You ain't nothin' ter look at special. I ain't gonna be trifled with no more. I'm th' wrong sort of man fer ye, be I? You don't like me, you don't? Wal, I'm a brown forester, I am! I'm a rough man. I hain't no Johnny Cake! Thar hain't no smooth skins from where I live! Give me my rifle, 'cause I'm gittin' out!

BURKE. Now, Lem, hold on!

MORRISON. Almost too late, Sally.

LEM. Sal likes ter be coaxed; that's what's the matter with 'er!
MRS. BURKE. Sal, fer your ma's sake?
SALLY. Lem said I ain't as pretty as Mis' Morrison! She ain't much ter look at, is she, Parson?
MORRISON. Well now . . .
LEM. Mis' Morrison's somethin' to see! A right choice eye-full. Yes sir! [*Advancing on* MRS. MORRISON.] You sure be, ma'am. Pretty as a young polecat! If I had a hundred posies I'd give 'em all ter you.
MRS. MORRISON. And not one to Sally?
LEM. I been plumb blind. Sal's spiled. Wusser'n pizen.
MRS. BURKE [*taking up the glove for* SAL]. She ain't spiled, Lem Lord. She's a good gal!
LEM. She's spiled! Ye never teached her ter make up 'er mind.
MRS. BURKE. Don't you dast talk to me like that!
BURKE [*approaching the quilt*]. Sally, ain't you gonna git married terday?
SALLY. Well . . . maybe, Pa.
BURKE [*brightening up*]. Thar! Then come out, Sally gal!
SALLY. But I'll git married whar I be, er not at all. If I ain't good enough fer Lem without this weddin' dress, he ain't gonna see it agin.
LEM. I never said nothin' 'bout her dress. . . .
BURKE. Whar ye be?
SALLY. Yes, Pa.
LEM [*solving the whole problem*]. I'll just come back in there, then. Me'n th' Parson.
SALLY. No. I don't want no one else in here.
LEM. No one at all?
SALLY. 'Less th' Parson wants ter come. . . .
LEM. Wal, by crickety! [*Advancing on* MRS. MORRISON.] Mis' Morrison, I reckon you're th' hansomus gal I ever see! No sir, 'tain't often a feller'll stumble onto a posie like you be. Wish I was th' Parson. Gonna be hard gittin' used ter Sal, after clappin' eyes onto you. [*The quilt moves violently.*]
SALLY [*wailing*]. Ma, Lem's insultin' me!

## LET'S GET ON WITH THE MARRYIN'

LEM [*grabbing* MRS. MORRISON *by the arm*]. Mis' Morrison, I'm tellin' ye true. . . .

MRS. MORRISON. Here, here! Something's got to be done! [*She gets away from* LEM, *goes to the table, and takes a large knife.*]

LEM [*starting back*]. Hold on! I never meant no harm!

MRS. MORRISON [*going to the quilt*]. I'll settle this right now. And it's an old quilt, anyway. [*She makes a slit in the quilt about half way up.*] There, Sally, you just put your hand through this hole! [*To* MORRISON.] Mr. Morrison, you may now join these young people in holy matrimony. And the quicker you join them, the better!

BURKE [*admiringly*]. Scat my—! Cleverer'n my red mare!

[*As they all watch,* SAL's *hand and arm appear through the rent in the quilt.* LEM *makes a sudden dash and captures her hand.*]

LEM [*loudly, in victory*]. Now you ain't gonna git away! Git ahead with th' marryin', Parson! I waited six years fer this!

MORRISON [*as they all laugh and crowd in toward the quilt*]. Gather round, friends!

[*He takes a stand upstage of* LEM *and between the clasped hands. Everybody gets ready for th' marryin'. Only* TIM *is left alone at the other side of the cabin, still fiddling with* LEM's *rifle.*]

MORRISON. Young people, we are gathered to join ye in matrimony, and I charge ye both that if either of ye knows of anything between ye, why ye should not be united in marriage, ye do now confess it.

[TIM *looks worried at this. He looks at the quilt, then at the rifle; raises the gun, takes a quick aim, and shoots. The cord which holds up the quilt breaks and causes a wild upheaval.* LEM, *startled, raises the clasped hands and knocks the* PARSON's *book away.* MORRISON, *surprised and overbalanced, falls forward.* SALLY, LEM *and* MORRISON *lie buried and entangled in the quilt.*]

BURKE [*bellowing*]. Tim!

MRS. BURKE. Laws-a-mercy!

LEM [*yelling*]. Anybody shot? [MRS. MORRISON *begins to extract them.*]

BURKE [*raising his hand to* TIM]. Tim, I'm gonna wallop ye so hard . . .

TIM [*backing away*]. Well, guess I want sister married off, bad as anybody. Parson said if there was somethin' between 'em . . .

[LEM, SALLY *and* MORRISON *rise.* LEM *is still holding to* SAL's *hand, the quilt still between them but trailing on the floor.*]

LEM. What ye waitin' fer, Parson? Let's git on with th' marryin'! I've got ye, Sal, and I ain't gonna let ye go again!

MRS. MORRISON. Shall I fold away the quilt before we continue?

LEM. Not on yer life, ma'am. I got no more time to waste. Let's git on, while we got th' chance. [SAL *begins to wail and pull away.*]

MORRISON [*seeing that haste is necessary*]. Lem, will you have this woman . . .

LEM [*cutting in on him*]. What else did I come here fer, Parson?

MORRISON. Wilt thou, Sally Burke, have this man to be your husband? [*Without waiting for her reply.*] I pronounce you man and wife. Lem, kiss the bride!

LEM [*beaming and joyful*]. Wal, wal, wal! I'm ready to do anything, Parson, but slap me if I know how. You show me, and I'll foller if it kills me.

BURKE [*laughing loudly*]. Go ahead, Parson. Give th' young feller a lesson!

MORRISON. Sally, let me be the first to . . . congratulate you. [*He gives her a sound kiss.*]

MRS. BURKE [*giggling*]. Ha, ha, ha, ha! [*The rest roar with laughter.*]

LEM. Wal, I vum if I don't do ditto! [*He approaches* MRS.

## LET'S GET ON WITH THE MARRYIN' 97

MORRISON *who backs away a little, but is evidently bound to be even with her husband.*]

BURKE. Oh, oh! [*He bursts into a roar of laughter as* LEM *succeeds in giving* MRS. MORRISON *a resounding smack, then stops laughing suddenly to see how* MORRISON *is taking it.* MORRISON *begins to laugh, and* BURKE *begins again as they all laugh except* SAL.]

MORRISON [*stopping his laughter and wiping his eyes*]. Now, folks, that congratulations have been given . . .

LEM. Ah, Parson! I know what yer thinkin'. . . . Want yer pay, eh? Wal, how much fer marryin'? Don't be afeared ter speak up!

MORRISON. Just anything, Lem. Anything at all. [*But he is interested, and so is* MRS. MORRISON.]

LEM. Brung ye a present. [*Gets his package from the chair, and they all crowd around to watch as he unwraps it.*] Here, Parson. Here's a muskrat skin. [*Hands it to* MORRISON *who takes it gingerly.*] Don't be feared of it, 'twon't bite! [*He roars with laughter.*] And here be two big cabbages. [*Hands them to* MRS. MORRISON.] Wish you was cookin' 'em fer me, ma'am! Wal, wal, wal! Sure been a fine marryin'! Shootin' and all! [SALLY *grabs him and begins to pull him toward the door.*] Quit haulin' me, Sal.

SALLY. You come on, Lem, 'fore I lambaste the life outta you!

BURKE [*as they all laugh*]. Don't take her long to ketch onto bein' a wife!

LEM [*hanging back*]. Don't know if I want ter go er not!

SALLY. You come on!

MRS. BURKE. You children go on. Pa 'n I'll bring things. [TIM *takes* LEM's *rifle.*]

MORRISON. Goodbye, young folks! Good luck! [*The rest call "goodbye," and "good luck."*]

LEM. 'Bye! [SAL *pulls him;* BURKE *whoops like an Indian; and to calls of "goodbye,"* LEM *and* SAL *exit.*]

MRS. MORRISON. There they go at last! [*She takes up the cloth-*

*ing* SALLY *has left in the corner and gives it to* MRS. BURKE.] Now, Mrs. Burke, you come to the meetings when you can get away.

MRS. BURKE. You bet I will!

BURKE [*to* MORRISON]. Thanks fer everything, Parson. [*In a low voice.*] Sure too bad it wasn't no clock. [*He bursts out laughing, and* MORRISON *joins in.*]

MORRISON. Oh, we got the usual thing.

BURKE. Well, come on, Lucy. We got a long trip home. Git on out, Tim, ye rascal!

MRS. MORRISON. Hold on. I almost forgot. Let's all have a drink on it first. I've got 'em ready.

MORRISON. I'll get them. [*He takes a tray with mugs on it from near fireplace and brings it to the table.*]

BURKE. Say! [*He grabs one, smacks his lips.* MORRISON *gives a mug to* MRS. BURKE *and* MRS. MORRISON. TIM *moves in to grab one, but receives a cuff from* BURKE. TIM *sulks.*]

MORRISON. Well, here's to the young folks! [*They gulp their drinks.*]

BURKE [*setting down his mug*]. Right good root juice, Parson. Well, we must be off!

MORRISON. Here, let me help you with that coat. Be seeing you soon, I hope.

MRS. BURKE. Sure hope so. 'Bye!

MORRISONS. Goodbye! [*The* BURKES *go out, waving and calling "goodbye."*]

MORRISON [*pausing a moment after the door is closed to wipe his face*]. Whew! What a marryin'!

MRS. MORRISON. I really think, Jonathan . . . after all . . . [*The door opens and* LEM *enters hurriedly, looking behind him.*]

LEM. Say, Parson, I . . . [*Fumbles in his pocket.*] . . . done paid you fer marryin', but here's somethin' fer a new quilt. Ten dollars! [*Planks a bag on the table and turns to go.*] And say, Parson, if I'd seen yer wife 'fore you was married, Sal could've gone ter th' dickens! [*He looks around quickly to see if* SAL *has followed him and is listening.*]

SALLY [*entering and grabbing* LEM *by the arm*]. Oh, I could, could I? [*She jerks* LEM *out, sticks her head back inside, makes a nasty face at* MRS. MORRISON, *and exits.*]

MRS. MORRISON. Well, husband Morrison, I don't know but if I'd seen that young man . . . [*They both burst out laughing together.*]

CURTAIN

# DONALDS O'ROURK

A Drama of Settlers and Iroquois on the New Frontier

*by*

LOUISE O'CONNELL

# DONALDS O'ROURK

IN A foreword to the original manuscript of *Donalds O'Rourk* the author wrote: "The main plot is taken from the story of Cornplanter, the very great Seneca sachem, and his putative father, David O'Beal, or O'Bale. It is recounted by W. L. Stone in *Border Wars of the Revolution*, and is referred to by Washington Irving in *The Life of Washington*. It is also mentioned in a speech delivered by Cornplanter to the Governor of Pennsylvania in 1822, which is transcribed by James Buchannon in *Sketches of the History, Manners, and Customs of the North American Indians*. I used this last only to confirm Stone's picture of Cornplanter's character."

"As I wished to use the tiny subplot of the salt wells, I placed the play on the shores of upper Cayuga Lake, although the main plot actually occurred on the Mohawk. But this change of locale obliged me to rename my otherwise historical characters, The Snake Weaver and Donald O'Rourk. The other characters are wholly fictitious. The long speeches of The Snake Weaver are broken bits of the still longer speech reported by Stone."

TIME: *An Indian Summer evening of about 1790, just after the Lakes Country was opened for settlement.*
PLACE: *A cabin in the forest, perhaps on the banks of Salmon Creek, not far from Lake Cayuga.*

## THE CHARACTERS OF THE PLAY

DONALD O'ROURK, *an old man.*
JOSHUA O'ROURK, *Donald's son, a frontiersman of thirty-five.*
GEORGE FERRY, *another frontiersman of twenty-five.*
MARY O'ROURK, *Joshua's wife.*
JOSHIE O'ROURK, *their lad of thirteen.*
THE SNAKE WEAVER.

Note: The script of *Donalds O'Rourk* has been so arranged that for a somewhat simplified production the section from the asterisk on page 115 to the asterisk on page 118, and the section between the asterisks on page 119, could be omitted.

# DONALDS O'ROURK

THE SCENE *is the* O'ROURK *cabin in the Central New York wilderness. In the center is a rough table; at right the hearth, with a settle extending into the room, and a stool. Against the lower left wall stands a keg of rum. Flitches of bacon and a bag of bullets hang near the fireplace; blankets, provisions and guns are stored under and back of the settle. The only entrance is a center door leading toward forest and sky.*

[JOSHUA O'ROURK *leans in the door, silhouetted against the sunset, which deepens from red to starlit darkness during the action.* GEORGE FERRY *moves to and fro between settle and table, where his long rifle lies, filling his shoulder-pack.* DONALD O'ROURK *sits on the settle within easy reach of the fire. After a moment* JOSHUA *turns from the door, joins* FERRY *and carefully loads a long rifle which he takes from behind the settle.*]

[DONALD O'ROURK *is nearly eighty, but his broad, stooped shoulders, gnarled hands, and quick emotions still evince primal vigor and hardihood. His age is shown by slowness of body and a dreamy absence of mind in which Past is confused with Present. His lightly-lined, dark face shows the upturned nose, long lip and jutting jaw of the Celt; his hair, in scraggly curls to his shoulders, is snow-white, as are his bushy and expressive brows. He wears fringed buckskin and moccasins; at his belt a sheathed hunting knife and Indian tobacco pouch. He speaks a soft Irish bass, here and there reminiscent of his long-forgotten brogue.*]

[JOSHUA O'ROURK *is thirty-five, and the frontier has made his father's son leaner, keener—the power replaced by a stringy,* enduring toughness. *His manner is deeply reserved, yet, like his movements, easy, and only awkward in revealing emotions. His youthful gaiety died within him as, one by one, his children died. He wears buckskins or rough frontier clothes, and moccasins; his hair long and bound in eelskin; coonskin cap; hunting-knife, powder-horn, and large pouch at his belt. Never more than an arm-length from him, his long rifle is an extra limb, as is* FERRY'S *to him, and old* DONALD'S *churchwarden pipe.*]

[GEORGE FERRY *is of the same frontier type although his ancestry is quite different; twenty-five years of age; sceptical and still capable of gaiety. Both younger men speak in the high, nasal whine of the backwoods.*]

JOSHUA O'ROURK [*with curbed impatience as he turns from the door*]. An' can ye recall no more o' the trail than *that*, da?

DONALD O'ROURK [*petulantly, as he stoops to the fire for a brand to light his churchwarden*]. Let be, lad, let be. . . . I can recall ary trail ever I trod. But me pipe is out.

GEORGE FERRY [*grumbling to* JOSHUA *as he proceeds with his packing*]. He be too old. He *can't* remember. Blazes by Sullivan's scouts! Weathered to naught long ago!

DONALD [*as he works at his pipe, half-forgetting it now and then in his reminiscent excitement*]. Me not remember? Man, dear, I c'n remember more'n ye'll ever live t' hear tell! Times past . . . back yon in Herkimer even th' old tale-tellin' parson come to an end of tales, an' him areadin' out o' a book was thick an' wide. . . . Ye come t' th' end o' books! But me, I niver can come t' th' end o' me tales . . . and evera one about meself too!

JOSHUA [*laughing a little*]. And were thy tales true by chance, da?

DONALD. True as Gospel print! Though did I tell ye half, ye'd not believe! Fer 'tis strange times I've lived, strange, an' mortal bad . . . fer days o' th' French wars was bad . . . but feasts an' dancin's was they to what come in th' War fer Independence. Aye, 'tis no wholesome sight t' see a Frenchy scalp an English; but better far 'n watch an Englishman scalp his blood brother! Did ye ne'er hear tell, lads, o' Jock McIntyre an' his auld father th' time when Mohawk Brant . . .

FERRY. Ye forget, old gentleman, we likewise lay at Cherry Valley!

JOSHUA. An' remember too much o' it too well! Can ye no remember some earlier days o' peace, perchance?

DONALD. Aye, hearding cattle in the fields o' Derry . . . a wee lad. . . .

FERRY [*trying to get out of* DONALD *some forgotten clue to their trail*]. Aye, aye, but som'at o' yer comin' to this Western Gate?

JOSHUA. An' findin' your valley?

DONALD. Aye, lads, seventeen I was. Woods-runnin' with Sandy McCune fer Sir William Johnson . . . following the Great Trail to the Senecas till we bogged in th' great marshes t' th' north . . . paddlin' down this lake's end . . . takin' th' trail south forninst a mortal high fall, an' turnin' t' th' right, trailin' through mostly oak and pines, to the little castle of the Cayugas. And there we lay th' night, and I mighty taken by the slim, brown maid . . . but let that bide th' while. . . . From there by dawn, trailin' south an' west, under th' swingin' sun till just at even, comes a side-valley facing south, a waterfall droppin' from its head, an' noon-tide heat turnin' to drenchin' dew. . . . Ah, there's the vale we need, my lads, an' there's yer trail. . . .

FERRY. Were there no landmarks 't th' mouth o' th' vale?

DONALD. Aye, a dead pine, bent north . . . 'tis easy marked . . . on top a pointed hillock half bechune th' swamp an' th' great hill th' valley cuts. Points like a finger to th' vale. Aye, there's the valley fer you lads to find . . . warm, rich, sweet, green and growin' in the sun. . . .

FERRY. A wild goose chase but worth a try!

DONALD [*finally puffing clouds of smoke*]. Wait, lad, I mind som'at else. . . . Not an arrow's flight north o' the trail leads to me fine, fertile valley, the great hill breaks into a naked cliff, where on th' stone they'd painted the Sign o' the Bear. Ye'll know that Bear sign, hunter? [FERRY *shakes his head.*] Here, then. . . . [DONALD *unties his hunting shirt to show an ensign tattooed on his chest.*]

FERRY [*respectfully*]. Ye'll be o' the Sign o' th' Bear, old gentleman?

DONALD [*retieing his shirt*]. Adopted, young hunter, by these same Senecas, when first I come into this Western Land . . . a loon-mad lad! Eh, the days that were, when I lay in the Longhouse as me own. . . . Aye, I recall th' valley facin' south, th' waterfall 't its head, th' slim, brown Injun maid. . . . [FERRY *and* JOSHUA *exchange looks as though they had heard this tale before;* JOSHUA *turning away a little as* FERRY *chuckles.*] Aye, 'n I told the maid, bein' loon-mad by nature, 'twas here I'd be buried. She answered 'twas Seneca country, an' I'd best speak to them o' my desire; a people both war-like and obligin'. She were a Priestess o' the False Faces, I mind me, wise an' witty beyont ary woman I've knowed. And she . . . eh? Well. . . . [*He dreams deeper, murmuring.*] Days I have lain in th' Longhouse as my own. . . . Yes, lads, me valley's facing south. . . .

JOSHUA [*still at work but turning to point toward* DONALD'S *chest*]. Yon's why I'm lief to go ahomesteadin' with you and Loder, Ferry, leavin' Mary and th' boy in land but yesterday were hostile.

FERRY [*nodding*]. That Sign on's chest'll guard 'em safer'n a regiment o' the line! [*He nods toward the rising moonlight outside.*] Yon's moon at last, O'Rourk.

JOSHUA [*looking out of the door*]. And here comes Mary and the boy. [*He backs a step in, leaving passageway.*] We be ready to start, Mary.

[MARY *and* JOSHIE *enter, a dripping bucket between them.*]

*Lovely once, ten years on the frontier have made her as strong and sinewy as her husband; bitter determination about her mouth is contradicted by resignation in her eyes and on her untroubled brow. She wears a full skirt of dull blue calimanco, with kerchief and apron, but neither hoop nor cap.*

[JOSHIE, *small for his thirteen years, is slender and nervous, but as controlled as his parents and far more so than his grandfather. He is dressed like the men, but wears no cap; instead of the knife, he has a deadly-looking trade tomahawk at his belt.*]

MARY [*speaking in a flat, even tone throughout*]. So soon? Maybe we were longer gone'n I thought . . . [*As she talks she moves swiftly about the cabin, taking blankets, bacon, and flour from various places to the table and helping* JOSHUA *and* FERRY *to finish packing and closing their two shoulder-packs.*] . . . Joshie, here, would have it he see a redskin peerin' from the bank above the spring, and nothin' would do him but go scoutin' after.

JOSHUA [*stopping his gun-loading to frown*]. Find any traces, son?

MARY. To be sure he didn't!

JOSHIE [*defensively*]. There were, too, dad! Mark of a moccasin on th' moss, the green of it still risin'.

FERRY [*also stopping*]. So?

JOSHUA. Don't like the sound o' this. . . . Any other trace, son?

JOSHIE. Not's I could find, dad, 'n I searched main close.

JOSHUA. Ye certain-sure? [JOSHIE *slowly nods his head.*]

MARY [*briskly*]. Were no mark on that moss, nor Indian on the bank! All childer's fancy from listenin' to da's old tales! Don't ye hold back on this, lads.

JOSHUA. What think, da?

DONALD [*reflectively*]. We-ell, may be a bit o' truth in Mary's sayin'. 'One swallow does not make a summer'; an' if lad saw som'at, 'twas no hostile, but a Seneca sneakin' through th' woods fer salt. Their secret wells be hereabouts.

FERRY [*in a tone of relief*]. That'd be it, o' course.
JOSHUA [*hesitating*]. We-ell . . .
MARY. On with your packin', and waste no fear on us.
FERRY. 'Tis four stiff mile to Loder's camp, and if th' moon should cloud, we'll bark our shins on ever' log betwixt here an' him.
MARY. Here's yer bacon. Two flitches, that leaves but one for us. [JOSHUA *suddenly begins measuring out a large portion of powder and ball.*] That means ye hurry back to get us more afore the trails close. I've no hanker for another winter on coon's grease.
JOSHUA. Joshie, bring the other rifles here to me.

[JOSHIE *drags two rifles, one by one, from behind the settle to the table, where* JOSHUA *starts to ram in powder, wadding, and ball,* JOSHIE *helping by holding the guns.*]

MARY. What be ye about, lad? Pack all the ball. Come mornin' I'll run more for da to hunt.
JOSHUA. I'd loaded two. But I'll load 'em all, an' leave ye four round besides. 'Tis all we can spare.
FERRY [*protesting*]. Heap more'n we can rightly spare! We'll have too few to hunt, an' they'll have not nigh 'nough fer defense, . . . grantin' they'll need 'em, which I doubt.
MARY. That last's the true word, George Ferry. Your haste'll be our best protection. Go get on, and get back, Josh, bringin' news o' the new homestead.

[*Again* JOSHUA *hesitates, and* FERRY *seizes the opportunity to sweep the extra pile of shot into the two bags that lie waiting for it. Then he tightens his pack, and* JOSHUA *slowly follows his example.*]

JOSHUA. Well, th' rifles be all charged, 't any rate. And first thing 'n th' mornin', Mary, run off them bullets.
FERRY [*swinging his pack to his shoulders and wriggling into its straps*]. Though small good'll one round do, if aught be needed. Here, yonker, lend a hand . . . [JOSHIE *jumps on the stool to help* FERRY.] . . . tighter, if ye've the arm. . . .

Sho, ye'll not strangle me! . . . I thank ye, kindly. [JOSHIE *jumps down, and* FERRY *turns to* DONALD.] Well, old gentleman, bid ye god-den and trust ye've news o' your green hidden valley 'fore day week.

DONALD. The trail lays clear, all clear . . . and beyont, the valley lyin' snug and soft in the southern sun . . . och! but the corn'll sprout up early there!

FERRY. Aye, so we hope. . . . Ready, O'Rourk?

JOSHUA [*being helped into his pack by* MARY]. Nearly . . . nearly. . . . [*He turns to put his hands on her shoulders.*] Be ye frighted, lass, by Joshie's seein' by the spring, I'll stay.

MARY [*impatiently*]. Nay, I'm not the one to hold ye back for childer's fancy! If ye go not in with the first parties, da's valley'll fall to some other settler. Good-bye, lad, get ye gone, . . . and quick. [*He stoops to touch her lips with his.*]

JOSHUA. Good-bye, lass. [*Turns to his father.*] Good-bye, da.

DONALD. Good-bye, son. . . . God bless ye on yer trail, which as I says . . .

JOSHUA [*cutting the old man off before he expounds again*]. Look sharp t' th' hogs, Joshie . . . don't ram the waddin' too hard, if ye take out the old rifle . . . give da his noggin' o' rum, an' no more. . . .

DONALD. Aye!

MARY. Aye, and no more!

JOSHUA. Now I *be* ready, Ferry.

[*With slinging stride, they go into the moonlight.* MARY *watches a moment from the door;* JOSHIE *drags pallet and blanket from behind the settle, strips off his fringed shirt, lays the tomahawk beside the pallet, rolls into the blanket, and composes himself for the night, his feet all but in the fire. While they talk* MARY *stirs about, redding up the men's litter;* DONALD *re-lights his pipe and sits puffing and gazing into the fire.*]

DONALD. He be a good son . . . my Josh.

MARY. And a good husband.

DONALD. He be all I've left . . . out o' nine that Rachel bore me.

MARY [*constrainedly*]. 'Tis the way o' things, da. Quick born, quick gone. . . . The Lord's will be done.

DONALD [*absently*]. . . . I sometimes think we be like the maples, Mary. Ten thousand winged keys they fly each spring, yet out o' all that multitude mayhap but forty seeds'll sprout, an' o' the forty but one saplin'll grow great enough to tap for sugar.

MARY [*her throat suddenly working*]. Aye, we be even so, da . . . save that . . . that . . . [*She sobs.*] . . . save that the trees cannot remember. . . . [*She suddenly sinks on the stool, fists to her mouth, her shoulders shaking convulsively. DONALD scrambles to his feet to go to her in puzzled distress.*]

DONALD. Why, what ails ye, lass? I meant not to grieve ye! I would not for th' King o' Spain's fair daughter!

MARY [*fighting her emotion and uncovering her working face*]. 'Tis that the pain o' losin' 'em . . . lasts a deal longer'n . . . the pain o' bearin' 'em! 'Tis six year . . . six year tonight . . . we laid little Donald away!

DONALD [*his hand on her shoulder*]. So 'tis, Mary! . . . so 'tis! I'd forgot.

MARY [*mastering her emotion and smoothing her face and hair*]. 'N Josh had forgot. But I'd no call to remind him. We've all troubles enough of our own without sharin' 'em.

DONALD. And you were right, lass. 'Tis ill travellin' on a heavy heart. [*Suddenly JOSHUA looms in the doorway, and steps inside with an apprehensive glance over his shoulder.*] Eh? Forgot som'at, son?

JOSHUA. Mary! Ye be weepin'! Then I'll not go.

MARY. 'Tis naught, Josh . . . and less'n naught! [*She rises.*] For why did ye come back?

JOSHUA [*putting his hands on her shoulders*]. Have ye hurt yourself? [*Looking at her searchingly.*] Or were ye frighted?

# DONALDS O'ROURK

MARY. 'Tis nothin'. Just an old pain chance words o' da's brought to my mind.

JOSHUA. Be ye certain-sure o' that, Mary?

MARY [*in surprise*]. Why, Josh . . . what else'd there be?

JOSHUA [*dropping his hands to glance uneasily at the door, as he speaks in hushed tones*]. 'Tis still as death under the moon. Not a breath stirrin'. Even the alders hang silent. Yet th' woods seem full . . . o' soundless rustlin's! Step ye out and harken, da. Ye've keener ears than I, even yet.

[DONALD *moves through the door;* JOSHUA *and* MARY *stand listening and only whisper.*]

MARY. Where's George?

JOSHUA. He be watchin' silent by the rock by the run. [*As* DONALD *returns.*] What be it, da?

DONALD. Naught, lad, need trouble ye. The woods be sometimes so; that's all mortal man can say of it. Get ye gone with free heart.

JOSHUA. But Mary were weepin'.

DONALD. Women will weep at times.

JOSHUA [*suddenly looking at his wife*]. 'Tis five year since wee Donald died. . . . Were that it, lass?

MARY [*she nods, but must correct him gently*]. Six years, Josh. . . . [*And presses her knuckles against her mouth, as he goes to put his arm around her.*]

JOSHUA [*awkwardly*]. Why, sweetheart . . . there, there! . . . Ye be sure that's all? There's no present fear?

MARY. Nay . . . truly.

JOSHUA [*kissing her again*]. Then fare ye well, lass. Ferry'll wait no longer. Bar the door well come night.

[*He goes out;* DONALD *goes half out the door, watching them go and listening, then shuts the door but does not bar it.*]

MARY. Did ye truly hear naught, da, when ye stepped without?

DONALD. Naught but the spirits o' the dead. Times, when

moon's full, th' woods be filled with 'em. Your heart was callin' on wee Donald . . . and the others. Cease your thoughts of 'em, an' they'll go back again.

MARY [*with weary impatience*]. Seems like I spend my life tryin' not to think of 'em. [*She has finished redding up and sits on the settle beside him, asking practically.*] Da, did ever ye traffic with The Snake Weaver?

DONALD [*shaking his head*]. He'll be a sachem new-raised since my time. Why do ye ask?

MARY. We've sore need o' salt, and have I not heard o' secret salt wells here?

DONALD [*nodding assent*]. Many a bucket o' brine I've seen brought out th' woods.

MARY. Know ye not where it lie?

DONALD. A Cayuga'd 've kept that from his clan-brother, an' they not o' the same nation! . . . Still, I doubt not th' Senecas'll trade salt with us in the bucket, if, meeting up with them, we treat 'em civil.

MARY [*her mouth pinched bitterly*]. 'Twill go again' my grain to trade e'en a bucket o' brine with them painted, stinkin', blood-thirsty varmints!

DONALD [*rebuking her*]. Now, lass! Ye'd not miscall 'em so, if ye'd lain in the Longhouse.

MARY. Mayhap, mayhap! But for seven mortal hours, I lay under a rottin' bearskin in my father's byre in Cherry Valley, while them redskins was massacrin' an' burnin' through that night.

DONALD [*this is an old argument between them*]. Ye'll never remember, Mary, *them* Indians had blue eyes. Blue eyes, an' orders from a noble lord in London.

MARY. Blue-eyed or redskinned, they killed ye just as cruel. [*A faint and distant cry offstage brings her to her feet, crying shrilly.*] What was that!

[JOSHIE *stirs uneasily and opens his eyes, while* DONALD *gets slowly to his feet.*]

DONALD. I heard naught. . . . Hark!
   [*As they hold breath, a long trilling cry comes off right.*]
MARY. Oh! 'Tis but a screech owl. They always give me the creeps.
JOSHIE [*rising to one elbow*]. That were no screech owl . . . were it, Grandad?
DONALD [*moving toward the door to bar it*]. No . . . it were too harsh. . . .
JOSHIE [*scrambling to his feet, grabs a gun and faces the door*]. The whicker of a coon, belike? *
   [*As* DONALD *bars the door the call comes again, nearer and from left.*]
MARY [*whirling to face it*]. Why, I thought 'twere over yon. . . .
   [*The call comes from off back.*]
JOSHIE. Now 'tis this side! [*The call comes in quick succession from left, right, and back.* JOSHIE *runs to* DONALD.] Grandad! What be it?
DONALD [*barely breathing the words*]. God . . . surrounded!
MARY and JOSHIE [*whispering*]. Redskins?
DONALD. Aye . . . redskins.
MARY [*very calmly.*] What shall we do? [*Wailing in quickly passing hysteria.*] What *can* we do?
DONALD. Little enough. But we'll do it. [*His years slip from him as he faces a crisis that is no new one to him.*] Joshie, get out all th' rifles. [*He peers through the loop-hole in the left wall;* MARY *helps* JOSHIE *lug the four rifles from behind the settle to the table.*] Mary, bring me the new one. [*She drags the rifle to him; he leans the muzzle in the loop.*] Can ye handle it, rested again' the loop? [*She presses the stock to her shoulder and sights along the barrel.*]
MARY. I think so.
DONALD. This be your post. [*He peers above her head into the moonlight.*] The woods this side be so far, I doubt they risk bein' picked in a run through the stubble. [*He moves toward*

*the table, speaking to himself rather than to the others.*] They can't be knowin' we've but one round, though must have marked we're short two men. . . .

MARY [*dropping her rifle with a crash*]. Josh! Josh and Ferry, da! Out yon. . . .

DONALD [*sternly*]. Let be! . . . We've no time, now, to think of aught save ourselves. [*She controls herself and picks up the rifle.*] Now, Joshie, you here. . . . [*He posts the boy with a second rifle at the right loop, taking an ax from under the settle with him.*] And here be the ax. . . . Oh, ye've your tomahawk. I'll keep the ax meself, then. [*As he carries it to the door, with one foot he hitches the stool along with him and then lays the ax upon it. He moves the two remaining rifles to the door, leaning one against each lintel. Then he crushes out the flame of the fire with quick dabs of his moccasins, leaving only the glow of the backlog. Finally he goes to the door, adjusts the peephole, thrusts a rifle through it. His voice comes with calm authority through the faintly glowing gloom.*] Now, listen close! We've four balls bechune us, so ever' one *must* tell. 'Tis tricky, by moonlight, so save your shot till ye *cannot* miss. That'll be four men's lives. Joshie must do one with his tomahawk, and I'll try for two with the ax. If there be more'n seven, th' good Lord deliver us! [*There is a long pause, then the owl cry sounds again from three sides.*] See aught, lass?

MARY [*doubtfully, weaving her head from side to side*]. It might be a breeze in the bushes.

DONALD. There be no breeze.

JOSHIE [*quietly*]. 'S creepin' through the weeds by the white birch.

DONALD. Hold, lad, till ye be sure of him.

MARY [*screaming*]. Da! Da! Comes two through the stubble! [*Her rifle slips and goes off at random.*]

[*A many-throated warwhoop rises from every side.* JOSHIE *shoots; shouts,* "Missed, by Golly!"; *darts to seize his grand-*

*father's spare rifle; and returns to his loop ready to shoot again.* Donald *calmly sights, and fires; then he throws aside the rifle, seizes the ax, and stands at the door, glancing hurriedly back over the room.*]

Donald. Mary! Mary! Th' cask. Bash it, quick! So they'll no get rum! [*But she sinks to her knees paralyzed by terror.*] Joshie, th' rum! Bash it in with your hatchet! [*But before* Joshie *can turn from his loophole* Donald *dashes to the keg, knocks the head in with a blow or two of his ax, tips the keg to empty along the joint of left wall and floor, and dashes back to the door.*] Drunken redskins'll no help th' case!

[*There is a long moment's silence.*]

Joshie. Have we scared 'em off?

Donald. Not them. But they've drawed our fire. . . . Listen. See aught?

Mary. Nothin' stirrin' this side. [*The owl cries sound again from all sides.*]

Donald. They was but testin' us. Steady. . . .

Joshie. Wait! There's a big buck standin' alone by the white birch. Shall I . . . ? He's movin' in!

Donald [*quietly*]. Let 'im get closer, lad.

Joshie. He's got his hand up. He's stoppin'!

Donald. Mayhap 'tis the signal to rush us. Hark! [*From outside a voice calls "Donald O'Rourk!"*]

Mary. Da! He's callin' *you!*

Donald. What in tarnation . . .

Voice. Put up your guns. We come in peace!

Mary. A trick to get in!

Voice. We come to speak with Donald O'Rourk. If he is within, open your door. No harm will come to you.

Joshie. He's close now. Shall I . . . ?

Donald. No! No! Listen!

Voice. It is The Snake Weaver who speaks. Open the door.

Donald. The Snake Weaver! [*To* Joshie.] Is he armed?

Joshie. His hands be empty . . . but there's a knife in his belt.

DONALD [*moving to the door*]. 'Tis our sole chance. . . .
MARY [*running to get between him and the door*]. No, no, *no!* Da, ha' mercy!
DONALD [*brushing her aside*]. We've but a shot bechune us . . . and I have lain in the Longhouse! [*He throws open the door and steps back.*]

[MARY *gasps hysterically and backs with* JOSHIE.* *As they stand,* THE SNAKE WEAVER *enters slowly but firmly. He is a tall, unusually broad Iroquois, rather past middle-age, in full ceremonial dress: buckskin leggings, fringed belt and pouch, the clan sign of the Deer on his chest, and over it, many necklaces, with a silver U.S. gorget among them. A scarlet blanket trails from one arm; a pair of heron feathers descend from the curiously gray scalplock.*]

DONALD [*in puzzled amazement*]. No paint! Nor firearms! Now, why in tarnation . . . [*Stepping forward and addressing the Chief.*] Listen, you sachem . . . carry ye white belts or black?
THE SNAKE WEAVER. Are you Donald O'Rourk?
DONALD [*cautiously*]. And if I be?
THE SNAKE WEAVER. The belts are white.
DONALD [*curiously*]. And if I be not?
THE SNAKE WEAVER. We go, like the snow under the March moon, as if we had never been. [*He waits in proud patience while* DONALD *meditates.*]
DONALD. Give me the belts, you sachem, for I am Donald O'Rourk.
THE SNAKE WEAVER. If your words are true, you carry a token of my father's clan, which is the Clan of the Bear. Show it to me, before I give the belts.
MARY. Da! You must . . . [DONALD *silences her with a gesture and opens his shirt to show the Sign on his chest.*]
THE SNAKE WEAVER. How! Good! The belts are white. [*In pantomime he delivers many imaginary belts to* DONALD *who*

*receives them in the same fashion, raising them high above his head.*]

MARY [*almost beside herself*]. Da, ask him—ye *must* ask him—what he has done with Josh and Ferry!

DONALD. Hush! This be ceremony, and women may not speak, save through the mouths o' men. White belts bind the settlers and the Council Fire, you sachem. Why come ye to the cabin of Donald O'Rourk with owl-cry and warwhoop?

THE SNAKE WEAVER [*folding his arms in the ritualistic manner*]. How! I am a warrior. I am a sachem. I am The Snake Weaver. With owl-cry and warwhoops I came to this lodge, for I feared if I knocked at the door the latchstring would be drawn in, and your ears closed against my words. [*During the subsequent "I am a warrior" speeches, he paces slowly back and forth across the stage like a speaker before the Council Fire.*] Listen, you Donald O'Rourk . . . I am a warrior. I am a sachem. Many are the scalps I have taken. Many are the prisoners I have burnt. I might have made you my prisoner, to be scalped and tortured, as is the custom in our warfare. . . .

MARY [*shuddering*]. Da! . . . Da!

* THE SNAKE WEAVER [*ignoring her, suddenly notices the spilt keg, goes to it quickly, turns it up, then back, seeing it is empty; he grunts first as though in disappointment, and then as in reluctant approval*]. It is well, Donald O'Rourk!

DONALD. It is well, you sachem.

THE SNAKE WEAVER [*beginning to pace again*].* But I came carrying no weapons, nor with painted face, nor have I let my young men paint theirs. For I bring white belts.

DONALD. It is so belts should be brought to one who lay as brother in the Longhouse many a winter long gone.

THE SNAKE WEAVER [*halting, folding his arms, and lifting his chin*]. I am a warrior. I am a Seneca. I am The Snake Weaver. I am your son.

Donald. H-wh-at? My son?

Mary [*awed*]. Da . . . yon's crazed!

The Snake Weaver. My mother was a Seneca, of the Clan of the Deer. They called her the Dog Tooth. . . .

Donald. My slim brown Priestess o' the False Faces!

The Snake Weaver. She kept your name green in her memory, and spoke to me of you. You are Donald O'Rourk. You are my father. I am Donald O'Rourk. I am your son.

Donald [*to himself*]. Could it be I have still *two* sons? She said naught to me! Nor later, when I passed that way in '54.

Mary. I'll warrant not! The lyin' Injun trollop!

Donald [*impatiently*]. Ye do not understand! Ye never do. In the Longhouse, the childer belong to the mother. The father be naught.

Mary. Then why be *he* here . . . claimin' naught of ye?

Donald [*puzzled*]. What the woman says is sense, you sachem. Why come ye, The Snake Weaver, claimin' kin with me, who though onct was som'at, be now so little?

The Snake Weaver. How! It is true. I am a Red Man, and a sachem among the Senecas. But I am your son. So I am white man. When I depart from the trail of my red brothers, with the white man's rum, [*He points to the cask.*] it is because I feel your white blood leaping in my veins. But, when I walk with my white brothers, I have no name. It is the custom of white men to take the name of the father. Give me your name, so men will not point saying, "There goes the Nameless One." Give me your name, O'Rourk, so I need not be ashamed. Give me, also, my father, your "blezzing," [*He lingers on the unfamiliar word.*] as is the custom of white men.

Donald [*suddenly wilting into old age*]. This be all too crooked a trail fer me to follow!

The Snake Weaver [*gently*]. I wished to see you, and greet you in friendship. . . .

MARY [*in bitter scorn*]. Why comes he whoopin' th' hearts out'n us to show his "friendship"!

DONALD. Again the woman says sense. It is not with war-cries white men claim kinship.

THE SNAKE WEAVER [*drawing himself up to his full height*]. I am a warrior, and a war chief. When men called me by my true name, many young men followed me on the warpath. Now, when I put on the horns, they listen and heed my words. I am not a louse to be crushed between your thumbnails. I am The Snake Weaver. I come to your cabin with my young warriors lest you hold me an old moccasin, fit only to be left rotting by the trail. I am a warrior whom many have feared. [*Becoming gentle.*] But you need not fear. You have been friendly to Indians. They are your friends. I respect you, my father. [*He bends to sweep his fingertips across the flaps of* DONALD'S *moccasins.*]

MARY [*angrily*]. Da! Surely ye be not creditin' yon?

DONALD [*slowly*]. Why, lass, beyond doubt he's white blood in his veins, and if his mother said 'tis mine, what call've I t' deny it? . . .

MARY. Ye'll be acknowledgin' the whole Six Nations, come they traipsin' to call ye "father"!

DONALD [*walking round and round the quaintly embarrassed sachem*]. Nay, look at his scalp-lock. Nary Indian e'er showed gray, at fifty odd. And his hands, heavy to strike a man or wield an ax, . . . no redskin ever'd hands like them.

MARY [*wailing*]. Da! 'Tis you that be crazed!

DONALD [*ignoring her words, his voice ringing with curious pride*]. And did ye note, lass, how's chin stuck out? That's straight from Derry. Sure, 'tis the mark of an Irish fighter! But he's his mother's eyes, that could see further'n most. . . . And that bold beak's from the Longhouse, too. 'Tis a better'n I could've give him. Sure, an' he's drawn th' best from th' both of us t' make him a man, an' a leader o' men!

Deny 'im? Me as have but one other left me? And he a son the King o' all Spain might take pride in th' claimin'!

MARY. And you, as've been a respectable married man, with a wife bore you nine, afore you laid her away!

DONALD [*quickly*]. There was no wrong! 'Twas all long afore ever I saw Rachel. And I and the maid was married, too . . . as things go in the Longhouse.

MARY [*savagely*]. Aye, . . . I know how they go!

[*Suddenly* DONALD *drops his head in his hands, the years overwhelming him.*]

DONALD. 'Tis . . . all so mixed-like! Were Rachel's husband th' lad as wintered with the Senecas? Was either of 'em th' man as scouted for Gen'ral Schuyler? Was he the old owl, dozin' but now in the firelight? Which man be I? . . . What be I? . . . Be I . . . be I . . . *me?* [*He thrusts out a hand, swaying blindly.* THE SNAKE WEAVER *takes the hand, and draws it down, with a curious gentleness.*]

THE SNAKE WEAVER. We of the Longhouse love our friends and our kindred, and treat them with kindness. If you choose to follow the trail of your yellow son, I will cherish your old age with plenty of venison.

DONALD [*coming out of the past, but still dazed*]. Eh?

MARY [*blazing*]. Da, how can ye hark to yon! With Josh, maybe, layin' scalped, not a stone's throw from the door.

[*For the first time* THE SNAKE WEAVER *acknowledges her presence, although he still addresses* DONALD *exclusively.*]

THE SNAKE WEAVER. My white brother is now far on his trail. And that trail is made clear.

DONALD [*to* MARY]. Ye see? They wear no war paint. . . . Where be me pipe? How can I ponder aught without me pipe?

[THE SNAKE WEAVER *spies and retrieves the churchwarden from under the table. He hands it to* DONALD *while* MARY *continues angrily.*]

MARY. And what be there to ponder, pray?

DONALD [*packing his pipe*]. The life in the lodges! The brave life I lived in the lodges . . . when I was young. [*He goes to the hearth, where* THE SNAKE WEAVER *holds a coal to his pipe.*]

MARY. And who'll hunt for us, if ye go back to 'em? Can Joshie handle a log by his lone, or bear in a buck, if be so lucky he's to hit one? When redskins come asneakin' in, am I one to pow-wow 'em, 'n offer belts and tokens? Is it ye'll leave your flesh an' blood to freeze an' starve an' at th' last be scalped, to loiter out your age in a dirty Injun lodge!

DONALD. Wait. Me . . . me pipe's not right lit yet. [*He stands leaning against the chimney, puffing gray clouds down into the fire.* JOSHIE *slips to the floor at the settle's end, where he now squats like an Indian, nodding sleepily.* MARY *looks anxiously at* DONALD. THE SNAKE WEAVER *waits in proud patience, arms folded. At last the old man knocks some ashes from his pipe and turns to* THE SNAKE WEAVER *with finality.*] Listen, you Donald O'Rourk, that ye be my son I well believe, th' more as I have lost many sons as tall and strong and straight as you be. Aye, in all fatherhood, I hold ye for me true-begotten son, an' as such shall ye be addressed and acknowledged. But I cannot live in your lodge. There be for each man a trail, a trail which he may travel but once. When I was young me trail led to the Longhouse of the Senecas. Now I am old I cannot go that way again. I must walk with me white childer till the end o' th' trail be reached . . . t' th' end o' th' trail! But, till then and after, I charge ye, Donald O'Rourk, to live in peace and friendship with your white brother, and to keep his squaw an' his childer under your arms. Then my blessing shall descend on both ye sons alike. . . . I have spoken. . . . Is it good?

THE SNAKE WEAVER [*gravely*]. It is good! If you wish to go to the new fields, my young men shall show you where the best ones lie. Is there more I may do for you . . . my father?

MARY [*calm and practical again*]. Salt, da,

DONALD. We be sore need o' salt for the winter's meat.

THE SNAKE WEAVER. Is the moon still clear?

MARY [*wonderingly*]. Clear as clear.

THE SNAKE WEAVER. Come then, . . . the squaw and the boy. My young men will show them the little well tonight. It lies but a long shot from where we stand.

MARY [*muttering to herself*]. Nay, but I must! I'd not swap a bucket o' salt for a bucket o' gold, and us winterbound in the wilderness.

DONALD. The . . . the belts are white.

[THE SNAKE WEAVER *takes* DONALD's *right hand and raises it above his own head.*]

THE SNAKE WEAVER. When the sun has risen, my father, I, Donald O'Rourk, will visit this lodge again. [*He steps to the door and gives the owl-call which is answered from without; then he turns to* MARY.] Come! With the boy. [*He steps lightly over the log-threshold and disappears.* MARY *casts a distrustful glance at* DONALD, *and taking* JOSHIE's *hand, follows.* DONALD *sinks wearily into his accustomed seat.*]

DONALD [*petulantly*]. Eh? Me pipe be out again! [*Once more he packs and lights it, watching the clouds of smoke in silence. Suddenly he sighs heavily.*] Aye, I'm old. That's it. . . . I'm old! Fit for naught, now, save to pot pigeons and chop firewood for the women and childer. . . . The trail comes to an end. . . . All trails come to an end . . . some kind . . . of an . . . end. . . . [*His head sags back and he sinks into the easy sleep of old age, the pipe fuming between his fingers.*]

SLOW CURTAIN

# A DAY IN THE VINEYARD

## Ballad and Folk-Say Among the Grape Pickers

*by*

E. IRENE BAKER and A. M. DRUMMOND

## A DAY IN THE VINEYARD

THE COLORFUL harvesting of the grapes in the vineyards of Western New York is the important event of the year for many Yorkers. And the talk, songs, and ideas of grape pickers make up this Chautauqua County ballad-play. The workers themselves, whose homely, proverbial sayings are common to farmers throughout the State, supply most of the setting; their day's work is the plot. The play's life-like and lyrical quality shows that "folk plays" need not always be "historical," but can reflect pleasantly the work and play of our own time.

A *Day in the Vineyard* is a singing-talking scene; but almost anyone can sing a simple ballad, and act and talk while he sings. Many groups find such ballad-plays more entertaining and festive than straight dramatic pieces.

The stage directions suggest a vineyard setting. But with colorful costumes, and a few crates to sit on, the play is effective without "scenery." The great popularity of Thornton Wilder's *Our Town* shows that audiences enjoy pantomimed action unencumbered by realistic setting. This style makes presentation easy: indoors, a bare platform or the end of a large room serves; outdoors, the lawn or picnic ground provides luxurious staging. Or the play can be made an episode in a pageant.

One of the characters, or an added character, can accompany the singing on a guitar, fiddle, accordion, or mouth-organ. Or an organ or piano with a supporting chorus can supply the musical background, while the actors perform the play and sing, too. The "girls" all sing. JASMINE and ADELAIDE have a duet, though any other two, excepting perhaps MYRA, could sing this. MYRA might accompany the duet and the later stanzas of the ballad on a guitar. The music is printed at the close of the script.

Your group might try this play and then compose a similar one, based on apple-picking, a quilting bee, a picnic supper, a square dance, or some other festival activity,—and on a song you like to sing.

## GRANDMA'AM'S ADVICE

My grandma'am lived on yonder little green,
As fine an old lady as ever seen;
She ofttimes taught me with caution and with care
Of all false young men to beware.
Ti di um dum dum dum didi id i air,
Of all false young men to beware.

These false young men, they will wickedly deceive,
But O my dear daughter, you must not believe;
They will coax and they will flatter till they get you in a snare.
Then away goes poor old grandma'am's care.
Ti di um dum dum dum didi id i air,
Then away goes poor old grandma'am's care.

There are many versions of this American adaptation of the Eighteenth-Century English song "The Old Maid"; see Emelyn E. Gardner's *Folklore from the Schoharie Hills*. University of Michigan Press, Ann Arbor, 1937.

The first that came a-courting was from yonder little green,
As fine a young gentleman as ever was seen;
But the words of my grandma'am were running through my head,
So I could not attend to one word that he said.
Ti di um dum dum dum didi id i aid,
So I could not attend to one word that he said.

The next that came a-courting was from yonder little hill,
He seemed to come with a right good will;
But not one fig for him did I care;
I told him to go, but I didn't care where.
Ti di um dum dum dum didi id i air,
I told him to go, but I didn't care where.

The last that came a-courting was from yonder little grove.
'Twas there I met with a joyful love,
Such a joyful love! O who would be afraid?
'Tis better to be married than to die an old maid.
Ti di um dum dum dum didi id i aid,
'Tis better to be married than to die an old maid.

O dear, what a fuss these old ladies, they do make;
Thinks I to myself, "It is all a mistake;
For if all the young ladies of young men had been afraid,
Why, grandma'am herself had died an old maid."
Ti di um dum dum dum didi id i aid,
Why, grandma'am herself had died an old maid!

TIME: *The present.*
PLACE: *A grape vineyard.*

## THE CHARACTERS OF THE PLAY

PEGGY, *she is fifty, and "married her husband to mother him."*
ADELAIDE, *an old maid; the others think she'll stay one.*
VERONICA, *about forty; married too young, and if she had it to do again, would wait till older.*
FLORA, *a vigorous fifty; is philosophical and efficient, with a baked-goods business.*
JASMINE, *in her late twenties; she is shrewd and sharp but good-natured.*
MYRA, *a pretty eighteen; she thinks she won't marry, but has a good heart and a romantic air.*
COUSIN KATE, *a motherly young woman of twenty-some.*
BABY ELLEN, *a real baby, or a dummy.*
THE HIRED MAN, *a reticent humorist of forty-odd who sings a little, and has a way with him.*
THE BOSS, *middle-aged, big, hearty, slow-speaking; he likes laughter and singing.*
THE BOSS'S WIFE, *the business end of the family, but pleasant, and buxom.*

# A DAY IN THE VINEYARD

THE SCENE *is a grape vineyard, showing one trellis parallel to footlights or the end-posts of several trellises. Grape-baskets are arranged at the front. A shock of corn, a boulder, or a growing tree might add to the scenery. Clothes are old and worn, but colorful.*

[THE PICKERS *arrive in the field. They carry lunches wrapped in newspaper or in paper sacks; one has a dinner pail, one a large basket, one a big jug of water. Perhaps* MYRA *has her guitar. Each picker has on a heavy wrap of some kind, for the morning though bright is cool. They place their lunches, jug, and basket under a tree. They arrange themselves, one humming the song brightly.*]

PEGGY [*yawns, shivers, looks about, gathering herself for work*]. Oh dear, oh dear! Work! [*To the one la-la-ing the ballad.*] You sound wide-awake as a marigold!

ADELAIDE [*sneezes*]. Ooh . . . I got up sneezing!

VERONICA. Sneeze before seven, company before eleven!

FLORA. Well, here comes the hired man with grape-shears.

PEGGY. With the grape-shears for—[*She yawns.*]—work!

JASMINE. Well, it's about the last of the grape picking.

VERONICA [*answering* FLORA *in low voice*]. Not so much to look at is he?

FLORA. No. They tell me he's a bachelor. Been working for them these ten years.

VERONICA. I'd hate to've been hanging since he was forty.

FLORA. Homeliest man I ever set eyes on! [*Points.*] Watch him stride along!

[*The* HIRED MAN *enters smiling broadly.*]
HIRED MAN. Good mornin' everybody!
PICKERS [*answering variously*]. Good morning!
FLORA. Where are our shears?
HIRED MAN. Right here you are, ma'am.
FLORA. I suppose you sharpened them last night. Mine wouldn't cut worth a picayune yesterday. They needed oiling, too.
HIRED MAN. Yep. I sharpened 'em all . . . *and* oil'd 'em. Let's see . . . six of you. Six pairs of shears. Here they are.

[*He brings the shears in a basket. He holds them in the palms of his hands and the* PICKERS *gather around him as each selects a pair. They test them by clipping them together. They start picking grapes while the* HIRED MAN *loiters and watches them work; he leans idly on one foot with hands on hips. They make a marked rhythm with sound of clippers; and, as they swing their bodies slightly to the rhythm, one, perhaps* MYRA, *sings the first verse of the song rather under her voice but with words distinct.*]

These false young men, they will wickedly deceive,
But O my dear daughter, you must not believe;
They will coax and they will flatter till they get you in a snare.
Then away goes poor old grandma'am's care.
Ti di um dum dum dum didi id i air,
Then away goes poor old grandma'am's care.
   [*And they all sing the Chorus.*]

HIRED MAN. Do they work all right?
JASMINE. Sure, for a fellow like you sharpening them.
HIRED MAN. So you didn't think I could sharpen shears?
JASMINE. I couldn't tell by the cut of your rig, what you were up to.
HIRED MAN. Handsome is as handsome does!
JASMINE. Maybe so!
HIRED MAN. How are the grapes, anyhow? How do you like this vineyard?

JASMINE. Better than the one over there by the woods. Not so many stick-tights. I got covered with stick-tights from head to foot over there. Itch! Woh! How they itch! I'd think the boss'd have you out there during your spare time doing a little scything.

HIRED MAN. Guess he thinks it don't pay. We did plant turnip seed in a few rows to keep the weeds down, for a' 'xperiment. Next year we'll maybe try buckweat over in that vineyard—[*Points.*] and millet—[*Points.*] in that one up on the side hill.

JASMINE. I see, just waiting around for the cork to bob! You know, you need something to keep you kind of busy. . . .

HIRED MAN. Me? Kind of busy . . . ? I'm busy as a one-armed . . .

JASMINE. Yes. You kind of busy. . . .

HIRED MAN. What d'you mean? [*Laughing.*] It's a poor job can't afford one boss!

JASMINE. Never send a boy on a man's errand.

HIRED MAN. Say now, honey draws more flies'n vinegar!

JASMINE. What I mean is, a bald-headed Dutchman like you should . . .

HIRED MAN. Should be going! Well, go on with your poppy show! I was just enjoyin' hearin' her sing. But I feel no call to stay and be nibbled to death by ducks!

JASMINE. Good-bye! Remember, we'll be here again tomorrow, rain or shine!

[*He backs away and stands singing, glancing at them and at the sky, and around at the grapes and ground.*]

    This life won't last forever
    And beauty will decay
    So take y'r troo love by the han',
    And lead 'er over the way.
[*Then goes, singing louder.*]
    F'r when I hunt fer squirrels

I hunt from tree to tree,
And when I kiss a pretty miss
I think she oughta kiss me.

FLORA [*watching him go*]. He's got a gait like a pair of bars!

JASMINE. Yeah . . . and a natural face long enough to eat oats out of a churn! Well, girls, let's swing to it!

[*They clip and move in rhythm, and sing the second verse.*]

The first that came a-courting was from yonder little green,
As fine a young gentleman as ever was seen;
But the words of my grandma'am were running through my head,
So I could not attend to one word that he said.
Ti di um dum dum dum didi id i aid,
So I could not attend to one word that he said.

[*And the Chorus.*]

JASMINE. Girls, who has the time?

FLORA. I have. [*Looks at watch.*] I have ten-thirty. Getting hungry, are you?

JASMINE. No, thirsty. I'm going to get a drink of cold water to tide me over until noon. The rest of you girls want any?

ALL. Yes.

[JASMINE *goes to the place where the lunches have been stored and returns with a water jug.*]

JASMINE. My turn first, girls! [*Drinks.*]

One, two, three
Out goes *she!*

[*And she hands the jug to* FLORA. *She wipes her mouth with a big handkerchief.*]

Monkey, monkey, bottle o' beer
How many monkeys have we here?

[*They pass the jug along; after they have finished drinking,* JASMINE *returns jug and comes back for her next line.*]

FLORA [*after drinking*]. I can never work until noon without a big drink of water in the middle of the morning.

## A DAY IN THE VINEYARD

VERONICA [*just finishing her pull, breathlessly*]. Me neither!

PEGGY [*points*]. Looks like rain over there! Clouds are darker'n a stack of black cats!

ADELAIDE. Rain! I was hoping the rain would lay off until we finished this vineyard.

MYRA. And this my first day of picking! I wanted to pick all day long!

JASMINE [*drily*]. Your *first* day is the last day of the grapes!

ADELAIDE. Now, back to drudgery again.

JASMINE. Let's swing into it!

[*All begin work again, clipping and swinging in rhythm, and sing the third verse.*]

The next that came a-courting was from yonder little hill,
He seemed to come with a right good will;
But not one fig for him did I care!
I told him to go, but I didn't care where.
Ti di um dum dum dum didi id i air,
I told him to go, but I didn't care where.

[*And the Chorus.*]

PEGGY [*excitedly*]. Oh girls! A red bird with a top knot, just beyond that post! See? What bird is he? There he flies!

MYRA. I know! That's a cardinal. Sometimes they call it Kentucky Cardinal. I remember that because I read a book once called *Kentucky Cardinal*. It told how this bird helped a love affair along. And was it interesting!

JASMINE [*drily*]. Did the lovers get married in the end?

MYRA. Yes, they got married in the end . . . and lived happily ever after, I guess.

FLORA. That's the way with all the stories, but not real life.

PEGGY. Now, now! Real life is what you make it. Just look at me! *I* married my husband to *mother* him. We get along *handsomely!*

JASMINE [*aside*]. The biggest drunkard ever you saw! Spends every nickel on liquor. That's why his *wife works*.

VERONICA. Well, I was married too young! Run off from high school one day. What a mess I got into! My advice is, wait till you're past twenty-one to get married—unless you want to live with your apron to your eye!

FLORA. It's all part of the game of life. I had a good job in an office, when one day along came a handsome salesman. We was love at first sight. He was making big money then. . . . Yes, big money. We got married. Then, the firm wouldn't keep married women any longer and I lost my job. And my husband lost his position . . . so we had to pare the cheese pretty close to the rind. We'd just bought a new car. So we went to selling various articles to small stores around the country. That went all right for a while. But, fin'ly we couldn't even make expenses. And as *he* says, "You can't live on wind pudding and air sauce." So we bought a farm on time, and moved on it, and planted a garden; and as soon as the radishes were big enough I took 'em to town and traded them in for a sack of flour and a few other groceries. That evening I baked some pies, some cookies and two cakes, and began peddling baked-goods the very next day. That was how I started this business of baked-goods.

ADELAIDE. If there's a will there's a way.

MYRA. *I'm* never going to get married!

ADELAIDE. After hearing all you girls talk, it does sound as though you ought to do some planning before you say "yes"! I read Dorothy Dix columns. Her advice is great. She says "feed the brute" is the number one rule! So that's what I'm going to do. Learn to cook!

JASMINE. Not a bad idea *anyway*. They do say a woman can throw out more on a spoon than a husband can bring in on a shovel!

FLORA. She'll be an old maid, sure as living!

JASMINE. There's worse things if you ask me . . . though maybe she don't know it.

PEGGY. I've figured it up. If I pick forty-two baskets of grapes

today, I'll have twenty-four dollars. Not so bad!
VERONICA. What are you going to do with all that money?
PEGGY. One thing, I'm going to buy my daughter Sylvia a new red velvet evening gown for the party they are having for the nurses at the Community Hall.
JASMINE [*drily*]. Silks and satins put out the kitchen fire!
PEGGY. Sylvia's going to be a nurse, not a hired cook! And then she wants some money to buy her new beau a birthday present.
ADELAIDE. I thought Jack O'Brien was her *steady*.
PEGGY. Well, Jack was. But Sylvia's interested in this other young man now. After thinking it over I thought it was just as well for Sylvia to get acquainted with more than one fellow. Sylvia's a sensible girl, and very much interested in her nursing career. Sylvia says that after she comes home for the last of her training, she's going back to New York and work in a hospital there indefinitely.
ADELAIDE [*thinking of nursing now, not of cooking*]. I think nursing is a wonderful profession.
JASMINE. Well, a career won't hurt any woman or girl. That is one thing I regret! I didn't finish normal school and teach . . . before settling down!
VERONICA. Here too! Wish I'd kept on with my music. Maybe I'd been somebody by now.
MYRA. Why, Mother, you are somebody!
VERONICA. Myra, you're going to keep on with your guitar lessons if I have to work my head and toenails off . . . and lock you in to your practice!
MYRA. Just as you say! Only I want a Spanish guitar and not a Hawaiian one. Everybody on the radio plays a Spanish one. And I want to learn to sing Spanish, too.
VERONICA. I don't see why you can't sing in Spanish . . . if you stick to it. You keep right on trying.
JASMINE. Yes sir, Myra, stick to it. I don't know that I can wait for you to learn Spanish, though. And just so you won't

get too high-falutin'! Adelaide and I used to sing duets when we were girls. Come on, Adelaide, suppose we try our voices once again!

ADELAIDE. All right! What will we sing? "Lily Dale"? or "Go Work in the Vineyard"?

JASMINE. Well, either one'll fit nice and sadly on all this "lived happily ever after"!

FLORA [*looking at her watch*]. It's twelve o'clock, girls, let's *eat!* . . . You can sing that duet while we're eating. My stomach thinks my throat is cut!

PEGGY. I could eat a horse and chase its rider!

JASMINE. All right, Adelaide and I'll sing while we're getting ready. You can't sing on a tight belt.

[*The girls drop their clippers and gather where they placed their lunches before beginning work in the morning. They pick off stick-tights as the conversation continues.*]

FLORA. Wheeew! It's hotter'n Dutch love!

ADELAIDE. Look at Flora! Not a single stick-tight on her. How do you keep so clean? I'm simply covered from head to foot!

JASMINE. Oh, I can't sit down! Somebody help me pick off the stick-tights!

ADELAIDE [*helping her*]. They stick like death to a nigger!

FLORA. Yesterday they pricked me so I wound newspaper around my legs. You'd be surprised how that helps!

VERONICA. I'll try that tomorrow!

PEGGY [*who has been sitting near the vines*]. That's a good idea!

MYRA. Come on, Peggy, nearer with us.

PEGGY. No I like it here. [*Pointing to work and to food.*] Where I scratch, there I peck. [*To* MYRA.] Here, young woman, your shoe's untied. . . . That's a sure sign you *will* get married.

[*The girls begin to eat lunch with a chattering of gossip.* JASMINE *and* ADELAIDE *sing the duet,* "Go Work in the

Vineyard." *At its conclusion, all applaud lightly, in various situations as to lunch, and so forth.*]

MYRA. I like that! [*Laughing good-naturedly.*] Still I want to sing in Spanish to a Spanish guitar.

ADELAIDE. Girls! do you dare me to go over to that tomato patch and help myself to a few tomatoes? They'd make lunch taste better.

VERONICA. Sure, go on!

ALL. Get enough for everybody!

[ADELAIDE *disappears.*]

VERONICA [*seeing* JASMINE *produce an egg*]. So! Jasmine! You got up in time to cook yourself an egg!

JASMINE. Don't you wish *you* had! I heard the alarm go off at five o'clock. So I jumped, started breakfast cooking, and fed the chickens and ducks. You should see my ducks, girls! We're going to have duck for every holiday this year!

PEGGY. This tea is strong enough to work by the day!

FLORA. I'm inviting myself to your house for every holiday dinner! I told my husband last night I wished he'd help me milk the cows during grape-picking time.

[ADELAIDE *reappears with several tomatoes; she passes them around with a salt shaker; each shakes salt on her tomato and eats it.*]

THE LAST ONE [*drops the salt and spills it to the right*]. Oooh! Spilled the salt! Company will come from that way! [*Points to right, where the* Boss *will enter.*]

FLORA. Say, Peggy, you were talking this morning about what you were going to do with your grape money! I'm going to buy a cow with *mine!* My husband says I'm crazy, and maybe I *am*, but honestly I want something to call my own, so I thought this was the time, opportunity and money! Just think, a cow all my own!

[ADELAIDE *is ruffling the grass with her hand, looking for something.*]

PEGGY. Lost something, Adelaide?
ADELAIDE. Looking for good luck.
VERONICA [*warningly*]. If you find a six-leaf it means marriage!
[ADELAIDE *finds a daisy, and plucks the petals.*]
ADELAIDE. Rich man, poor man, beggar man, thief,
Doctor, lawyer, Injun chief. . . .
[*Squeezes the seeds in her fist, throws them in the air, and catches them on back of her hand; and holding up two seeds stuck together.*] It says it will be twins!
VERONICA. Well, well, *well, Adelaide!*
JASMINE. Isn't it time to get back to work, Flora? I don't know whether that rain'll hang off or not!
FLORA [*looks at watch*]. Oh, we can take a minute.
MYRA. I hope I don't have to make my *living* picking grapes! This outdoor work is too much for *me*.
VERONICA. Oh, I *like* grape picking for a while . . . maybe *not* as a steady diet!
PEGGY [*looking at the newspaper in which her lunch was packed*]. Girls, I've just come across a poem about grape picking! Want to hear it?
GIRLS. Read it!
PEGGY [*reads poem*].

I gathered grapes today from tangled vines beside a way-
 side path;
And when in Winter, we take jelly with our meat,
My mind will fly to this sweet spot,
Before my eyes will hang the clusters, blue as summer
 skies;
The blue jay's cry will ring again,
And red winged blackbirds rush above my head.

That was written by Edith Wanmer in the *American Agriculturalist!*
VERONICA. That's not a bad poem! [*The others agree.*] I couldn't write one half as good.

## A DAY IN THE VINEYARD

FLORA [*looking at her watch*]. Come on, ladies, up and at it!
[*They rise and prepare to resume work again; one whistles the tune of the song.*]
[COUSIN KATE *enters with* BABY ELLEN.]
JASMINE. Why, hello here! [*Advances to the* BABY.] She's the dearest little thing I ever saw. I'd like one just like her. Didn't you say she had a twin brother that died? How much did he weigh?
COUSIN KATE. Four and a half pounds.
JASMINE. And you say this baby weighed three and a half pounds! My, wouldn't they have been cute now?
VERONICA. She's the sweetest *thing!*
ADELAIDE. The *darling!*
[*The girls gather around admiringly.*]
FLORA. Those two little dimples!
MYRA. See her *smile!*
VERONICA. Do we expect to finish this job today?
JASMINE. Not at this rate. Hey, look! There comes the boss! I'll bet he wants us to finish up this afternoon. Girls, let's show him a thing or two!
GIRLS. [*in glee*]. Sure!
JASMINE. Lazy folks work the best
   When the sun is in the west!
[*They start to work with increased energy and swing, singing the fourth verse.*]

The last that came a-courting was from yonder little grove,
'Twas there I met with a joyful love,
Such a joyful love! O who would be afraid?
'Tis better to be married than to die an old maid.
Ti di um dum dum dum didi id i aid,
'Tis better to be married than to die an old maid.

[*The* Boss *enters.*]
BOSS. Well, girls, [*They greet him.*]—do you suppose with that south wind it'll rain before night?

MYRA. The moon last night was red as blood: that means dry.
VERONICA. We're going to be *done* at half-past three!
BOSS. Half-past three! Well . . . you'll be done at half-past three . . . or else not! [*He looks at the sky and then off south.*] Off on the hill the leaves are turning up white, that's a sure sign of rain. You can *see* the wind bringing it.
JASMINE. Half-past three! By that time we'll be ready to be paid off! . . . Say, Boss, I bet you fifty cents, half-past three is quitting time!
BOSS. Just as you say. I'll take it. If you're through by half-past three, it's fifty cents bonus for the hurry! My wife will be here then with your pay.
JASMINE. See that you're ready to pay up! You know:
> Lazy folks work the best
> When the sun is in the west!

BOSS. Don't you worry. I'll stick to my bargain. [*Mumbles to himself.*] Can't be done . . . can't be done. . . . [*Chuckles as he leaves.*]
FLORA. Three o'clock! Step on it, girls! Why don't you sit down and wait for us, Kate?
MYRA. Here! [*And gives* KATE *something bright to dangle before the baby.*]

[*They swing into it, singing the fifth verse, spacing lines of verse out to get in speeches after the successive lines of the song.*]

O dear, what a fuss these old ladies, they do make;
ADELAIDE. Come on, girls, fifty cents, waiting!
Think I to myself, "It is all a mistake";
MYRA. Five more minutes!
For if all the young ladies of young men had been afraid,
ADELAIDE. We'll make it!
Why, grandma'am herself had died an old maid.
PEGGY. Sure. Three minutes to go. . . .

Ti di um dum dum dum didi id i aid,
Why, grandma'am herself had died an old maid!

VERONICA. One more minute . . . and *here*, my friends, comes the *last* bunch of grapes from the vines for *this* year! [*Holds it up.*]

[*They repeat last two lines of verse as they finish the picking with a flourish.*]

ALL [*variously*]. There you are! Done! Wheewh! Now where's that boss?! The grapes are over for this year!
[*They come down, drop shears in basket, and generally settle themselves, pulling at sleeves and shaking out their clothes; they rest and look to see if the* BOSS *is coming.*]
JASMINE. Well! Look who's coming! The slab-sided Dutchman again! And with a gun!
[*The* HIRED MAN *comes with a gun.*]
JASMINE. Who are you going to shoot?
HIRED MAN [*grinning*]. A cottontail!
JASMINE [*teasing*]. You can't shoot!
[*The* HIRED MAN *laughs and shoots; goes for the rabbit; holds it up and laughs.*]
PEGGY. There, Adelaide, 's a good provider for a good cook!
[*The* HIRED MAN *throws his rabbit over his shoulder and starts to leave, singing.*]

>And when I hunt fer rabbits
>I hunt from tree to tree,
>And when I kiss a pretty miss
>I think she oughta kiss me!

PEGGY [*calling after him*]. Tell the boss we're done.
FLORA. And don't you want to take the shears?
HIRED MAN. I'll tell him. He'll be taking the shears in the car. Here they come now . . . right on the dot!

[*The* Boss *and his* Wife *enter.*]
Jasmine. Well, we did it!
Flora. Three twenty-eight. Grapes picked! No rain *yet!*
Boss. Good work, girls! You win the bet. Here's the fifty cents. [*He hands it to* Jasmine.] You can have a good time on all that! [*Laughs.*]
Jasmine [*taking it*]. Dirty hands make clean money! [*Laughs.*]
Boss. And now the missus'll pay you off.
Boss's Wife. You girls give me the number of baskets you picked. And maybe you—[*To the* Boss.]—better give Kate ten pennies for Baby Ellen's bank on that bet.

[*The* Wife *summons the pickers by name one after the other to be paid off. Each picker hands a slip of paper, receives her cash, and counts it while the next is being paid. After each has counted, the* Wife's *question: "That right?" is answered with: "That's right!" before she calls up another.*]

Boss. Not a bad idea. Here you are, Kate, for Baby Ellen. [*He counts out ten pennies while* Wife *is paying off the girls; and simultaneously to* Kate.] How about the missus and me taking you and Ellen home in our car? The girls'll fill that Ford pretty tight. And we'd enjoy havin' you.
Cousin Kate. Thanks, we'd like that, wouldn't we, Ellen?
Boss [*poking a finger playfully at* Baby Ellen *and laughing to try to make her laugh*]. Ti di um dum dum dum didi id i aid! Let me carry her, Kate. Come on here, Miss Ellen, upsey, daisey!

[*These two group actions are finished simultaneously.*]

Boss. Well, girls, that finishes the grape picking for this year. Good work, and good-bye. Bet you another bonus next year! [*Laughs.*]
Jasmine. We'll win it, mister.
Boss's Wife. Well, Ellen, you going with us? That's nice, Kate! Good-bye, girls.

[*The girls all variously reply: "Good-bye!", "Good-bye,*

# A DAY IN THE VINEYARD

Ellen!", "Good-bye, Kate!", "Good-bye!"]

Boss. I guess we'll all make it home before it rains. [*Kicks the basket of shears.*] I'll have to send him back for these after all. Come on, Miss Ellen. Ti di um dum dum dum didi id i aid!

[*The girls' "good-byes" have strung along and amount almost to cheers and a Chautauqua salute at the exit. The girls pick up their things, preparing to leave.*]

MYRA [*sighing gratefully*]. Well, that's over for this year!

JASMINE. No more grape picking till next grape-picking time. Of course, you can start before the *last* day *next* year!

[*They sing the fifth verse of the song, slipping in a spoken line after each line of the verse.*]

O dear, what a fuss these old ladies, they do make;
MYRA. What'll we do with the fifty cents bonus?
Think I to myself, "It is all a mistake";
FLORA. Let's add a bit to it and go to a show. . . .
For if all the young ladies of young men had been afraid,
VERONICA. No! Buy peanuts. . . .
Why, grandma'am herself had died an old maid.
PEGGY. Candy'd be better. . . .
Ti di um dum dum dum didi id i aid,
JASMINE. I suggest a party at Flora's house. . . .
Why, grandma'am herself had died an old maid!

ADELAIDE. No party after all this dirty work. . . .

[*The* HIRED MAN *returns for the shears.*]

MYRA. I have it . . . the boss's idea. . . . Let's put it in Baby Ellen's bank!

[*The girls exclaim cheerful assents: "Why not?", "Good idea!" and so on.*]

JASMINE. It's unanimous. Here it is, Myra, you take it. [*Hands over the money.*]

HIRED MAN. Well! for *women* that's an *idee*! I'll add a nickel myself. [*And digs out the money for* MYRA.]

JASMINE. Good for you, Dutchman! I'll call our bet paid.
  [*He laughs good naturedly and pats her on the shoulder. It has darkened and a faint roll of thunder is heard.*]
HIRED MAN [*commencing to pick up shears, basket, and jug*]. Come on, girls. It's goin' to rain full-grown frogs in a minute. I'll bring along the picnic for you. Duck for your car.
  [*The girls gather together to start to run for the car, turning up collars, etc., looking up toward stage right at the rain. Small flash of lightning and a sharp clap of thunder. They squeal a little and run. We hear the wind and rain commencing to roar toward us.*]
HIRED MAN [*gathers up basket, jug, and shears, hunched up against the wind and rain*].

>     And when I hunt fer rabbits
>     I hunt from tree to tree,
>     And when I kiss a pretty miss
>     I think she oughta kiss me.

  [*As he sings* JASMINE *dashes back.*]
JASMINE. Say, let me help you with some of these!
  [*They face each other just as she takes the basket from him and he finishes his ditty; they look at each other, then laugh and kiss quickly over the basket.* JASMINE *dashes out laughing, and he follows singing.*]

>     And when I kiss a pretty miss
>     I think she oughta kiss me!

  [*As he exits stage is darkening; a long roll of thunder comes up with roaring sound of rain; lightning flashes.*]

THE END

# GO WORK IN THE VINEYARD
*(Adapted from the old Gospel Hymn)*

Go work in the vine-yard there's plen-ty to do, The
har-vest is great and the lab-'rers are few

There's weed-ing and fenc-ing and clear-ing of roots and
plough-ing and sow-ing, and gath-'ring the fruits.

There are sheep to be tend-ed and lambs to be fed, the
lost must be gath-ered, the wea-ry ones led.

There are fox-es to take, there are wolves to de-stroy, All
(Go to Chorus)

*(over)*

a-ges and ranks we can ful-ly em-ploy.

CHORUS Work _____ go work _____
Go work in the vine-yard, go work in the vine-yard, go work in the vine-yard, there's plen-ty to do. Go work go work The
work work work work The har-vest is great and the lab-'rers are few.

## THE HIRED MAN'S SONG

For _____ when I hunt for squirrels I hunt from tree to tree And when I kiss a pret-ty miss I think she oughta kiss me oh _____

# CHENANGO CRONE

A Drama of the Horse-Runners and Outlaws

*by*

EDWARD KAMARCK

# CHENANGO CRONE

ORGANIZED GANGS of horse-thieves and hoodlums for over a century troubled the New York countryside. Some of these, like Cowboy Claudius Smith and his henchmen of Revolutionary War infamy, are still remembered and give color to the folklore and balladry of the State. The atmosphere and subject-matter of *Chenango Crone* are drawn from the stories of a number of these New York outlaws, and can be considered typical of the horse-running gangs that operated and were in the news and courts of Central New York during the decades before the Civil War. In so generalized a treatment, of course, no names of actual persons have been used.

*Chenango Crone* is a melodrama; but in the dark recesses of Nine Mile Swamp, just off the Cherry Valley Pike near Waterville, where the storied Loomises lived, tragic melodrama was the stuff of life. And at length, led by a strange and controversial figure, Constable Filkins, the people of the countryside marched, and crushed and scattered the outlaws. The story and the play have as essential background and motivation the unrest of the period, brought to a climax by the end of the War and the return of the Northern soldiers to their homes. The theme of son against mother is a device supplied by the author to lend a touch of universality to this York State drama.

TIME: *About 1865, late afternoon of an autumn day.*
PLACE: *The dark recesses of a swamp in the Chenango Valley.*

## THE CHARACTERS OF THE PLAY

ZACK MCILLHERRON.
DAISY.
TERA MCILLHERRON.
CLINT MCILLHERRON.
RINEY MCILLHERRON.
THE DUTCHMAN.
GRIFFIN CHILDERS.

# CHENANGO CRONE

THE SCENE *is a well-furnished cabin, with skins on the floor and skins bedecking the walls. There are several shotguns and rifles, of the Civil War period, suspended along the walls. A door at the back leads to the outside; two windows at the back give glimpses of a dark tangle of cedars and vines. A door at stage right leads to* TERA'S *room.*

[We see ZACK MCILLHERRON, *a big, rough, crude man of about thirty-five, sitting propped up on two chairs next to the edge of a table. He has been wounded, and his legs are swathed in blankets.* DAISY, *a pretty girl of about twenty-one, is doing some household tasks. We hear her singing as the curtain opens.* ZACK *is listening in rapt attention—almost childlike and naive in his interest. He holds a newspaper in his hand clumsily, as if he had suspended reading when she began to sing.*]

DAISY [*singing the old American ballad, "The Brown Girl"*].

>  Lord Thomas had a long broad-sword,
>    It was wonderfully long and sharp.
>  He cut the head of the Brown Girl off,
>    And kicked it against the wall.
>
>  He pointed the handle toward the sun,
>    The point toward his breast,
>  Here is the going of three true loves,
>    God send our souls to rest.
>
>  Go dig my grave under yonder green tree,
>    Go dig it wide and long;

> And bury Fair Eleanor in my arms,
> And the Brown Girl at my feet.

DAISY [*after finishing the ballad*]. My brother taught me that when he was on leave from the War. He died at Bull Run, couple years ago. Ye liked that, Zack?

ZACK [*moved with sincere appreciation*]. It's purty.

DAISY [*proudly*]. I got lotsa songs. . . . [*Pointedly.*] Some real sweet ones 'bout love, too.

ZACK. Ye gotta sing 'em for me, Daisy. All of 'em!

DAISY. Yew sound as if ye never heard singin' afore.

ZACK. Never did, much.

DAISY. Ain't that funny? None of ye ever did, from what I kin see. Yore maw, she most chews me up when I starts singin'. All you McIllherrons is like that—hard, with no joy of livin' in ye. 'Bout the only thing any of ye takes pleasure in is those big, black Civil War guns. [*Points to the guns on the wall.*] All the time cleanin', and makin' 'em shiny. I'm afeared of 'em. Keep feelin' they're goin' to go off when I ain't lookin' 'n maybe shoot me in the back. [*She shudders.*] Wouldn't like that much. Well, they all warned me afore I hired out here. "Ye'll come to no good, Daisy," they said. "Them McIllherrons is a bad lot, 'n Bear Swamp is the most God-forsaken place in all the Chenango Valley." . . . 'N yet . . . [*She pauses, and then softly, looking at* ZACK *intently.*] I ain't at all sorry I come here. [ZACK, *flustered, casts his eyes down. He begins studying the newspaper at his elbow.* DAISY *starts humming and busily resumes her work.*]

ZACK [*putting the newspaper down with a puzzled look and finally shamefacedly offering it to* DAISY]. What do the noospaper say? Read it ter me agin, Daisy!

DAISY [*surprised*]. What! Ye want to hear it agin? I've read it 'bout three times already!

ZACK. Read it fer me!

DAISY. Wouldn't ye rather hear another song? [*Suddenly

*smiles.*] Oh, I'm smart ter ye. Ye just like ta hear yer name writ in the noospaper! [*Coming toward him.*] Don't ye?

ZACK [*handing her the paper*]. Spell me that part what says I'm a roothless, unprinc . . . unprinc . . . [*Can't pronounce it.*] Yew know the part I mean!

DAISY [*wearily*]. Ye oughter have it all knowed by heart now! [*Taking up the newspaper, she reads in a mechanical voice, slowly and deliberately.*] "Zack McIllherron . . . the lee-der of . . . the . . ."

ZACK. Lemme see the letters! [*She comes close and accidentally bumps his leg. He growls.*] Look out fer my leg!

DAISY. I allus fergit which one it is 'at's got the bullet in it! [*Coyly.*] Did I hurt ye, ye pore boy? [*She tries to caress him.*]

ZACK [*drawing away, growls*]. No! Go 'head 'n read it! [*He is afraid of her femininity. He regards it as a menace.*]

DAISY [*continuing to read, she points the words out to* ZACK *as he strains over them*]. ". . . the lee-der . . . of . . . the no-tor-ious . . . McIllherrons of Bear Swamp . . . is a roothless . . . " [*Pauses over the word.*] Don't know what it means, but it sure sounds like a right purty name fer *yew*. . . . [*Continues.*] "is a roothless . . . [*She mouths the word lovingly.*] . . . un-prin-ceepuled . . . killer!" [*She glances at him coyly and half smiles.*] Humph! . . . [*She continues.*] ". . . nooly . . . elected . . . constable . . . Griffin Childers told the . . . *Deauville* . . . *Times* . . . yester-day. He . . . 'n . . . his . . . gang . . . de-zurve nothin' better'n hangin'!" [*She finishes quickly, putting the last three words all together. Then proudly.*] Ain't so hard if youse eddicated 'n knows your letters! [*She sees him still looking at the paper.*] Ain't that enuf?

ZACK [*still training his eyes on the paper*]. What else does it say?

DAISY. Oh, fer lands sakes! Do ye wants hear the rest of it agin, too? How the townsfolks gonna have a meetin' in the town hall today fer to celebrate Childers' election! [*Smiles.*] Don't say nothin' 'bout yew in that part!

ZACK. Childers' 'lection! [*Grumblingly.*] They wouldn't be celebratin' that if maw had her way.

DAISY. Whaddey mean?

ZACK. She wuz aimin' on me fer to be constable.

DAISY [*laughing*]. Yew? A McIllherron as constable? Yew ain't a-foolin' me?

ZACK [*a little hurt*]. I ain't foolin'.

DAISY. Don't seem as if folks would like that much.

ZACK. We'd a made 'em like it.

DAISY. But 'stead the soldier boys come back from the war 'n elected one a their own kind 'n cheated our Zack outa bein' a nice constable. Ye pore boy! Well, 'at's what ye git fer bein' a bad old outlaw. I kin understand now why ye git so mad every time ye hear the name Childers. 'Specially since he wants to hang yew all.

ZACK [*angrily*]. Childers's a goddam trouble maker! He's got folks stirred up. Ain't no tellin' what he'll lead 'em inta doin' 'gainst us! [*Then significantly.*] Wisht I wuzn't all shot-up here like I am.

DAISY [*playfully*]. Why? Do ye mean you'd hurt him or somethin'?

ZACK. Reckon I would . . . plenty!

DAISY [*laughs*]. Why yew roothless, un-prin-ceepuled killer, yew! [*Smiles coyly.*] Guess they don't know ye like I do or they wouldn't say that!

ZACK. Huh?

DAISY. They wouldn't call ye no roothless killer, if they knowed . . . how . . . ye wuz scairt of wimmen.

ZACK. Ain't scairt of no wimmen.

DAISY. Ain'tcha? [ZACK *is conscious of her charms, but he is awed by her advances. He watches her as warily as a suspicious animal. She smiles at him.*]

ZACK [*growls*]. What ye drivin' at?

Daisy. Ye ain't afeared . . . of . . . me . . . [*She comes close to him.*] . . . or are ye? [*She lifts her head challengingly.*]
Zack [*overcome*]. Goddam!! [*He suddenly kisses her fiercely.*] Yew're . . . purty . . . awful purty!
Daisy. Like me a leetle bit?
Zack. Yeah. [*He kisses her again.*] A little bit.
Daisy. I like yew lots! Since yore old woman first tuk me on here. 'N since then more 'n more. [*Reproachfully.*] Ye never paid no 'tention ter me. [*Teasingly.*] The rest of 'em, they sure noticed me.
Zack. They? Who?
Daisy. Yore brother Clint; the Dutchman . . . 'n some of the others . . . even little Riney!
Zack [*suddenly becoming possessive and jealous*]. Did . . . any of 'em touch ye, any?
Daisy. No! I wouldn't let 'em! Cuz I liked yew! [Tera McIllherron *appears at door at stage left, unseen. She is old, slightly wizened, and hobbles about on a staff. She stands there silently and listens attentively.* Zack *holds* Daisy *in his arms, regarding her passionately and avidly.* Daisy *runs her hand through* Zack's *hair.*] After ye got shot 'n had to stay home I could tell ye had come to like me. Just knowed it from the way ye looked at me, 'n the way ye follered me aroun' with yore eyes!
Zack. If Clint, or the Dutchman, or anybody else starts messin' round with ye, jest . . . tell 'em . . .
Daisy [*hanging on to his words and leading him on*]. What, Zack?
Zack. Jest tell 'em yew're my woman!
Daisy. Oh, Zack! [*She kisses him. Then slowly and wheedlingly.*] Will ye mebbe marry me, sometime?
Zack. Marry ye?
Daisy. I'd sing fer ye the rest of yore life. I'd be yore wife . . . Mrs. Zack McIllherron. Wouldn't ye like that? [Zack

*doesn't answer.*] I know the McIllherrons is known fer not botherin' much 'bout marryin' when they wants a woman. But yew're diffurent. I kin see that.

ZACK. I ain't never had a woman afore. Yo're the first.

DAISY. Wouldn't be no servant girl no more. The old woman couldn't boss me none, or beat me with her stick!

ZACK. She don't beat ye so hard.

DAISY. She does, Zack . . . somethin' awful . . . when yew're not around . . . on my back 'n shoulders. Wanna see the marks? [ZACK *is startled at her immodest offer.*]

ZACK. Marks? Ye mean all over yore purty body? [*The idea is horrible to him.* DAISY *nods.*] I'll marry ye, Daisy!

TERA [*Comes forward quickly and starts beating* DAISY *over the shoulders.*] Oh, no ye won't. Want to be Mrs. Zack McIllherron, do ye? So ye can sit around 'n let me work fer ye! You lazy hussy! Slut! Witch! Git outa here!

ZACK [*in surprise*]. Maw!

DAISY. What's the matter? Zack! [*Appealing to him.*]

ZACK. Have ye got a wildcat in ye?

TERA. Git!

[DAISY, *frightened, runs out of the door at stage right.* TERA *limps after* DAISY, *beating her.*]

ZACK [*fiercely*]. What the hell's wrong with ye? What fer did ye beat her?

TERA [*returning from the door*]. What fer? Cuz she's nothin' but a whore!

ZACK. Don't ye call her that!

TERA. I wuz standin' here 'n I seed her a-seducin' ye there, tryin' to get ye to marry her.

ZACK. She waren't seducin' me. She likes me, 'n I like her!

TERA. Likes ye? Ha! Ye never did know nothin' 'bout wimmen. Allus told ye, ye should keep way from 'em. [*Pause.*] I seed her a-playin' up ter Clint 'n Rett . . . 'n . . .

ZACK. Yew shut up!

TERA. 'Ceptin' they knows enuf not to marry her!

ZACK. I'll marry her if I feel like it!

TERA. Ye ain't if I say ye ain't! I know what happens when a man whut's been afeared of wimmen all his life like yew, gets mixed up with one. She ties 'em round her little finger 'n gives 'em crazy idears like leavin' his old maw, 'n such.

ZACK. Keep outa my bizness! [*Pause.*] Yew 'n yore bossin' ways! 'Ats the cause of all this trouble we're havin'! Yew makin' Clint kill that tin peddler, cuz yew needed some noo pans! [*Scornfully.*] Shoulda knowed like I told ye that wuz goin' too far . . . 'specially with these fellers comin' back from the war . . . that folks wuz too gingered up 'bout the Dutchman killin' old Mose . . . that we wuz doin' too much at once 'n not givin' 'em a chance ta cool down. But no, yew wuz right, ye said. But ye didn't figger that everybody in Hubbardsville seed 'im start out from there 'n knew too durn well he passed this way!

TERA. Ye don't know what yer talkin' about! [*Starts back for her room.*]

ZACK. 'N that wuz jest the thing that broke the mule's back. It's all yore fault Childers wuz elected, 'n the blood'll be on yore hands when the last one of us is hanged!

TERA [*turns around and surveys* ZACK *with anger*]. Ye never wuz one to say much. Ye oughter stay that way! Cuz when ye starts talkin' yer talkin' runs away with ye!

ZACK. Ye dunno nothin' 'bout nothin' . . . 'n yer allus makin' us do things yore way! When we wuz little, ye'd send us ta the store at Deauville 'n say, "Fetch me somethin' extry on the side!" 'n beat us if we didn't steal somethin' 'n fetch it home to ye, 'n ever since ye been bossin' us, 'n we got so used to it, we let ye go ahead!

TERA. When yore maw tells ye to do somethin', it ain't bossin'. It's the right she gits fer bearin' ye.

ZACK. Well, I'm a man . . . fer ten years I been one . . . 'n

I'm durn sick 'n tired of takin' orders from that stick! [*Points to the staff. Then simply and firmly.*] I'm gonna marry Daisy!

TERA [*stubbornly*]. Ye ain't gonna marry nobody, now! [ZACK *doesn't answer but looks at her defiantly.*] I say ye ain't! I say ye ain't! [*In her anger she raises her staff.*]

ZACK. Better not touch me with that! . . . Old witch!

TERA. Calls me a witch, will ya? [*She starts beating him.* ZACK *sits quietly and regards her stonily.*] Ye been needin' this fer a long time! But ye growed up 'n got big on me. But now ye can't hit yore old maw back!

ZACK. If I catch holt a that I'll beat ye dead!

TERA [*in vicious pleasure*]. Ye can't beat yore maw back! [*Continuing to lay into him.*]

[DAISY *appears at the door of stage right, sees the struggle and runs to* ZACK's *aid. She grabs* TERA *and pins her around the arms.*]

ZACK. 'At's right, Daisy! Help me git the stick from her!

[TERA, *surprised, struggles vainly.* ZACK *and* DAISY *wrench the staff free from her hand.* DAISY *has it in her hands.*]

ZACK. Beat her with it. Beat the old . . . [*Stops.* TERA *reaches into her old coat pocket and takes out a revolver.* ZACK *sees it.*] Maw, put that away! [*To* DAISY.] Watch out fer the gun, Daisy!

[TERA *turns around on* DAISY. DAISY, *startled and frightened at the appearance of the gun, drops her stick and retreats in terror to the back door.*]

DAISY [*in terror runs outside.* TERA *goes to the door. We see her back to the audience. We hear* DAISY's *voice outside*]. I'll tell everythin' I know! All about yore killin's 'n stealin'! Don't shoot!

[TERA *shoots twice. There is a slight scream and then silence.*]

ZACK [*speechless at the swift pace of events. There is a pause*

*in which* TERA *puts the gun away, comes back, picks up the staff, and stands staring at* ZACK. ZACK *speaks with quiet, intense hatred*]. Ye killed her, Maw? [TERA *doesn't answer, and then* ZACK *fairly screams at her*.] Ye killed her, didn't ye?
TERA [*quietly*]. No.
ZACK. Don't lie to me! I know ye did! [*In despair*.] The only woman I ever had!
TERA [*quietly*]. I only scared her.
ZACK [*after a pause. He gets doubtful*]. What are ye tellin' me?
TERA [*continuing in the same quiet, emotionless manner*]. I didn't harm a hair of her head. [ZACK *looks at her dubiously and doesn't say anything*.] Believe me, Zack, nary a bullet teched her! [ZACK *stares fixedly before him. Pause.* TERA *watches him for a moment; then speaks for the first time with pity and womanly emotion in her voice*.] Zack, it hurts me awful to fight with ye like this. Yew wuz my first born, 'n I allus liked ye best. Wuz so proud of ye when yew came into the world . . . so small 'n purty . . . like a bear cub . . . we called ye that. We knowed ye'd grow up ter be as strong 'n big as a full-grown bear! [*She tries to caress him*.]
ZACK. Keep yore hands off me! What's got inta ye, anyhow?
TERA [*gently*]. Don't say that ter me, Zack. [*Pause*.] It hurts me powerful to see ye wantin' ta get married 'n leave . . . 'n I gits so mad when ye sets yerself up against me. [*Pause and then weakly*.] I'm old, 'n lonely, 'n miserable. Don't seem like there's nothin' in this world left fer me. . . . I allus thought I wuz diffurent from other wimmen. Usta think I could put down a lotta feelin's I had inside me . . . chicken-hearted feelin's I called 'em . . . feelin's like havin' love fer yore paw, 'n fer yew 'n the rest of 'em . . . 'n takin' pride 'n joy in fixins round the house. But I had to do that, Zack, so misery 'n hunger couldn't touch me none. When yore paw died I found myself all alone with a lotta young 'uns—'n no way a providin' fer 'em. It wuz a hard lot fer a young girl . . . 'n it wuz lonely here in the dark swamp

with no one to talk to. We wuz awful pore . . . gettin' enuf fer ye all to eat wuz all I thought about . . . way we starved all the time! 'Twuz corn bread 'n taters from one end of the year to the next . . . 'n I so wanted ye to grow up big 'n strong. 'Twuz a man's work I had on my shoulders, 'n I had to be as hard as a man. But all the time I had gentler feelin's inside o' me here, a-fightin' with me 'n a-wantin' ta come out. I never larned to give way to 'em like wimmen should. I wantcha ta like me, Zack, ta like me like a son should like his mother. [*Pause during which* ZACK *looks at* TERA *strangely.*] I'm tired out. Soon my old bones are goin' to be laid down in the Chenango hills with the rest of the dead McIllherrons . . . but afore then I want a little of what every woman should have . . . love fer her young 'uns 'n love from 'em.

ZACK [*laughs*]. Maw, that sounds jest a little queer comin' from yew! [*A little viciously.*] Ye allus been so hard 'n ornery.

TERA. I'll make some supper fer ye, Zack. What would ye like? Shall I kill a chicken fer ye?

[*The back door opens, and* CLINT, THE DUTCHMAN, *and* RINEY *come in.* CLINT *is about thirty, small, built chunkily and close to the ground; he is the most intelligent of the group and the best able to express his thoughts.* THE DUTCHMAN, *a member of the gang, is a German immigrant; he speaks little, and with a very noticeable accent.* RINEY *is about seventeen, tall and sparely built. They all carry saddlebags.* THE DUTCHMAN *has a jug of whiskey.*]

CLINT. 'Lo, Maw! Zack! We're back from Albany! [*They exchange greetings.* THE DUTCHMAN *merely nods.*]

RINEY [*Proudly*]. I went 'n got myself one a them noo barlow knives to scalp Injuns with. See, Maw! [*Shows it.*] It's sharp enough to shave with, too. I been tryin' it. [*Applies it to his smooth cheek.*]

CLINT. Better watch out it don't shave yore head off. Albany's a booming town, Zack, now that the soldiers are back. Hell, looks like an army hit town. They're swarmin' round like bees . . . a-drinkin' away their war pay in the saloons and a-whoopin' it up fer Lincoln, Grant and Southern women! [*Chuckling.*] Some a tha stories they tell me about them "belles of Dixie" makes me kinda sorry I didn't jine up the time that draft feller come around, 'stead a chasin' 'im away *unpolitely* the way I did. [*Laughs.*] He sure wuz scairt. [*He stops, his interest attracted by* TERA's *unusual conduct. With awkward tenderness she has put a hand on* RINEY's *shoulder.*]

TERA. How's my little boy been? [*The men watch with acute interest.*]

RINEY [*surprised*]. Huh? [*She kisses him and tries to fondle him with her old, work-worn hands. He pushes her away, revolted by this display of affection.*] Goddam it, Maw! 'At's a hell of a thing to do!

CLINT [*with a whoop*]. Well, gol durn . . . if she didn't go 'n kiss ye! [*They roar with raucous laughter. Mockingly.*] My leetle boy! [*The men laugh while* RINEY *stands humiliated. To* TERA.] Ye wouldn't call 'im that if ye could see all the likker he kin put away!

TERA [*angrily*]. Shut up! Every last one a ye!

CLINT [*still chuckling, changes the subject*]. Well, we had a purty good trip. Got ourselves plenty a hard cash there! [*Throws two saddlebags, one stuffed with bills, on the table.*] Nigh over two thousand! Who said there waren't no money in stolen hosses? Had to do some foxy tradin', though . . . oughter seen how hot they were after them roans from Healy's farm. 'At's dam good horse-flesh. Sorry ye waren't there to do the tradin', Zack. Seein' as yew wuz the one what wuz shot-up gettin' 'em.

ZACK. Ye ain't any sorrier than I be that old man Healy ain't able to see what good prices they fetched. He wuz right proud of 'em . . . while he wuz *alive!* [*The men laugh coarsely.*]

CLINT. Got all the things ye wanted, Maw . . . in the saddlebags . . . brought ye some of that extry special im-ported English smokin' tobaccy fer yore pipe. [*Goes to the saddlebag on the table.*] Put that barlow knife away 'n git the horses in tha barn, Riney, 'stead a lettin' 'em stand there. 'N might look over Blackjack's leg. He wuz limpin' a little accounta that stone he wuz hit with. [RINEY *goes out.* CLINT *assumes a serious note.*] Didn't wanna say anythin' in fronta the young 'un, but Goddamit, Maw, things have gone just too far. I ain't ashamed of tellin' ye I wuz scairt stiff fer my life today ridin' through Deauville. Folks yellin' 'n hootin' when they seed us; Blackjack gettin' hit with a big rock whut wuz meant fer my head; fellas takin' pot shots at us from nowhere; 'n on all sides men starin' at us with blood in their eyes. It ain't never been like this afore.

TERA [*contemptuously, goes to window*]. Yer all feelin' like a young girl.

CLINT. Think so, do ye? Well, lissen to this. There are lots a men in Deauville today from along Bear Path Road 'n all around . . . some in uniform, too. 'N yew know why they're all there? *To celebrate Childers' election to be constable!* 'N what fer should they be doin' that if it tain't cuz he's the first constable they've had in over five years what's had guts enuf to stand up to us and say to everybody in sight, "I'm gonna free the Chanango Valley from the bloody rule of the McIllherrons." Them's his 'xact words, too, cuz they were yelled at us a hundred times today in Deauville.

TERA [*glancing out of the window, quietly*]. There's the devil whut ye jest been mewlin' about.

CLINT. Huh?

TERA. There's yore fancy constable all dressed up in his uniform up there on the road, a-ridin' down into the valley.

CLINT [*looking*]. Well, gol durn—Childers! He's like a bad dream or somethin'. Must be on his way to town. Do ye reckon he'll be cocky enuf to stop in here?

TERA. I ain't scairt of 'im if he does. [*Turning to saddlebags on table.*] What's this stuff ye bought me here? [CLINT *comes back to the table and opens up the saddlebag. Hands* TERA *her tobacco.*]

CLINT. Three dollars the feller wanted fer it. 'Twaren't worth it, so when his back wuz turned . . . I just *tuk* it. [*Laughs.*] Some chawin' tobaccy, Zack? [*Throws him a piece. He gives* THE DUTCHMAN *some. Takes some himself.* TERA *lights her pipe. The boys chew and spit profusely. They're all in deep contemplation thinking about* CLINT's *words.* CLINT *stretches himself in his chair, kicking out his riding kinks.*] 'S good to be home. Wuz hard riding. [*Pause.*] Aw, to hell with Childers. Lemme have that jug, Dutchman!

[THE DUTCHMAN *has been cleaning a gun at the table. He gets up and hands him the jug.*]

TERA [*sitting in the corner, puffing away on her pipe, watching* CLINT]. Where are the rest of ye? Didn't ye all come back together?

CLINT [*with the jug tilted to his mouth, looks at her out of the corner of his eye. After a moment he puts the jug down*]. The rest are still in Albany.

TERA. What?

CLINT. Only Riney, me, 'n the Dutchman have come back.

TERA. What are ye tellin' me?

CLINT. We had a few drinks at the saloon. . . . Everybody got to feelin' high, 'n what with all the hell-raisin' goin' on in town, there wuz no makin' 'em come home. The fellers thought it would be kinda unpatriotic not to stay around and help the boys in blue celebrate the freein' of the niggers. Yew know the way it is, Maw, when a bunch a young fellers git to-gether. .

TERA [*springing up from her chair in anger*]. Ye fools! Ye call yoreselfs growed men, but ye ain't any smarter than three-day colts! Jest can't keep away from yer likker 'n wimmen, kin ye? I tole ye ta come right back as soon as ye sold them hosses.

CLINT. Know ye did, Maw.

TERA. Way folks is roused up 'gainst us, we need all the men we got.

CLINT. Tole Rett the same thing, but he wouldn't listen none . . . wuz dead drunk, 'n rest of 'em stayed cuz he did.

[RINEY *runs in at the back door. He is pale with fright.*]

RINEY. Somethin's wrong with Daisy! Found her lyin' on the side of the road by the barn. She's all shot-up 'n bleedin' somethin' awful.

ZACK. What's that?

RINEY. Wuz crossin' the road to water the horses at the crick 'n there she wuz . . . so pale 'n bloody! Ye gotta come quick, Maw!

ZACK [*he and* TERA *stare at one another.* ZACK *in a quiet voice*]. So, yew wuz lyin' ter me!

CLINT. Did ye have some trouble here?

RINEY. Come on, afore it's too late!

CLINT [*to* TERA]. Go 'n help her, Maw!

TERA [*they are all looking at her*]. I'm stayin' here.

CLINT. What?

[RINEY *has left the back door open, and* CHILDERS *appears.* ZACK *stares at* TERA *intently. There is a moment's silence.*]

RINEY. She's bleedin'! We gotta git to her afore . . .

CHILDERS [*he is small, thin, sandy-haired and wears a Civil War uniform*]. There's no hurry now . . .

[*They all turn around in surprise.*]

CLINT. Childers!

CHILDERS. She's dead.

[*There is a long pause during which they regard him with cold hostility.*]

ZACK. It ain't so healthy to be pryin' round here.

CLINT. Why ain'tcha down to yer town meetin', Mr. Constable?

CHILDERS. Wuz jest a-goin' there. Stopped by fer ta give ye the bad news. Thought ye might wanna know.

TERA. We're grateful to ye. [*Watching him warily.*]

CHILDERS. Her old maw is gonna be awful broken up 'bout it. [*He pauses and then adds significantly.*] Lots of the folks in town are goin' to be, too. . . .

TERA [*impatiently, cutting in*]. We don't know nothin' 'bout it.

CHILDERS. Nothin'?

CLINT. Yew heard her.

CHILDERS [*with bitter sarcasm*]. Reckon her death wuz an "accident," then.

CLINT [*grunts suspiciously*]. Huh?

CHILDERS. We've had lots of "accidents" like that round here. Reckon this ain't nothin' special fer me to git riled up about . . . is it?

CLINT [*ominously, as he begins to suspect that* CHILDERS *is double-talking*]. Accidents like what?

CHILDER. Like that tin peddler that wuz found dead. Remember, you tole everybody it wuz an "accident." Then Mose, that hired man of yourn, who got himself killed by a scythe . . . "accidently."

[THE DUTCHMAN *starts up. He drops the gun he is cleaning on the floor and glares viciously at* CHILDERS.]

CLINT [*puts a restraining hand on* THE DUTCHMAN'S *shoulder and says belligerently*]. Listen, Childers . . .

CHILDERS [*cutting him off*]. Trouble with most folks is they're jest natcherly suspicious. Anythin' out of the ordinary happens 'n right away they starts lookin' fer the person that done it. They don't seem to realize that "accidents" kin jest happen . . . "accidents" like horses disappearin', men being found dead, wimmen being raped, stores being robbed, farmers losin' wagons, hogs 'n cows. . . . [*Pause.*] A course ye kin understand folks bein' a leetle riled up when these "accidents" have been goin' on without let-up fer ten years.

TERA [*cutting him off*]. Yo're a meddlin' fool! It's gonna git you in trouble.

CHILDERS [*smiles bitterly*]. Trouble? Mean mebbe I'll have an "accident"? [*Smiles and shakes his head.*] Ain't gonna be no more of them things. Folks round here is takin' Fate in their own hands now. Especially us men what just come home from the war. For five long years we been killin' 'n being killed 'cause we all wanted decency 'n freedom in this country. Now that's over with 'n we all figgered on comin' back 'n doin' some peaceful farmin'! But we see we can't put our guns away. The awful stories our wimmen folks been tellin' us 'bout the killers from Bear Swamp, 'n what we've seen with our eyes in the last couple weeks, has made our blood boil more than any stories Gerrit Smith or Greeley could tell us 'bout the enslaved black man. 'N we see the Civil War ain't over—not yet in the Chenango Valley.

TERA [*aroused*]. Git outa here! Git outa my house!

CHILDERS. I'm gittin' out. [*Takes several steps towards the door and stops.*] It would be kind of terrible if mebbe you folks had an "accident". . .

TERA [*raises her stick*]. Git out!

CHILDERS [*retreating and continuing*]. . . . like gittin' hung or somethin' mebbe! [*He exits.* TERA *is aroused to anger. The rest are astonished by the sheer audacity of the man.*]

CLINT. Listen to him, will ye?

ZACK. Mighty cocky little feller.

TERA [*shaking with anger*]. He's gotta be taught to know the fury of the McIllherrons. He's gotta larn there is still men here to be feared. [*To* CLINT.] Git yore gun! [*He stares at her in surprise.*] Git yore gun!

CLINT. Want everybody from that town meetin' up here burnin' with revenge?

TERA. Git yore gun!

CLINT. In town, today . . . there wuz somethin' in those folks' eyes. It wuz dangerous. They're like people that's had to stand too much, 'n now ain't gonna stand no more.

TERA. Ye never shied of anythin' like this afore. I'm tellin' ye ta go!

CLINT [*scornfully*]. You've made us go too far already.

TERA. Are ye goin'?

CLINT. No!

TERA [*stares at him in anger; then turns to* THE DUTCHMAN]. Will yew go?

THE DUTCHMAN [*still cleaning and repairing his gun, snorts in disgust and shakes his head*]. Nein!

TERA [*frustrated, she casts about*]. Wish Rett wuz here. He ain't grown yeller. [CLINT *laughs derisively.*] He kin still call himself a man. [*Pointedly at* CLINT.]

CLINT. Are ye so sure? Wanna know somethin'! Wuzn't figurin' on tellin' ye. But the reason Rett 'n the rest of 'em wouldn't come back from Albany is not cuz they were dead drunk! [*Pause and slowly.*] It wuz cuz they're tired of yore cussedness and yore bossin' ways!

TERA. Yo're lyin'!

CLINT. Ask the Dutchman! [THE DUTCHMAN *nods an affirmative.*] They said they waren't comin' back to be hung!

TERA [*suddenly*]. Riney!

RINEY. Maw, not me! [*Frightened, he pales with fear.*]

TERA. Git yore gun!

RINEY [*whimpering*]. I'm scared.

TERA. Git after 'im afore he gits to that meetin'.

CLINT [*surprised*]. Ye gonna send the *young-un?* Have ye gone plumb outa yer head?

RINEY [*pleading, fearfully*]. I ain't never done nothin' like this, Maw. I'm scared!

TERA [*picks a gun up and puts it in* RINEY'S *hand*]. Git out! Git out afore I lams ye! [*Raises her staff.* RINEY *takes the gun and silently walks out.* TERA *turns from the door. They all look at her silently. She goes to the table, picks up the saddlebag full of money, takes it under her arm, and goes to the door of her room. She turns around and surveys them with a faint smile of scorn on her face*]. Goin' in fer a spell to rest my tired old bones. Reckon yew won't need *me* none. Yew wimmen oughter be able ter git yore own grub. [*She goes into her room.*]

CLINT [*staring after her*]. Goddam! She's like some kinda wild animal! No feelin's! [*He restlessly walks around the room.*]

ZACK [*after a pause*]. Give me that jug, Dutchman. [THE DUTCHMAN *gives it to him and he drinks.*]

[THE DUTCHMAN *continues to clean and repair his gun.* CLINT *gazes out of the window.*]

CLINT [*after a pause*]. It's gettin' dark. The pines 're black against the light sky. Soon everything will be black. Look at them sycamores lifting their white arms . . . as if they were prayin'. [*The light begins to dim rapidly in the room.* THE DUTCHMAN *gets up and lights several kerosene lamps, one on the table. After a pause.*] Through the trees there I kin see torches and lights down in town. Looks like a heap of excitement there tonight. The shadows are deep 'n dark out there in the hills. The valley looks real scary at night . . . like as if it had a spell on it. Maw tole me a story 'bout it when I wuz a young 'un. They say a preacher come into the valley once to start a church. He talked to the people 'bout the sins of man 'n such, long 'n hard, but no one would listen to 'im. So he ups on his horse 'n leaves. But 'fore he left the valley, he got up top that ridge near the far side of Unadilla Creek 'n looked down out over the valley 'n said, "The curse of God be on ye. May ye never find pleasure in his sight." 'N they say that God forgot 'bout the Chenango Valley, 'n the devil's been raisin' hell here ever since. [ZACK *has been drinking steadily, putting the jug down and then lifting it to drink again; he gets grimmer by the moment; his eyes staring glazedly, he sits at the table sunk in his own thoughts. After a sigh,* CLINT *exclaims nervously.*] This waitin's awful. Wish somethin'd only happen.

[CLINT *walks fearfully around the room. Outside it is now completely dark, and the room too is dark except for the eerie light from the smoky kerosene lamps. At the table it lights up the drunken face of* ZACK *and the cold, emotionless face of* THE DUTCHMAN *working over his gun.*]

CLINT [*at the window, talking half to himself*]. It's a funny thing . . . last couple months I been feelin' I wuz gonna die soon, 'n that *she* would be the cause of it.

ZACK [*half tearfully to himself*]. Daisy wuz a purty gal . . . could sing good.

CLINT [*peering out into the darkness, a note of fear in his voice*]. Fer all we know there might be a mob gettin' organized fer a hangin' down there now!

ZACK [*pause*]. And she killt her . . . like killin' a canary. [*He lets his head fall across his arm on the table.*]

CLINT [*getting panicky*]. Zack! [*Goes to him quickly and shakes him nervously.*] Zack! We gotta do somethin'! [ZACK *looks up at him blankly.*] Gotta git afore they come!

ZACK. What's matter?

CLINT [*in steadily rising panic*]. They'll be up here, all of 'em, that whole town meetin'!

ZACK [*gradually catching* CLINT's *panic*]. Huh?

CLINT. Do ye wanta die like a trapped critter? With death starin' ye square in the eye no matter how hard ye fights! [ZACK *coming out of his drunk, shakes his head in fear.*] We'll be surrounded, 'n they whoopin' like Injuns . . . settin' fire to the house . . . puttin' ropes around our necks!

[THE DUTCHMAN *rises nervously.*]

ZACK [*sobered*]. We gotta go!

CLINT. Yeah.

ZACK [*nervously*]. Give me a slug of that stuff first! [*He downs some liquor.*] We'll take that swamp road 'n lose ourselves inside a half an hour. Light that lantern, Dutchman! [*Points to a lantern in the corner.* THE DUTCHMAN *goes to it hurriedly.*] We'll be needin' it! It's dark as tarnation in Bear Swamp! [*To* CLINT.] Three horses ready in the barn fer us? [*Looking around to see if they're properly prepared.*]

CLINT. Reckon there are! [*He breathes heavily in excitement.*] C'mon! Fer God's sakes!

ZACK. All right! Give me a hand, Clint, 'n let's be goin'.

CLINT. Right! [*He hurriedly picks up* ZACK *and starts bearing him toward the door.*]

ZACK [*in a whisper*]. Be as quiet as ye kin!

[THE DUTCHMAN *is at the door waiting. Suddenly* TERA *appears at the door at stage right. She takes out the gun from her old coat and holds it on them. Watches for a moment.*]

TERA. Reckon yew oughter stay. [*They stop, startled, and look around to see her.* THE DUTCHMAN, *seeing her, slips out of the door.*] Dutchman! [*Pause.*] Git back inta here! [*Shamefacedly* CLINT *brings* ZACK *back into the room and deposits him in his chair.* ZACK *is smouldering with anger and frustration.*] So ye would go 'n leave yer old maw, would ye? Ye kin jest sit here, 'n not stir unless I lets ye.

[*There is a long pause during which the two men stare at* TERA. *Suddenly there is a fumbling at the back door, and* RINEY *hesitantly comes in. He is haggard and frightened. He stumbles into the room and stands there with his shotgun hanging at his side.*]

RINEY. Maw! . . . [*He is crying.*]

TERA. What happened?

RINEY. Ye shouldn'a made me go.

TERA [*grabs him by the arm*]. What happened?

CLINT. Tell us 'bout it!

TERA. Did ye do like I told ye?

RINEY. No! [*Hysterically.*]
TERA. What?
RINEY. I mean yes . . . er . . . no! Didn't kill 'im, if that's what ye mean, but I tried. I tried, Maw! Ye can't beat me, cuz I tried. Wuzn't my fault I wuz scairt. Follered 'im all the way ta town, 'n I jest couldn't bring myself to it . . . this wuz the first time! Rode right inta town behind him. There wuz lots of excitement there tonight . . . hundreds of soldiers 'n farmers . . . hollerin' 'n cheerin' when they seed Childers, 'n they wuz yellin' 'bout us, how Childers wuz gonna clean the McIllherrons out 'n hang the last one of us. At first they didn't recognize me cuz it wuz dark, 'n then some of the men seed me, 'n I got scairt . . . they were a-callin' my name when I rode by . . . everybody wuz millin' around 'n yellin' 'bout Childers, 'n callin' after me, 'n we wuz gonna git hung . . . 'n I had to shoot Childers . . . 'n yew'd beat me if I didn't . . . it wuz all goin' round 'n round 'n I got all mixed up in my mind, 'n I shot the gun at Childers! Jest shot . . . didn't aim er nothin' . . . didn't hit nobody.
TERA. Shot at 'im in front of everybody?
RINEY [*nods*]. Most everybody in town seed me. Started to yell how one of them McIllherrons jest tried to kill Childers in cold blood 'n stuff like that, 'n started chasin' me 'n raisin' a big fuss, 'n . . . [*He breaks down hysterically.*] Lots happened I can't remember. All I know is I jest 'scaped with my life.
CLINT [*bitterly to* TERA]. I guess ya finally went 'n done it!
RINEY [*sobbing*]. 'N I lost my barlow knife, too.
CLINT. Only one thing left . . . to git! Git afore it's too late.
   [*Several shots are heard, and the door suddenly opens.* THE DUTCHMAN *appears, frightened, breathing heavily. His clothes are ruffled, and he is scratched and bleeding.*]
THE DUTCHMAN. Gott in Himmel! Dey kome. Dey kome!

CLINT. Who?
THE DUTCHMAN. Childers mit der soldiers und farmers! Efferybody!
CLINT [*terror stricken*]. How close?
THE DUTCHMAN. Efferyvere! 'Underts! Manner mit guns . . . pitchvorks . . . clubs. Dey are mad, awful mad. Oh, mein Gott, it is schrecklich! Schrecklich!

[*An undertone of voices is heard far off in the distance.*]

CLINT. I just knowed it would happen like this! [*Pause.*] Listen to 'em!!
THE DUTCHMAN. Zum Fenster hinausschauen!

[*They all go to the window and peer out. The undertone of voices from the distance comes nearer and nearer. Undifferentiated shouts are heard: "Set fire to the house 'n burn 'em out!" "Come on out, McIllherrons!" "Ye got the whole Union Army against ye." "Whoopee! We're fightin' the Civil War in our own back yard!" Several shots ring out.*]

RINEY [*crying in despair*]. I don't wanna die, Maw!

[THE DUTCHMAN, *completely demoralized, is mumbling brokenly to himself, like a child in his utter lack of control.*]

RINEY. Look! Ain't that Childers in the moonlight under the big oak! He's wavin' a flag.
CLINT. A flag! Hell! It's his shirt on a stick!

[CHILDERS' *voice is heard from the distance,* "*McIllherrons! McIllherrons!*"]

RINEY. Listen!
CHILDERS [*from the distance*]. McIllherrons! McIllherrons! Ye haven't got a fightin' chance! Ye better surrender! Promise ye a fair trial if ye come out now! If you don't, it's a fight to the finish. Better surrender!

[*They all look at one another with the relief of hope on the men's faces.*]

CLINT [*grasping at the chance like a drowning man*]. Give up?
THE DUTCHMAN. Ja! Ja! Ja! [*Cringing with fear, his whole body moves rhythmically in his assent.*]

RINEY. They won't *kill* us then!

CLINT [*starting for the door*]. I'm gonna tell 'em! [*Starts for the door, but* TERA *slams him viciously over the shoulder with her stick. He gives a cry of shocked surprise and pain. She goes quickly to the door, opens it, and shouts out into the darkness.*]

TERA. Git outa here! We're gonna fight till the last one of us is dead . . . 'n lots a yourn, too! Watch out I don't put a bullet through yore head, Childers! [*The men see all hope collapse.*]

CLINT [*mutters*]. She must be plumb crazy.

[TERA *returns to the room.*]

TERA [*her back is half turned to* ZACK, *and she addresses* CLINT *and the others.* ZACK *has secured the gun* THE DUTCHMAN *has been cleaning and repairing during most of the play. It is now bright and shiny, ready for use*]. Reckon I tole 'em.

ZACK. Reckon ye did.

[TERA *turns to him, and he shoots the gun. She falls to the ground with a faint cry and reproachfully mutters,* "Zack." *The men stare at her.* RINEY *sobs quietly.* ZACK *signals* CLINT *to surrender. After* TERA'S *speech of defiance the excitement outside increases to a frenzy pitch. Shots ring out faster.* CLINT *takes the lighted lantern from the floor, goes to the door, and opens it. The shots outside sound louder as the door opens.* CLINT *waves the lantern in the open doorway. The shots cease. He puts the lantern down and walks into the night, his hands extended into the air.* THE DUTCHMAN *follows* CLINT *out. And then* RINEY, *sobbing.* ZACK *sits alone in the room, staring at the body of the dead woman. There is a heavy, hollow silence in the room; all excitement and noise have suddenly ceased as if a radio had been turned off. There is a pause of several seconds.*]

**CURTAIN**

## THE BROWN GIRL

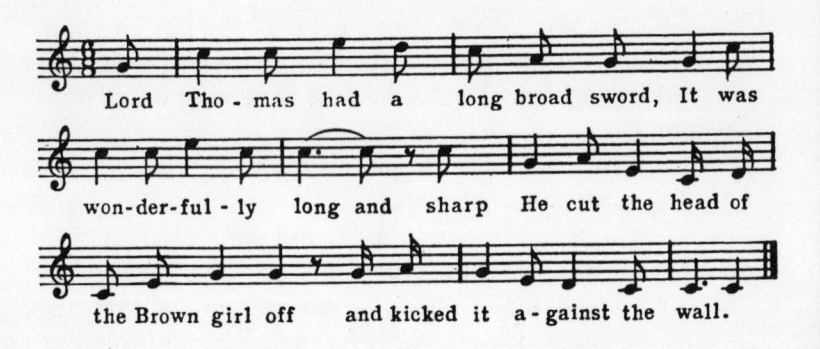

Lord Thomas had a long broad-sword,
   It was wonderfully long and sharp.
He cut the head of the Brown Girl off,
   And kicked it against the wall.

He pointed the handle toward the sun,
   The point toward his breast,
Here is the going of three true loves,
   God send our souls to rest.

Go dig my grave under yonder green tree,
   Go dig it wide and long;
And bury Fair Eleanor in my arms,
   And the Brown Girl at my feet.

A more complete version of "The Brown Girl or Fair Eleanor" is to be found in Carl Sandburg's *The American Songbag*, Harcourt, Brace and Co., New York, 1927.

# RAISIN' THE DEVIL

## Parson Dow Scorches a Schoharie Convert

*by*

ROBERT GARD

## RAISIN' THE DEVIL

LORENZO Dow, generally called Ren Dow, was one of America's famous itinerant preachers. Although he was not the most violent of the loud preachers of the westward expansion, his uncanny powers, long hair, wild gesticulations, and eccentric gait made Dow perhaps the most widely known of his kind.

Stories about Ren Dow crop up all over New York State; but Schoharie County produces the best Dow yarns. Emelyn E. Gardner, in her book *Folklore from the Schoharie Hills*, recounts this pleasing tale: One day while riding past the cabin of a couple of doubtful and unchurchly reputation, Dow thought he spied through the window a recent convert disappearing into an alcove off the sitting-room. Dismounting quickly, Dow reached the cabin just in time to see his recreant disciple slipping into an empty barrel and being hidden under loose spinning-tow by his hostess. Answering his peremptory knock at the door, the flustered woman ordered Ren to leave at once; her husband was due at any moment and would be furious if he found she had let a preacher into the house. Ren refused to leave, pushed in to a chair in the alcove, and sat there until the husband arrived. Incensed at the unwelcome visitor, the infidel husband challenged the preacher's powers and demanded scornfully, "Kin ye raise the dead?" Ren replied, "Yes, I kin! But better still I kin raise the Devil!" And quickly striking a match, he touched it to the barrel. The tow blazed, and like a flash a wild-eyed and disheveled figure bounded out and fled terrified from the scene. The startled husband, convinced that Dow could make good on his words, joined the church and made his wife join.

This tall tale lends itself readily to dramatization and, in the form of the comedy *Raisin' the Devil*, has been widely produced throughout New York and adjoining States.

TIME: 1825, *late afternoon in summer.*
PLACE: KING MILLER'S *cabin, near Schoharie, New York.*

## THE CHARACTERS OF THE PLAY

JENNY MILLER, *the daughter of the horse-thief, King Miller.*
BILL SPARKS, *a young blood of the country-side.*
REN DOW, *a tall, somewhat grizzled, travelling evangelist; he has a slight limp and carries a cane.*
KING MILLER, *a notorious horse-thief; sly and whiskered.*

# RAISIN' THE DEVIL

THE SCENE *is the main room of* KING MILLER'S *cabin near Schoharie, New York. The room is sparely furnished: a couple of rough benches; a center table upon which stands a small jug of cider; a large barrel with bung-hole in its side, in a corner of the room; a couch along a part of the left wall. Doors are right and left, the left door leading outside, the right door to another room of the cabin.*

[BILL SPARKS *is trying to pull away from the clinging hands of* JENNY MILLER, *a pretty girl of twenty.*]

BILL [*in a frightened voice*]. Let me go! I'm scared!
JENNY [*after a struggle, pulling him onto the couch*]. Sit down, Bill. Here, have some more cider. [*She starts to get the cider-jug from the table.*]
BILL. I can't! I . . . I shouldn't even be here!
JENNY. I'd like to know why not?
BILL [*hesitating*]. Well, you're a . . . I mean, your father's a . . . a . . .
JENNY [*without much interest*]. Yes, I know. Pa's a hoss thief. [*She pulls* BILL *down beside her.*]
BILL. Yeah, that's it, and I don't think . . .
JENNY [*stroking* BILL'S *shoulder*]. What Pa does hasn't got anything to do with you'n me. Come on, Bill, let's you'n me get friendly.
BILL [*as an owl hoots outside*]. What's that?
JENNY. Only an old hoot-owl! What you so nervous about, Bill?

BILL. You sure it's all right with your pa if I come here to see you?

JENNY. Well, Pa did say he wouldn't have any young fellers foolin' around here; but shucks, Bill, Pa never meant nothin'.

BILL [*rising and edging away*]. Yeah, he never meant nothin', I suppose, when he took that shot at Henry Vrooman. Henry ain't dared to go out alone at night since.

JENNY. Well, if Pa did shoot at you, it'd only be to scare you, Bill.

BILL [*not at all anxious to be scared in that way*]. Uh-huh, I see. Well, maybe I'd better go.

JENNY [*rising and catching him*]. No, no! Don't go! Why, we're only just startin' to get acquainted. Drink some more cider! You know, Bill, it's mighty nice to have a young feller come 'way out here in the woods to see me. You know, me and Pa don't get out much, daytimes.

BILL. You're *sure* your pa ain't anywheres around now?

JENNY. I told you he was out in the woods.

BILL [*wiping his face*]. I'm kind of nervous. 'Course, I wasn't brought up in the woods to be scared of night-hawks, but . . .

JENNY. You're not afraid of *me* are you, Bill?

BILL. Noooo, not of you.

JENNY. Then let's forget all about bein' afraid. Drink your cider.

BILL [*takes a nervous pull from the jug. After a moment, uncomfortably*]. You know Ren Dow, th' preacher?

JENNY. Th' travellin' evangelist? Sure, I saw him once. Him they call th' Peter th' Hermit of America, or some such.

BILL. That's right.

JENNY. And I heard a funny story about him once, too. Seems Ren was drivin' his sled through the snow, and he met a feller comin' t'other way. There wasn't room for 'em both to pass, so Ren he got up in his sled and shook his fist and said, "You git out of my way, or I'll sarve you as I did a feller back aways!" Well, Ren looked so fierce that the other feller wallered right out into the deep snow and back to th' trail again. Then he come up behind Ren, and he said, "Say, Ren, how'd you sarve that other feller?" And Ren, he said, "Well he wouldn't turn out for me, so . . . I turned out for him!" There, ain't that a good story, Bill?

BILL [*nervously*]. Uh-huh.

JENNY. And Ren Dow must make a fortune out of that snake-oil of his, even if he won't take a cent for preachin'!

BILL. Yeah. Well, last Sunday Ren come here to Schoharie and started preachin' on that little knoll east of the Court House, and . . .

JENNY [*as* BILL *hesitates*]. And what?

BILL. And . . . I . . . I . . . let him convert me!

JENNY. Aw, honest?

BILL. I sure did! Nobody coulda held out against him. It was either come or be damned! There wasn't no hangin' back, 'cause Ren, he said there wasn't but one kind of hell, and that was the hot kind! After that, the whole caboodle just walked to 'im, and give themselves up.

JENNY. They did?

BILL [*just a shade accusingly*]. An' you'n your pa's about the only ones ain't been converted here in Schoharie.

JENNY. I wouldn't mind bein' converted, Bill, but th' old man's tougher'n harness leather that ain't had no oil!

BILL. And that's what I mean! You see, it don't look so good, me comin' to see a gal that ain't even been converted.

JENNY. Nobody knows you been comin' to see me, do they?

BILL. Well, you see . . . I went and confessed it to Ren Dow; and he said I'd better mend my ways!

JENNY. Well, some's good and some's bad. Me'n Pa's just naturally bad. Have a little more cider?

BILL. I don't reckon I'd better.

JENNY. Look here, Bill Sparks, you think I'm pretty, don't you?

BILL. Sure, Jenny, I think you're pretty, but . . .
JENNY. An' *you* ain't mad 'cause Pa's a hoss thief?
BILL. 'Course that don't matter much to *me*, only, supposin' someone was to catch me here? I . . . I ain't afraid of *livin'* folks, but Ren Dow said th' Devil'd get a feller if he didn't take care about the company he was seen with. Said th' Devil was right lively hereabouts, too.
JENNY. Oh, so I ain't good enough for you, ain't I?
BILL. I never said that! Gosh, Jenny, I'm so mixed up. My morals is all twisted outta shape.
JENNY. I guess I don't understand you at all!
BILL. Well, I'm a convert. I reckon I'm a Christian!
JENNY. Oh, so you're a Christian! Well, I don't want you to do anything against your will, so maybe you'd *better* go.
BILL [*rising eagerly*]. You see what I mean, Jenny?
JENNY. Well, I wouldn't want to force nobody to stay with me.
BILL [*on his way*]. Then I'll just be going. [*He grabs his hat, then hesitates.*]
JENNY. Why don't you go, then?
BILL [*not in such a hurry after all, now that he has won his point*]. I was just thinkin' maybe I'd drop in tomorrow to say hello, if you was sure your pa'd be away. [*Hastily.*] 'Course, I couldn't stay.
JENNY. You needn't come at all if it's goin' to hurt your conscience.
BILL. It ain't that I don't want to see you, Jenny; but sometimes when I get to thinkin' about th' Devil, like ol' Ren Dow told about, I get plumb outta my head. Ren said the Devil had a big pitchfork, and a tail of fire, and that he come with snakes and wild beasts, all abreathin' fire!
JENNY. Then I don't blame you for gettin' scared, Bill. All right, you can come ridin' by, and if Pa ain't home I'll give you a signal, like always. And say, Bill . . . [*She lowers her voice.*] . . . if I was you, I'd look close after that fine hoss of yours. Pa's sure took an almighty shine to her.
BILL. To my hoss, Queen?

JENNY. Yeah. I tried to talk Pa out of it, but he said as how he didn't like you anyway, he guessed he'd just try to get your hoss.

BILL. He come right out and said he didn't like me? Whew!

JENNY [*laughing*]. You know Pa.

BILL. Say, someday the folks around here are going to get mad, and then they'll do your pa like they done that Mister Van Alstern that murdered Sheriff Huddleston and stole his hoss. . . . They'll hang him! Then maybe he won't be so smart! My hoss! Lawdy! Well, I'd better go see if he's where I tied him. Goodbye, Jenny.

JENNY. Goodbye, Bill.

BILL. You . . . give me a goodbye kiss 'fore I go?

JENNY. You was converted, wasn't you?

BILL. Yeah, but . . . [*Looking around to see that nobody is near.*] . . . it ain't a sin to kiss a gal if she wants to be kissed!

JENNY [*flirting*]. Who said I wanted to be kissed?

BILL. Well, nobody. Only the way you been actin', I . . .

JENNY. You can just go and kiss that hoss of yours goodbye, instead!

BILL [*starting toward her*]. Aw. . . . [*He is brought to a dead halt by a loud "Hallooooo" from outside.*]

JENNY. Somebody's comin'! [*She runs to the door and peeps out.*]

BILL [*transfixed and shaking with fright*]. Is it your pa?

JENNY. No. It's . . . it's Ren Dow! Ren Dow himself! I can tell by the way he limps and whips the grass with that long cane of his!

BILL [*uttering a loud cry of despair and wishing for the firm rock of salvation*]. Ren Dow?

JENNY. And big as life! Where's your hoss, Bill?

BILL. Hid in th' woods! [*He looks around desperately for a hiding place.*] Where'll I go? I dasn't let 'im find me! [*He runs toward the bedroom door.*] I'll just go in here!

JENNY. No, no! [*She gets in front of him.*]

BILL. No? Why not? I got to, I tell you. Ren Dow'll put the Devil onto me if he finds me here.

JENNY. Not so loud. Pa's asleep in this room!

BILL [*who has been struggling to get into the bedroom*]. Huh? Oh m' God! [*He darts back to the center of the room.*]

JENNY [*running to look out the outside door*]. Ren's acomin' close, now!

BILL [*whispering hoarsely*]. Help! Help!

JENNY. And I guess you'll be meetin' that Devil right soon, Bill. My gracious, do you suppose Ren's comin' to try and convert me'n Pa?

BILL [*wailing*]. Lost!

JENNY [*hastily turning from the door*]. Hold on a minute, Bill. If it ain't beneath your dignity, you could get into that flour barrel, yonder. It's big enough for you, and as it's gettin' dark, like as not Ren'd never see you at all!

BILL [*darting to the barrel*]. I'd rather stay in it a week than face Ren Dow!

JENNY [*running to help*]. Get in, then. Here, I'll hold the top off for you. May be a little flour still in it, but that won't hurt you any!

[BILL *is no sooner stowed away than there is a loud knock at the door.* JENNY *smooths her dress and hair and goes to open.* REN DOW *enters suspiciously. He is a tall, somewhat grizzled, keen, travelling evangelist; he is past middle age, has a slight limp, and carries a long, stout cane; his black clothes are worn with much travel; a paper sticks from his coat pocket; he wears a black hat. He looks the place over with obvious displeasure before he turns to* JENNY.]

DOW. You Jenny Miller?

JENNY. Sure am. And I know you, too. You're Mister Ren Dow, aren't you?

DOW [*half smiling*]. I reckon I be.

JENNY. Well, won't you sit down, Mister Dow?

DOW. Your pa to home?

JENNY. He's away right now. [*She pulls out one of the benches.*] Come sit down.

Dow. Uh. [*He sits stiffly.*] So your pa's away, is he?

JENNY. Yeah. [*After a long, uncomfortable pause.*] You . . . was wantin' him for somethin' special?

Dow. Yep.

JENNY. Somethin' I could do?

Dow. I reckon you could, if you had the conviction! [*He pauses, looking at her fixedly.*] I been conductin' service over in the knoll east of the Schoharie Court House. I ain't seen you'n your pa there. I come to persuade ye.

JENNY. Well, Mister Dow, me'n Pa, we don't go into sassiety much.

Dow. I said nothin' about sassiety! That's somethin' th' Devil worked up. [*Fixing her with his eye.*] Young woman, does your pa fear the Lord?

JENNY [*innocently*]. Why, I reckon he does. He never goes out on Sunday without his shotgun!

Dow [*starting back*]. Huh? Eh? He don't, eh? [*Taking the whip-hand again.*] Hunts on Sunday, does he?

JENNY [*a bit flustered*]. Will you have a glass of cider, Mister Dow? It ain't much hard.

Dow [*smelling the jug*]. Harder'n stone. Well, might have one mug of it.

JENNY. We ain't got a mug, Mister Dow. Guess you'll just have to tip the jug.

Dow. All right, all right! [*He takes a long, gurgling pull at the jug.*] Ummmmm. [*He puts the jug back on the table and looks intently at* JENNY.] When's your pa comin' home?

JENNY [*glancing cautiously at the bedroom door*]. Well, I dunno. You real sure you want to see 'im?

Dow. I want to have a talk with him.

JENNY. Pa ain't long on religion.

Dow [*dryly*]. Huh! As if I didn't know that. What d'ye think I'm here for, girl? I never come on no pleasure call.

JENNY. I was just tellin' you, Pa don't like preachers.

Dow [*composed*]. Like as not.

JENNY. And Pa said if ever a preacher come around here he was goin' to kill 'im!

Dow [*interested but not much moved*]. Oh. [*There is a short pause.*]

JENNY. Well, ain't you gonna leave?

Dow. I'll just wait a spell for your pa.

JENNY. But I just told you . . .

Dow [*exploding*]. Pshaw! I come here to convert King Miller, and I'm gonna do it! I'm gonna leave Schoharie with a clean record of convertin' every man, woman, child, and livin' beast, and nothin's gonna stop me short of the blazes of hell, which . . . [*He fixes* JENNY *with his eye.*] . . . is where you'll end up, young woman, 'less you turn from the trail o' enequity you been followin' an' repent! Girl, do you want to be a Christian?

JENNY [*frightened*]. Ju . . . just what does it mean, Mister Dow?

Dow. It ain't what the Baptists says it is!

JENNY [*wide-eyed*]. No?

Dow. No. An' it ain't what the Presbyterians says it is, neither!

JENNY [*hopefully*]. No?

Dow. No! [*Bringing his hand down hard on the table.*] It's what the Methodists says it is, and don't let anybody tell you different! [*Getting up and raising his eyes on high.*] When I was a boy I was a wicked swearer: but in the dead o' night I fought two devils on a sea o' ice; and one was weak and t'other was strong; an' th' weak one vanished in a cloud o' flame; and th' other one . . . [*He is interrupted by a loud, terrified groan from* BILL *in the barrel.*] What's that?

JENNY [*standing up*]. That must be Pa!

Dow. But you said he wasn't here! [*He starts toward the corner where the barrel is.*] Sounded like it come from over here.

JENNY [*getting in front of him*]. No, no! It was Pa, I tell you!
Dow. But you said he wasn't here!
JENNY. I was only tryin' to save your life. Pa's asleep in there. [*She points to the bedroom door.*]
Dow. Then I'll wake 'im up! [*He starts toward the door.*]
JENNY. No! Pa's awful when he wakes up. He might just shoot without thinkin'.
Dow. Bah! He wouldn't shoot me. [*As* JENNY *hangs onto him.*] Young woman, you are tamperin' with the Lord's business.
JENNY. You better go, Mister Dow. Come again tomorrow.
Dow [*looking toward the bedroom door*]. Sleepin' in the daytime! [*In disgust.*] Another sin against King Miller!
JENNY. Pa does most of his work at night. I guess he's got to sleep sometime.

[Dow *breaks away and goes into the bedroom.* JENNY *puts her hands over her ears and stands center, awaiting the uproar.* Dow, *however, returns immediately.*]

Dow [*severely*]. Young woman, falsehood is a cardinal sin!
JENNY [*trembling*]. You still alive? Pa must not be feelin' well today.
Dow. There is no one in that room.
JENNY. What? [*She runs to look.*]

[Dow, *left alone, walks to barrel, looks it over curiously, turns as* JENNY *comes back into the room.*]

JENNY. Well, for goodness' sake, Pa ain't there!
Dow [*savagely*]. Where is he?
JENNY. You might as well go home, Ren. Pa ain't hardly ever in after sundown.
Dow [*with great firmness, sitting down on a bench*]. I have come to see King Miller. I will see him if I have to wait until tomorrow morning. He has sinned. . . . [*He is interrupted by a loud "Whoa girl, whoa Queeney" from outside.* Dow *rises, faces the door.* KING MILLER *enters. He is a whiskered, sly fellow of fifty, slouchily dressed.*]
KING [*lurching in*]. Howdy, Jenny!

JENNY [*severely*]. Pa, where you been?

KING. Nowheres. What you got to eat, Jenny gal? [*Seeing Dow.*] Who's this here? Some feller acourtin' ye? Haw, haw! Got yerself kind o' an old one, didn't ye, gal?

JENNY [*trying to motion her father to be silent*]. Pa, I thought you was asleep.

KING. Fooled ye, I did. Crawled out th' winder 'bout two hour ago. [*Approaching* Dow.] Well, feller, I don't allow no courtin' of my gal, so you pack!

Dow. Sir, my name is . . .

JENNY [*quickly*]. It's all right, Pa. He just dropped in to tell me how-de-do.

KING [*turning away*]. Well, git! And you, Jenny, git me somethin' to eat.

Dow. My name's Lorenzo Dow. You King Miller?

KING. Yeah. Now feller, you'd better git, afore I lose my temper. I kin see you're a stranger, but I reckon a gal's good lookin' as mine'd draw 'em from a long ways off. Now I'm lettin' ye go, and ye'd better. . . .

Dow. Miller, I came to see *you*.

KING. I swored I'd kill th' first feller asked fer her hand!

Dow. I ain't askin' for her hand. I'm askin' for you!

KING. Fer me? Oh, ho! ho! ho! What'd ye want with me?

Dow. I been tryin' to tell you, Miller. I'm Lorenzo Dow, the great preacher.

JENNY. Oh, oh! [*She puts her hands over her ears.*]

KING. Dow? Preacher? [*He recognizes the name.*] Th' travellin' evangelist, b'God! Here in m'house! [*Yelling.*] Jenny, git my gun! [JENNY *clasps her father.*]

JENNY. Hold on, Pa. Don't kill 'im!

KING. Lemme go, Jenny. [*To* Dow.] You snake, snuckin' in here behind my back. I'll fix you!

Dow. King Miller, I'll either convert ye, er kill ye. Will ye come peacefully before the sight of the Lord, or will I have to use more unpleasant means to wash away your sins?

KING. Threatenin' me, are you? Oh, ho! Lemme go, Jenny!
Dow. Listen to the words that'll make you a saved man. [*Clearing his voice.*] King Miller . . .
KING. Quit callin' me King Miller. King's good enough fer my friends and my enemies! It don't sound good when you say 'em tergether thataway.
Dow. Tonight I ride on to Schenectady, and before I go I will convert every man, woman, and child in this town. Miller, you are the last.
KING. I'm givin' ye a last chance, Dow. Get out! Scat! If there's anything I can't stand to have around me, it's one of you preachin' fellers.
Dow. I thought you'd resist, Miller, so I came prepared. [*Takes a paper out of his pocket.*] Before I came here I went to the Court House and had myself sworn in as a deputy sheriff. I had, at the same time, a warrant made out for your arrest on a charge of horse stealing—a charge which, I am surprised to find, ain't ever actually been made out against you before.
KING [*sobered a little*]. Me, a thief? Haw, haw! Jenny, please git me my gun. [*But he does not struggle to free himself.*]
Dow. I got plenty of proof. How you been usin' Gebhardt's Caves as a hidin' place . . . what you done up on Schoharie Crick. I may as well tell ye right now that the citizens o' this town was fixin' to come in a body and hang you up to a tree over east of the Court House, but I saved you. I pled with that righteous passel o' men to let me touch you first . . . to see if I couldn't save you, Miller, and to keep my record in Schoharie one hundred percent! I won this great boon for ye, Miller. Now, what is your answer? Will ye repent in th' sight o' th' Lord, or will you go with me to th' jail to face a charge for which you will doubtless be hung? . . . To say nothin' o' roastin' through all eternity on th' coals o' hell!
JENNY. He's got you, Pa!
KING. Lemme see that warrant. [Dow *shows it to him.* MILLER

*reads slowly.*] "Fer stealin hosses. To wit: June 1st, from Dave Keppel, one black mare. . . ." [*He stops, puzzling out the next words.*]

Dow [*impatiently*]. Signed and attested to!

KING [*continuing*]. ". . . signed and attested to by Dave Keppel. From Abraham Keyser, one gelding, an old mare with foal, and two mules. . . ." [*Excitedly.*] That there's a lie! They was asses!

Dow. Make your choice.

KING [*plaintively*]. Now ain't you kind o' takin' advantage o' me, Parson?

Dow. It's for your own good, Miller. What'll it be?

KING. Well, I . . . I reckon you'll just have to take me along, Parson.

Dow [*starting back*]. What?

JENNY. Take it easy, Pa!

KING. I hain't givin' up my belief fer nobody.

Dow. But man, it'll mean th' noose!

KING. Maybe so. But ain't this here America? Ain't a man got a right to think as he sees fit? I reckon you can hang me up, Parson, fer I hain't givin' up my freedom of believin' fer nobody er nothin'. Why, that's what our grandpappies fought fer in the Revolution, waren't it? Tim Murphy, and Boyd, and . . .

JENNY. Told ye he was tough, Parson!

Dow [*very impatiently*]. Miller, I got no time to waste. Dark a'most now. What'll it be?

KING. Let's go to the jail, Parson. [*Plaintively.*] Never thought my old friends'd turn agin me like this!

Dow. But man, think! [*He is earnest and confused now that his scheme has broken down.*] You got no right to be an infidel! What'd it take to make you change your mind?

KING [*serenely*]. One o' them miracles.

Dow. A miracle?

KING. And that ain't possible. So let's go.

Dow. Hold on. Ain't you never heard o' John Sommers?
King. He 'nother preacher?
Dow. He was took blind. Stayed blind for twenty year. Then one morning he prayed to th' Lord fer his sight, and it come back to 'im.
King. Lived over'n Sharon, didn't he? Done some preachin'?
Dow. He did.
King. Biggest liar I ever knowed! Now, I lived about fifty-five year, Parson, an' all that time I hain't seen a single miracle I knowed of. An' that's where all you fellers' arguin' falls down. Feller I once knowed, preacher too, said he could raise th' Devil any time he wanted; but far's I could see he couldn't raise nothin' but th' roof, and he sure took that off whenever he opened his mouth.
Dow. Raise the Devil, eh?
King. 'Tain't never been done, and 'twon't never be done— 'cause, Mister Ren Dow, there ain't no Devil! If there had a been, he'd a got me long ago. Come on, let's go.
Dow. If I raise the Devil for ye, Miller, would ye freely confess your sins in th' sight o' th' Lord?
King [*smugly*]. Sure thing.
Dow. Miller, I will raise the Devil for you. Right here in this room.
King. Huh?
Dow [*in a deep, impressive voice*]. I will raise him!
King. You're bluffin' me, Parson. [*But he looks around nervously.*]
Dow. Miller, ain't you feared to meet th' Devil, face to face?
King [*laughing feebly*]. I ain't feared to meet any devil you kin raise.
Jenny [*hiding her eyes*]. Pa, he's goin' to do it!
King. He's bluffin'. All preachers is bluffers!
Dow [*in a hollow, awe-inspiring voice*]. I . . . will . . . raise . . . him!

[*Sound of a very loud and terrified groan from the barrel.*]

KING. Seems like I heard somethin'. . . .
Dow. I will raise the Devil that is lurking in your house, and I will drive him away. And if he ever returns . . . [*Another groan from the barrel. Dow turns toward it.*]
KING [*more and more feebly, and edging toward the door*]. Oh, ho, ho, ho, ho.
Dow. Stand still, Miller. [MILLER *halts as though shot.* Dow *in a deep voice.*] Devil, I command you to arise, and to heed the warning of a man of faith. Do not come nigh this house again, until it is cleansed of sin. I will raise you, Devil, into a ball of flame, and I will flog you as you flee! [Dow *slips his cane into the bung of the barrel and gives a sharp thrust and twist.*]

[BILL SPARKS *lets out a wail of terror and pain; bursts off the lid of the cask; and covered with flour, rises like a wraith; clears the rim of the barrel with a bound; and rushes toward the door, shouting and moaning at each step.* Dow *pursues him with surprising quickness, whipping him plentifully to the door and outside it.* KING *stands with mouth wide open, too frightened to move.* JENNY *holds back laughter with difficulty.* BILL *vanishes; his cries may be heard floating back through the darkness.*]

Dow [*re-entering*]. Miller, you have seen the Devil.
KING [*falling on his knees*]. By God, you done it, Parson!
Dow [*arranging his coat*]. Do ye freely confess your sins in th' sight o' th' Lord?
KING. I does, Parson.
Dow. And ye'll give up stealin' hosses?
KING. Yes, Parson.
Dow. And swearin'?
KING. Yer dam right, Parson.
Dow [*to* JENNY]. And you, young lady, you'd better mend your ways; or the Devil'll get you, first thing you know. You go to the meetings.

JENNY. Devil'll get me if I do, Parson. But I'll sure go if Pa'll let me.
Dow. King Miller, will ye let this gal go to th' meetin's?
KING. I'll flog 'er good if she don't, Parson.
Dow [*sighing*]. Then my duty's done. I must go now to the Schoharie Court House and perform a marryin'. Then to Schenectady. Then to Albany. I hear that they are cities of the ungodly! I see hard work ahead. Goodbye!
MILLERS. Goodbye, Ren!
 [Dow *exits, waving goodbye with his cane.*]
KING [*slowly getting up*]. What a preacher! [*He goes cautiously to the barrel; thrusts it with his toe; looks into it, sniffing the air.*] Whew! [*He mops his brow.*] Any o' that hard cider left, Jenny? Ren Dow never said nothin' 'bout hard cider, did he?
JENNY [*giving him the jug*]. No, Pa.
KING [*shaken*]. It ain't every day a feller sees th' Devil in person!
JENNY [*wistfully*]. No it ain't, Pa.
KING [*scratching his head*]. Jenny, somethin's botherin' me a little bit.
JENNY. What is it, Pa?
KING. Well, I been wonderin' if repentin' means turnin' back somethin' that was . . . borreyed before a feller gits religion.
JENNY. What's on your mind, Pa?
KING. Well, I was out in th' woods behind th' house, 'long earlier this afternoon, and I run onto that Sparks feller's mare. You know, th' one I took such a fancy to? It an' me just naturally sort of went away together. Jenny, you reckon I'd ought to take it back?
JENNY. I don't guess I'd bother, Pa. [*She throws on a wrap.*]
KING [*joyfully*]. You wouldn't? Where you goin', Jenny, gal?
JENNY. Well, Pa, if I can find Bill Sparks before Ren Dow per-

forms that marryin' he spoke of . . . well, it'll be a *double marryin'*, and that Queen hoss of Bill's 'll be in the family! 'Bye, Pa. [JENNY *exits.*]

[KING *gazes after her a moment, shakes his head, sits down on the bench, and takes a long swig of cider.*]

**CURTAIN**

# FAMILY COOPERATIVE

Neighborhood Comedy Spiced with
Agricultural Economics

*by*

ELLA L. THURSTON

(Adapted by Robert Gard and A. M. Drummond)

# FAMILY COOPERATIVE

The demand of the metropolitan areas of the State for fresh milk makes dairy-farming the great agricultural industry of New York. But the constant difficulties of the control of production, and the dissatisfactions and disputes over the rates paid to farmers for their milk, have resulted in repeated milk strikes, sometimes unfortunately accompanied by a bit of violence. These vital questions of disposal and price-fixing naturally lead to deep differences of opinion throughout rural New York; and often communities are divided, neighbor turned against neighbor and brother against brother.

*Family Cooperative* is a domestic comedy set before this tense background. The play makes no pretense of offering a solution for the difficult intricacies of the milk situation. But it does suggest, in mellow and humorous fashion, that neighbors who have grown up as friends together had best not sever their friendly relations in the undue heat of argument; and that cooperation in the home, and between human hearts, eases the problem that's over the hill. And it makes its point so warmly and laughably that you can consider *Family Cooperative* a neighborly comedy, with just enough agricultural economics sprinkled on to salt and pepper it.

Time: 1919, *an evening in summer.*
Place: *The living-room of the* Haines *farmhouse, Oneida County, New York.*

## THE CHARACTERS OF THE PLAY

Judith Haines, *a large, well-meaning farm woman.*
George Haines, *a prosperous York State farmer with strong convictions.*
Hilda, *George's old maid sister.*
Tom Baker, *a neighboring farmer with convictions as strong as George's.*
John Buell, *Baker's young nephew.*
Martha Haines, *the Haines' pretty daughter.*

# FAMILY COOPERATIVE

THE SCENE *is the living-room of the* HAINES *farmhouse. A door right leads out-of-doors. A door up center leads to a stair. There is a center table with easy chairs on either side, and a lighted lamp. A radio stands against the left wall.*

[JUDITH HAINES *is seated at the center table sewing.* GEORGE HAINES *enters right, in his sock-feet, carrying his shoes. He crosses directly to the radio and fiddles with the knobs.* JUDITH *watches him, shakes her head, and returns to her sewing.* GEORGE *gets a station playing jazz, turns away in disgust, but leaves the radio playing.*]

JUDITH. Now, George! It's 'way after time for the news.
GEORGE [*grumbling*]. Ought to put the news on later. I thought there might be something on about the milk strike.
JUDITH. The strike's written up here in the paper. [*She takes a folded paper off the table, hands it to him, and points to the place.* GEORGE *snatches the paper and, going to the chair left of the table, makes himself comfortable, sighs loudly, places his shoes carefully beside the chair, and turns to his paper.* JUDITH *goes to the radio and snaps it off, as* GEORGE, *having lifted the paper and read for a moment, suddenly dashes the outside page to the floor.*]
GEORGE [*suddenly thumping chair arm with his fist and roaring.*] Judith, if Porter and his gang of milk-dumpin' rioters go any further, something'll have to be done. They'll ruin all us honest farmers.
JUDITH [*nervously patting his arm*]. Now, George, don't think about it tonight. Everything'll turn out all right.

GEORGE [*grunting*]. Can't help thinking about it, when all our bread and butter's at stake. [*Settles back in chair and turns a page.*] Well, well! John Buell has sold that prize three-year-old heifer of his for eight hundred dollars.

JUDITH. Yes, Martha told me about it this morning.

GEORGE. Eight hundred! She's not worth it. Tom Baker must have helped John slicker somebody!

JUDITH. George! Don't say things like that. John's a fine, steady boy, and after he and Martha are married . . .

GEORGE. John's not going to marry our Martha, Judith.

JUDITH [*shocked and surprised*]. Not . . . not marry her?

GEORGE [*defiantly*]. No sir! [*He returns to his paper.*]

JUDITH [*flustered and helpless*]. But . . . but whatever is the matter? I thought it was all settled.

GEORGE. No girl of mine's going to marry into old Tom Baker's family. John's his nephew, so . . .

JUDITH. Now, George! Have you and Tom had another quarrel?

GEORGE. He's went and joined up with Porter's milk-dumpers! That's plenty for me!

JUDITH. But *John* hasn't done anything. He hasn't joined up with Porter, has he?

GEORGE. Well, he's got bad blood in him.

JUDITH. Oh, George!

[*The telephone jangles.* GEORGE *goes to answer it.*]

GEORGE [*savagely*]. Hello? Hello! Yes, this is George Haines. Who? Hey? Tom Baker? Well, what the hell do *you* want? Yes, I'll talk with you, if you'll talk *right*. Yes, come on over if you want to. But don't fix to stay long! [*Slamming the receiver on the hook.*] That was old Tom. He's coming over. [*Grimly.*] Wants to straighten everything out. Well, he'll have a mighty hard time doin' it.

JUDITH. I . . . I just don't know what Martha'll do when you tell her. She has everything all ready. Her linen, china, and . . .

GEORGE. I've already told her. Late this afternoon.

JUDITH. Why, she didn't say a word to me! Poor child!
 [HILDA *has entered during the telephone conversation and has seated herself across the center table from* JUDITH. HILDA *also has some needlework.*]
HILDA. I think George did right! I'd steer clear of Tom Baker! He's got a determined eye, and I wouldn't give him too much leeway, I tell you!
GEORGE. Aw, you don't often trust anybody, anyhow! [*Then jocosely.*] Guess that's the reason you never snared a man!
HILDA. I could have, and don't you forget *that*, George Haines! 'N what's more, I could have had old Tom Baker himself, years ago, if I'd of given in to 'im!
JUDITH. George! Hilda! Please don't argue! [*To* HILDA.] Don't brag, Hilda! You can be thankful you're as well off as you are! Poor Martha! I'd better go find her. [*Starts to rise.*]
GEORGE. Let her alone. She'll get over it!
HILDA [*to* JUDITH, *bitterly*]. Thankful, I suppose, that someone provides a shelter over my head?
JUDITH. I'm sorry, Hilda. I was thinking about Martha. Oh, George . . . [*She is interrupted by a knock at the door.*]
GEORGE [*smiling grimly*]. That'll be old Tom! [*Goes to open the door. A man some years older than* GEORGE *enters.*]
GEORGE. I thought it was you. Well, come in!
TOM [*stepping inside*]. Howdy, George! [*Puts his hat on a chair near the door and advances.*] Hello, Judith! [*Half turns to* HILDA *as though only just seeing her.*] Why, howdy, Hilda!
HILDA [*turning away spitefully*]. Howdy yourself!
JUDITH. How . . . how are things going, Tom?
TOM [*laughing*]. Things better be going pretty fine, or they'll be forced to!
JUDITH [*as* GEORGE *stands silent*]. Well, have a chair, Tom.
TOM. Thanks, Judith. Don't care if I do. [*He sits.*]
JUDITH [*floundering*]. We can all be thankful we got chairs to sit in these days. [HILDA *snorts.*]

Tom [*looking at* George]. We could all have plenty if we'd do the right thing about the milk situation. Now, I came over tonight to patch up our quarrel and make you see things *my* way.

George. I'll see things your way if you'll stand by the League!

Tom. To hell with the League. It's Porter's plan we got to stick to if we want our rights! We got to *act!*

George [*jumping up and pounding the table with his fists*]. Porter? Man, you're crazy! Those rioting, milk-dumping ignoramuses!

Judith [*helplessly trying to make peace*]. I . . . I thought you men were . . .

Tom. And it's cooperation, or bust!

George [*approaching and shaking a fist*]. You call "cooperation" this dumping of milk and stopping of income?

Tom. Certainly, cooperation! And if you Leaguers had any sense . . .

George. Why, man, cooperation's what the League's built around! You been a Leaguer long enough to know that!

Judith. Well, I think we'd ought to be thankful . . .

Hilda [*attacking her*]. For what? Thankful when a mess of nitwits like Tom Baker dump your milk, and kill off your cows?

Tom. You'll all be thankful when we Porter men set a stable milk market.

George. You can't fight this outfit with clubs or guns or fists! [*He shakes his own fist.*] You got to use brains, and decency! Go over it all sensibly, find out the best way, and . . .

Tom [*cutting him off*]. Brains! Decency! Common sense! Yeah! But when folks don't use 'em for themselves you got to force 'em! And there's some that ain't got sense of any kind!

Hilda [*looking at* Tom]. That's a true word, Tom Baker!

Tom. You got a hard tongue, Hildy, and you ain't slow to use it.

GEORGE. And how many of your Porter men are really milk producers?

TOM. I for one. And none of my milk gets dumped, 'cause I don't take it where I can't get the best price, and what's more . . .

HILDA. How many of your dirty gang ever owned a cow? Some of 'em wouldn't know the difference between milking a cow and a four-legged kettle!

JUDITH [*helpless to stop the arguing*]. Well . . . well, I'll go and get you all some pie! Please, everybody, remember we're all old neighbors! [*She exits.*]

TOM. Neighbors or no neighbors, I stick to Porter!

GEORGE. Yes, and you'll dump your neighbor's milk, and wreck his truck, and do anything else to stop him. Probably even kill him!

TOM. If it was for his own good to stop him, I'd stop him!

GEORGE. By God, that's a threat!

TOM [*heatedly*]. Maybe it is! Maybe you'll be the next man to lose a mess of milk! [*Going toward door.*] Any night!

GEORGE [*roaring*]. No blundering fool of a gangster'll dump my milk! I'm through arguin' with you, neighbor or no neighbor. And as for your nephew, John, marryin' my daughter . . . well, your nephew can go to blazes!

TOM [*yelling*]. I feel the same! Won't have no *Haines* blood in my stock! [*At the door.*] Somebody'll have to slap some sense into you. Maybe I'm th' one to do it!

GEORGE. Yeah? [*He makes a dive for* TOM, *but* TOM *has quickly stepped out and closed the door.* GEORGE *tears the door open and runs out.* HILDA *continues her needlework, not much concerned with the argument.* JUDITH *re-enters with a pie.*]

JUDITH. Oh, has Tom gone?

[GEORGE *comes back in, still angry.*]

GEORGE. Got away from me in the dark. Old criminal! Well, he better not come around here again!

JUDITH. Oh, George, you had another quarrel! What'll poor Martha do?

GEORGE. He better not dump my milk!

JUDITH. Neighbors and friends might be more important than a few cans of milk. You ought to be thankful . . .

HILDA [*exasperated*]. For what? I suppose if you were sitting on a chair, and the world dropped right out from under you, you'd still be thankful for the chair.

GEORGE. Tom Baker! Ranked with those ruffians! I tell you, there's no knowing what's in the blood. It's funny how two men can think so differently on the same subject, and each be dead sure he's right. I mean Tom and me. Both strong for cooperation, yet far apart as the two poles!

HILDA [*ruminatively*]. Yes, 'tis funny how Tom and I can believe the same about a thing, and yet be so far apart! [*As they look at her.*] I . . . I mean, well, just anybody!

JUDITH. My goodness, Sister, what's got into you, jabbering like an old hen after a brood of chickens!

HILDA [*regaining composure and taking up her work*]. Why nothing, Judith. I was just thinking how different people are, that's all. [*She rises, holds up her work, inspects it.*] Guess I'll run down the road to Mary's for a little while.

JUDITH. Don't stay too late!

HILDA [*carelessly*]. Guess I'm old enough to stay out late as I please. But I won't be late. [*As she exits.*] 'Bye!

JUDITH. Goodbye, Hilda.

GEORGE [*as* HILDA *goes*]. Where's Martha?

JUDITH. She went out right after supper. [*She goes to him, attempting to smooth things out.*] George, you ought to be thankful that Martha has chosen such a fine, steady fellow as John, rather than one of those wild, drinking young men you see about town.

GEORGE [*crustily*]. Yes,—and I might have grandchildren who'd take after Tom Baker, instead of me! I tell you, Judith, you're thankful too many times for too many things!

# FAMILY COOPERATIVE

The more I think of old Tom tying up to that crazy crowd, the more disgusted I get, and I tell you once for all, no daughter of mine's going to marry any kin to a weak-minded man like that!

JUDITH. I . . . I just don't know why Martha didn't say something to me!

GEORGE. Don't you worry about Martha! She'll cooperate! Why, she's always talking about cooperation in schools, religion, and government, and *families!*

JUDITH. I don't know as she'll call it cooperation if you go against her!

GEORGE. 'Course she will. I made it mighty clear that John Buell couldn't come here any more. You'n she'll both thank me in the end. Don't forget that!

JUDITH. That's what Tom said to you, George.

GEORGE. Don't you quote Tom Baker to me! [*Starts for the stair door.*] I'm goin' to bed. If I stay down here you'n my neighbors'll badger me to death! [*At the door.*] I'm gonna take things in hand around here and run 'em right! [*He exits.*]

JUDITH [*alone*]. Oh, dear! [*She begins to tidy up the room.*] I suppose things *might* be worse!

[MARTHA *enters.*]

MARTHA. Worse than they are? How?

JUDITH [*going to* MARTHA]. Oh, Martha, your father told me what he said to you. . . .

MARTHA. He said too much! The idea of Dad *forbidding* me to get married, or anything else! I'm old enough to take care of myself!

JUDITH. Now, Martha, be reasonable. Don't go against him, and he'll get over his spell of ill-nature. He just can't stand anyone not seeing eye to eye with him. Have a little patience and thing'll turn out all right.

MARTHA. All Dad's talk of cooperation! [*Suddenly laughing.*] It's really funny, isn't it! [*She comes to* JUDITH *and puts her arms around her.*] I guess you and I are the only ones left to really cooperate around here. Dad talks all the time about thinking things out calmly, but he's more ready for a fist-fight than anyone I ever saw!

JUDITH. Your father's mostly bluff, Martha. Doesn't mean one-half what he blusters!

MARTHA. Well, Dad's mighty like a dictator while he's blustering, and I don't like it.

JUDITH. Oh dear, where will all this milk trouble lead us? I'll be thankful when it's all over, and people can really be friends again. [*Sighing.*] But I guess anything worthwhile has to go through some struggle to prove itself.

MARTHA. Nobody's going to run my life!

JUDITH. Oh, Martha!

MARTHA. You go on to bed. Everything'll work out somehow. You're probably dead tired.

JUDITH. Isn't there something I can do, or say, that'll . . . [*As* MARTHA *shakes her head.*] . . . Well, your father's probably snoring his head off by now. [*Taking up her pie-pan from table.*] I'll put this pie back in the ice-box. Nobody seemed to want any. [*Sighing.*] There's no great loss without some small gain. There'll be enough for dinner tomorrow. [*Coming to* MARTHA.] I hope you'll be reasonable and not quarrel with your father. Have a little patience, and . . .

MARTHA. I'm not going to quarrel with Dad.

JUDITH [*relieved*]. Oh, I'm so glad! Maybe you'd better give up seeing John. [*Looking at* MARTHA *for reassurance.*] For a while, anyway?

MARTHA. That's just what I'm not going to do.

JUDITH [*disappointed*]. Oh, dear, you've always been so sensible and dutiful before! [*Brightening.*] But maybe you'll think better of it tomorrow!

MARTHA. Now don't you fret, Mother. Whatever I do, I'm sure I'll not regret it.

JUDITH. I hope not. [*Shaking her head and turning to go.*] Dear, dear, dear, dear! Good night, Martha.

MARTHA [*kissing* JUDITH *affectionately and laughing*]. You funny old mother, you!

JUDITH. In the end, things will mend! [JUDITH *takes her pie and exits through the stair door.*]

MARTHA [*calling after* JUDITH]. Good night, Mother. [*She listens a moment, moves after her mother and closes the door softly, waits a moment more, then goes softly to telephone, rings a number.*] Hello! Is this Reverend Davis? This is Martha Haines. I've made up my mind, and I'd like to have you marry John and me this evening, like we talked of this afternoon. You understand how things are? Sure Dad'll be sore, but he's got it coming. Yes, I *am* sure it's what I want to do. All right, John's got the license and we'll be over right away. John's coming for me in his car. Goodbye! [*She hangs up the receiver, goes to the stair door, listens, moves into the hall, and returns immediately with her hat and coat. She goes to the mirror, puts on her hat, gazes at her reflection.*] Quite a bride! No satin, no veil, no orange blossoms! [*She bows to herself, turns away.*] You're bound for a jolt, Dad, but maybe it'll jar your ego loose!

[*There is a rap at the right door.* MARTHA *opens it to admit* JOHN BUELL, *a young farmer, still dressed in his working clothes.*]

JOHN. Say, what's the rush, Martha? I got the license and beat it right over. Didn't even have time to change my clothes. What . . .

MARTHA. Not so loud. [*Leading him to the sofa, where they sit.*] Everything's in a terrible mess. Dad and your Uncle Tom had a knock-down quarrel, and now Dad says I can't marry you, and . . .

JOHN. Quarrel? But Uncle Tom and George Haines have always quarreled! What's that got to do with us?

MARTHA. Dad says Tom Baker threatened to dump his milk or something.

JOHN [*whistling*]. So that's it! Porter and his crowd! They've hooked Uncle Tom at last! I was afraid of it.

MARTHA [*unbelieving*]. You don't mean Tom Baker's really deserted the League and gone over to that rotten Porter gang, do you?

JOHN. Looks like it.

MARTHA. But if somebody did dump Dad's milk, he'd think it was Tom Baker did it, then where'd we be? I mean, instead of being a cooperative family, we'd be a competitive one! And I want cooperation, if I have to fight for it!

JOHN. I'm sure it's not in Uncle Tom Baker to actually damage anyone's property. He loves to bluster and boss, just like your dad.

MARTHA. Yes, and I want Dad to have a lesson he'll never forget. I love Dad, John, and I'd do any reasonable thing on earth for him . . . but this notion of his that I can't marry you, just because . . . Oh, I'll show him he can't trample on other people's rights just because he can't force people to think as he does. I've made up my mind to stand on my own feet and make my own decisions. And I want to get married tonight. Right now!

JOHN. Now?

MARTHA. Is it all right with you?

JOHN. Well, well . . . sure! But . . .

MARTHA. I've already arranged with Reverend Davis to marry us.

JOHN. You have? But aren't you kinda rushing things? I mean, I'm not . . . [*He looks at his clothes.*]

MARTHA. It's now or never.

JOHN. Well . . . let's go. But, gosh, Martha, I just come in from the cow barn! Can't we go by home so I can put on my new suit?

MARTHA. We haven't got time! Besides, if anybody ought to

doll up to get married, it ought to be me! You look like a dairyman, you are a dairyman. So what's bothering you?

JOHN. Nothing, only I always thought . . . gosh . . .

MARTHA. Oh, come on! We're wasting time! [*She pulls him to the door.*]

JOHN [*as they go out*]. Okay, Okay, but gosh . . . [*As they go* HILDA's *voice is heard outside.*]

HILDA. Martha! John! Come back here! Quick! All right, don't then! But you'll be sorry! [HILDA *enters from right, turns in the door, and calls once more after the fleeing* JOHN *and* MARTHA.] Come back! [*She turns into the room, out of breath and waving her arms excitedly.*] George! George Haines! Help! Help! [*Comes to center, waving arms.*] We've got to beat 'em! George, aren't you coming? George, can't you hurry, for once! [*She goes to the stair door and shouts.*] And you'd better put your pants on! You might have to go amongst folks!

[GEORGE *rushes down in his night-shirt and rubber boots, holding a shotgun.*]

GEORGE. Where is he? Where's the burglar?

HILDA [*panting for breath*]. George, I was over to Mary's, and we was listening on the phone, and we heard somebody calling Tom Baker. Those Porter men are coming through the whole community tonight and dump every League man's milk. Then, in the morning, they're going to gather at the Kelly Creek bridge and dump the milk from every truck as the men are on the way to the plant. [*She sinks exhausted into a chair.*]

GEORGE. That so? Well, we'll see about *that!* I'll balk 'em! [*Pausing suddenly.*] How'll I do it, though? 'Less I shoot 'em?

[JUDITH *has followed* GEORGE *down, and holds his overalls.*]

JUDITH. No, no! Don't fight. Somebody'll get hurt! [*Her eyes grow wide with a sudden idea.*] Wait! I'll tell you how!

GEORGE. By bein' thankful? Pshaw! You've never had a single constructive thought on this milk question!

JUDITH [*suddenly forceful*]. Maybe not! It's been a mighty queer jumble, with people talkin' and arguin' every-which-way!

HILDA. If you're so smart, tell us how!

JUDITH. When it comes to defending my property, I'm as ready to do it as anybody!

GEORGE [*already on his way to the door*]. Yeah? Well, I'm going!

[JUDITH *grabs him by his night-shirt tail and drags him back.*]

JUDITH. Wait! You go right out and get Hank to load up our milk, and then go right on and get everybody to take theirs too . . . right down to the plant. Then all of you get your milk off to the plant an hour earlier in the morning. . . .

GEORGE. Now there's an idea! Didn't think you had it in you, Judith. I'll beat it now! [*He starts to dash away, but* JUDITH *still has hold of his night-shirt and drags him back.*]

JUDITH. Wait! You know that old road down through Carter's sugar grove?

GEORGE. Sure, but . . .

JUDITH. In the morning, get all the men to go by that, then right on across our south pasture and out on the Kelly Road, two miles beyond the bridge. You'll get by the dumpers that way, and all the satisfaction they'll have'll be empty hands and guilty minds!

GEORGE [*excitedly*]. Just what I was thinkin'! I'll tell 'em how to do it! [*He exits.*]

JUDITH [*as he goes*]. Wait! Your pants!

GEORGE [*sticks his head back inside*]. Throw 'em to me. I'll slip into 'em on the way! [JUDITH *throws the overalls.*]

HILDA. And you leave that shotgun with me, George Haines! [HILDA *runs and gets the gun from* GEORGE *as he catches the overalls.* GEORGE *disappears.*]

JUDITH [*sinking into a chair*]. I'll be thankful when things get back to normal again!
HILDA [*tartly*]. I'm thankful that for once, something has jogged you out of your eternal thankfulness!
JUDITH. Hilda, don't you think it's strange that Martha hasn't heard all this disturbance and come down? I'd better go see . . . [*Starts to rise.*]
HILDA. Don't worry about her! I met Martha and John as I come in, and they was runnin' like they was going to a fire! Yes, sir! If I know our Martha, she's going to figure out her life in her own way!
JUDITH. But what if John'd turn out to be like his Uncle Tom? Just as George says?
HILDA [*bridling*]. Well, he could turn out a lot worse. When it comes to having his way, Tom Baker isn't a bit worse than George Haines!
JUDITH. Why, Sister! What's come over you! Standing up for Tom Baker when you've always said the meanest things about him!
HILDA [*confused*]. I wasn't standing up for him. . . . I . . . well . . . you can't kick a man when he's down, can you?
JUDITH [*hastily*]. It just seemed a bit strange, that's all.
HILDA [*flourishing gun*]. But I'll tell you this, Judith Haines, if I caught Tom Baker around here meddling with our milk, I'd just ride him down the road on a rail. That's what I'd do! I'd give him a ride on a good sharp rail!
JUDITH [*smiling*]. How? With Tom holding one end of the rail and you the other?
HILDA. Hush, Judith! [*A light flashes across the window curtains.*] There's a car coming down the road! [*She goes to the window and pushes back the curtains.*] It's slowing up! Come, Judith, look! It's turned in down by the old barn. I'll bet somebody's snooping around!
JUDITH [*going to the window*]. Dear me! I wish George was here!

HILDA. Well, I'm going to do a little snooping, too! I aim to find out who that car belongs to!
JUDITH. Something might happen to you, Hilda. Don't do it!
HILDA. Something'll happen if I get my hands on 'em! [*She starts for the door.*]
JUDITH. You give me that shotgun! [*She snatches it from* HILDA.] I won't have you shooting anybody! And don't go farther than the yard!
HILDA. I'll go as far as I have to. [*She exits.*]

[JUDITH *goes to the window, peers out, then comes to the table. She suddenly becomes conscious that she is holding the gun, almost drops it, and holding it very gingerly, thrusts it away from her.*]

JUDITH. Oh dear, oh dear! [*Sinks into a chair.*] Here I am all alone in the house with a gun, and heaven-knows-what prowling around outside! [*A noise like a door being kicked is heard outside.*] Oh! [*She clasps her hands in fear, and the gun clatters to the floor.* JUDITH *rises very nervously and comes center. Sounds of commotion come nearer, scuffling, gasps, muffled cries. The door bursts open.* HILDA *tumbles in, pulling on the cords of a bag which is over a man's head. Two or three neighboring farmers follow and surround them, helping* HILDA.]

HILDA [*wildly excited, to* JUDITH]. I got 'im!
MAN IN BAG. Let me get this bag off! I'll explain!
HILDA. Oh, you'll explain, will you!
A FARMER. You got aplenty of explainin' to do, feller!
HILDA. Call the troopers, Judith! He wants to explain!
MAN IN BAG. Sure, call 'em quick, 'fore this wildcat kills me!

[GEORGE HAINES *enters.*]

GEORGE. What's the excitement? You catch one of 'em?
HILDA. I saw this one sneakin' away from the barn, so I stole up behind 'im and threw this clothes-pin bag over his head.
A FARMER. We helped bring 'im in. Heard there was trouble brewin'!

GEORGE. Why'd you waste time bringin' him in here?
HILDA. So his friends wouldn't rescue him.
GEORGE. Shoulda strung 'im up!
HILDA. Go on, Judith, call the troopers!
   [*Suddenly the man has freed his hands and jerks the bag from over his head.*]
ALL. Tom Baker!
GEORGE [*stepping menacingly toward him*]. Tom Baker! I thought you were one of those hoodlums Porter brought in from out of town. Well, it'll be a hundred times worse for you than them! You come here to dump my milk, and you'll pay, just as if you really did it!
JUDITH. Tom Baker! After we bein' such good friends and neighbors all these years!
TOM. Let me explain. . . .
HILDA [*almost weeping*]. Tom Baker! And after I'd thought so much of you all these years!
TOM [*taking a step toward her*]. Thought so much of me? Why . . . when? How? Why, Hildy!
HILDA. Don't you Hildy me!
TOM. But I can explain. . . .
GEORGE. Yeah, Tom Baker! You can't explain to me! When you go out of here with the troopers you can do your explainin' to them. As for me, I hope never to lay eyes on you again! It's just mighty lucky Martha didn't marry that worthless nephew of yours, that's all! [MARTHA *and* JOHN *enter.*] What's this? Martha, I told you . . .
MARTHA. Dad, John and I are married.
GEORGE. Huh? Married? Well, you can both go to blazes! [*He turns away.*]
JUDITH. Now, George, it's too late to do anything. . . .
GEORGE [*wheeling on* JOHN]. After this rascally uncle of yours came here to dump my milk, do you expect me to welcome you as a son-in-law?
JOHN. Uncle Tom didn't do it! I know he wouldn't!

TOM [*shaking off his captors*]. Hey, let's quit all this foolish talk! I'm going to have my say right here and now! [*To* GEORGE.] George Haines, you let these young folks alone! And get this: I didn't come here tonight to dump your milk!

GEORGE. Then what did you want? Snoopin' around . . .

HILDA. *Sneakin's what he was doin'!*

TOM. I got to thinking on the way home, earlier in the evenin', what fools we were! Here we are, both you'n I, wantin' cooperation in dairying, yet we're both quarreling over how to get it.

GEORGE. Just what I been sayin'!

TOM. Some of Porter's men called me on the telephone. Guess they figured I'd go the whole way with 'em; but when it come to the show-down I knew I couldn't practice any violence against my friends and neighbors. I came over here tonight to stop those Porter fellers from molesting you or any other dairymen. But I found you'd stolen a march on everybody, and had your milk already headed toward town.

GEORGE. Figured out how to trick you, myself!

HILDA. Now, George . . .

GEORGE [*grudgingly*]. Well, me and Judith figured out how to do it.

TOM. And I guess that's about all, except when I started away from the barn, a cyclone or somethin' hit me, and here I am. *And* set to be reasonable. [*Holding out his hand to* GEORGE.] Want to shake and be friends?

GEORGE. I'll shake hands if you'll talk straight!

TOM. We could be mighty good friends if you'd listen to reason!

[*They shake, both serious for a moment, then suddenly both break into laughter. Everybody joins in. After a moment* TOM *turns, sees* HILDA, *becomes serious. Others become silent too.*]

TOM. Well, Hildy . . .

HILDA [*without waiting for him to finish*]. Sure I will, Tom. Woulda married you long ago, if you'd *asked* me, and not told me I was *going* to! We Hainses got plenty of spunk! [*She puts her arm around* MARTHA.]

TOM. Dog-gone! [*He beams happily and advances toward her.*]

JUDITH [*pushing* HILDA *into* TOM's *arms*]. I declare, we'd all ought to be thankful . . . for everything! [*Everybody laughs.*]

CURTAIN

# OVER FOURTEEN: AND SINGLE

Courtin' by Decree Beyond the Genesee

*by*

LAUREN WILLIAMS

(Adapted by A. M. Drummond)

# OVER FOURTEEN: AND SINGLE

The problem of love and marriage on the early frontier could often be reduced to the simplest terms: there were no girls to love, or marry. Of course, many families moved into the new lands, and groups of families sometimes travelled westward in great caravans—though generally after exploratory trips by the men. But it was the common practice for the younger men to go solo into the wilderness and hew out a farmstead for themselves before sending back East for their girls. If they had left no girls behind them, these young pioneers could only labor to better their holdings and wait, with what patience they could muster, for the westward trek to bring some within reach. Rapidly as the country seems to us to have been peopled, these young settlers often waited years before taking a wife and beginning a family. But they seem to have endured their plight with fortitude, and sometimes to have showed true Yankee ingenuity in attempting to make the wilderness hamlets attractive to unattached females.

They say that the five young bloods who first settled Farmersville, in the present Cattaraugus County, remained too long for their peace of mind the hamlet's most eligible bachelors. They therefore organized in town-meeting a "Confederacy" which voted this resolution, binding thereby their goods and chattels and their matrimonial prospects, *to wit*:

> "That if any single woman who is fourteen years of age shall come to reside in our village, and no one of this Confederacy shall offer her his company within a fortnight thereafter, then, and in such case, our Board shall be called together, and someone shall be appointed to make her a visit, whose duty it shall be to perform the same, or

forfeit the disapprobation of the Company, and pay a fine sufficiently large to buy the lady thus neglected a new dress."

It is to be hoped that this desperate and generous offer lured eligible maidens to the early Farmersville Village and that the young men had eventually a choice of good wives and true. Our historical researches to date do not enable us to say what their luck really was. But the preservation of the old record furnishes a pleasant idea for a comedy of courtin' in the Genesee Country—a comedy surely not more extravagant than the entanglements likely to result from a Farmersville Resolution.

TIME: *A late summer afternoon in the year 1820.*
PLACE: *The cabin of* RICHARD TOZER *in the town of Farmersville, Cattaraugus County, beyond the Genesee.*

## THE CHARACTERS OF THE PLAY

OLD JOHN, *a humorous, racy ancient, speaks the* PROLOG.

PETER TEN BROECK, *a tall, square-built, capable young farmer.*
PELEG ROBBINS, *stocky, red-cheeked, and skittish.*
LEVI PEET, *a huge fellow with a great black beard, but shy.*
ROSS PARISH, *the youngest farmer-bachelor, and fair-haired.*
PRUNELLA PRESCOTT, *"over fourteen, and white, and single."*
NELL TOZER, *Tozer's wife, and elder cousin of Prunella.*
RICHARD TOZER, *a jovial farmer of Farmersville.*

*And* OLD JOHN *comes on to speak the* EPILOG.

# OVER FOURTEEN: AND SINGLE

### THE PROLOG

[*Spoken before the curtain by* OLD JOHN, *an octogenarian frontier farmer who hobbles on a cane but whose eye retains all the sparkle of youth.*]

Hi, there! [*Shaking his cane.*]
Young fellow in the far back row,
Think I can't see an' know
You got yer arm around that gal?
Well, well, well!
Mighty nice asettin' close
To the one and only!

Last night you kissed another,
But you c'n trust me not to tell
'Cause men had better all agree
To keep such failin's under cover!

Yeah! Courtin' gals is lots of fun,
'Speshly when there's more than one
Dangling on your string.
When I was 'bout your age, by cracky,
Sparkin' gals sure kept me happy
As anything!

But did you ever stop to think, young men,
Just what we'd do *without* wom-en?
The Ladies, men, I say God bless 'em,
If there weren't none we sure would miss 'em.
Yes, sir! Yes, sir!

And that's just why I durst
Come here tonight to say—
In pretty rusty verse—
That long ago there was a day
When New York West was a wild frontier
With no young women; only wolves, 'n bears, 'n deer!
Young bloods that then fer profit an' fer fame
Struck out acrost th' Genesee new land t' claim,
Right soon found out that life was kinda slender—
Ye can't make happy homes without th' fem'nine gender!
An' lots o' young bucks without gals to court
Was in sad sitooations of that sort!

'N the five brash lads, so th' records tell,
Who settled th' village of Farmersville
In th' eastern part of North Cattaraugus
When faced with th' problem *this* voted in caucus:
"That 'f a lady'd come t' *their* town t' reside
They'd promptly apply t' make 'er a bride!
If said lady was over fourteen, 'n single, 'n white,
They promised a lover within a fortnight!"

Now, lads—*and* ladies!—such rash action shows
Sure as the dickens
How poor, in them frontier days
Was th' marital pickin's!

So while our show tonight may not be wholly true—
'N historical inacc'racies may rile a seryus few—
You gotta admit, take 'er late er soon
When such a moil entraps young men
Why, by the great horn-spoon!
Most anythin' might happen!

So let th' play perceed
An' treat it like a friend.

'F th' plot works as 'tis planned,
I'll see you at the end!

An' thank you kindly fer now!
  [*He exits, and the curtain opens on the play.*]

## THE PLAY

THE SCENE *is the log cabin of* RICHARD TOZER, *in the year 1820, in the town of Farmersville, Cattaraugus County, New York. It is summer; so there is no fire in the stone fireplace at the left. The late afternoon sun sifts through the open window in the left of the rear wall and falls on the rude table toward the right of the room. Three rough-hewn chairs are about the table. The outer door, opening onto the woods, is in the right rear wall. A small door at the right leads to the kitchen lean-to. A door below the fireplace enters the bedroom. A stool by the fireplace and a bench at the right of the room complete the furniture.*

  [PETER TEN BROECK, *a large, square-shouldered, earnest young man, is seated at the table examining a Holland Land Company chart. He is dressed in the rough homespun of the period.*]

  [*After a moment,* PELEG ROBBINS, *a stocky man with very red cheeks, peers in the doorway, looks nervously around, and then, seeing* PETER, *enters mopping his face with a bright new red handkerchief.*]

PELEG. Hot day, ain't it?
PETER [*drawling*]. Is that so?
PELEG. Sure is.
  [*The men act deliberately and speak laconically.*]
PETER. Mebbe your body-heat's up a bit.
PELEG [*wiping his face*]. Why should't be?
PETER [*pacifying*]. Just my notion, that's all.
PELEG. I ain't n' more excited 'n you be.
PETER. I reckon. Just holdin' the house till Tozer gets back

from the falls with grist, an' Black John brings Nell up from th' turnpike coach. [PELEG *snorts in disbelief.*]

PELEG. We ain't all ice blocks like you.

PETER. 'Pears not.

PELEG. W'at you workin' over that Holland Land Company map fer?

PETER. Just pickin' good tracts for a man to settle on . . . *and* raise a fam'ly mebbe.

PELEG. Takes a cold-blooded guy t' count such chickens afore hatchin'!

[PETER *is silent;* PELEG *sweats some more, and goes to door, and peers out.*]

PELEG. Seems they oughtta've come in b' now!

PETER. Take what mind you got off it, Peleg.

PELEG. I ain't worried—not a bit! [*Sweats and wipes his face.*] It don't matter none to me.

PETER [*smiling*]. No. What's the contraption round yer neck?

PELEG [*feeling it guiltily as he comes back from the door*]. Just a old cravat I packed 'long from the East.

PETER. Quite a touch for you, ain't it?

PELEG [*with an aggressive attempt at "savoir faire"*]. Well, Pete, I guess a *mite* o' gentility 'll be welcome to a lady as is far from home. We don't want her t' think we're all bears.

PETER [*smiles, rises, goes to the door, and glances out*]. Speakin' of bar, look 't what's comin'. Levi Peet! [*He laughs as he turns back toward the fireplace.*]

[LEVI *appears in the doorway where he pauses a moment without expression. He is a big fellow, his face almost completely enveloped in a black beard. A new black hat perched on his scraggy head is ludicrously incongruous with his rough clothes. More incongruous still is the bouquet of wood-flowers he holds awkwardly in one huge paw.*]

PELEG [*after a pause in which they survey him,* PELEG *flips his cravat with a bit of envy*]. W'at you got there, Levi?

LEVI [*shortly*]. Where?

PELEG. 'N yer hand.
LEVI [*sheepish but dogged*]. Just sumpin' I picked.
PETER. 'T's right smart o' you, Levi. Ladies is fond of posies, I reckon.
LEVI [*smiling with sudden delight*]. D'ju think so?
PELEG [*surveying the beard thoughtfully*]. Mebbe 'f you didn't have s' much underbrush t' go with them flowers . . .

[ROSS PARISH, *a younger man with curly blond hair and shirt open at the throat, enters inconspicuously and crosses to the bench.*]

PETER. Hello, Ross.
ROSS. Hello, Peter.
PELEG [*looking at* Ross *distrustfully*]. What you doin' here, Ross? *You* ain't thinkin' o' gittin' hitched too, be you?
ROSS [*looking up with a boyish smile mixed with a blush*]. Well, I don't know. Maybe I ain't an' maybe I am!
PELEG. Well, y' better not be! Ye ain't old enough yet t' know the things necessary fer a husband.
ROSS [*scratching his chin with a grin*]. Don't you reckon I could ketch on?
PELEG. I don't mean nothin' like that! I mean you're t' young to make a steady home fer a woman. Ain't accoomoolated 'nough worldly goods t' take on a wife an' family—not on that dinky farm of yourn by the crick.
PETER [*moving back to the table and map*]. Guess Ross'd hold his candle with most.
PELEG. Well, Ross'd better not be gittin' ideas! There's us as has waited longer fer wives and been here taming the woods longer'n him. 'N we ought t' come first!
LEVI [*strongly*]. Yeah. You gotta respect a man's age. 'N I'm th' oldest. [PELEG *glares at him.*]
PETER. Now, see here, you men. We can't quarrel over who's to marry the first girl that's come to our village. It's been hard enough for all of us young baches living three-four years alone out here on t'other end of civilization, with nary

society 'n families ner pretty girls to court, 'n nothin' to do but clear timber an' try to beat out a few fertile acres! But we gotta remember we're gentlemen, *and* we're friends . . . and we can't get into any silly fight over women—'specially not when there's only one.

PELEG. But we oughtta settle th' thing according to *justice!* We oughtta make a list 'cording to who has . . . what was that word you used . . . accordin' to who has priority rights.

LEVI [*emphatically*]. 'N that's me! I'm th' oldest!

PELEG [*whirling on him*]. I don't mean age, yu billy goat! I mean who's been here an' worked th' longest. An' that's me!

PETER [*quietly*]. Or me, Peleg. Remember I come up a summer before you.

PELEG [*silenced*]. *You* ain't thinkin' of marrying are you, Peter?

PETER. Why not?

PELEG. I thought you was foolin' me, what you said 'bout th' map. You never said before you was thinkin' of it. I thought . . . well, I thought you didn't *want* to git married.

PETER [*laughing*]. Mebbe none of us'll want to marry when we see the girl. D'ja ever think o' that?

LEVI [*blankly*]. No. Why not?

PETER. Mebbe there's a lot t' bein' married you fellows've forgot. If she's fat or ugly, or's got a nasty tongue . . . maybe you'd wish you'd stayed single!

PELEG. Tozer's wife says she was a right handsome gal when she last seen her.

PETER. She was just hopin'. Girl was two years old when Nell Tozer last saw her. Mebbe she's one of Nell's cousins they just wantta get married off.

LEVI [*dumbly*]. I don't believe it. I swear she's as purty as a pitchur.

Ross [*stretching his arms vigorously and running both hands over his hair to smooth it*]. She sure's a pretty name all right! Prunella!

PELEG [*looking at Ross viciously*]. Now, I tole you, you young poppinjay, don't you be getting no *idees!*

PETER. Wait a minute, Peleg. Remember we ain't th' ones decide what *man* does th' marrying. That's up to th' lady ever' time.

PELEG. This here's diff'runt. We voted a agreement!

PETER. Nothin' in our agreement forces the lady to nothing she ain't willing for.

PELEG. *Somebody* gits to marry 'er!

PETER. Only if she's willin'!

PELEG [*scratching his head*]. Read out that agreement we voted, agin.

PETER [*taking a document out of his wallet*]. This is the statement 's I took it down in our last town meeting—and as, by *all* of us, signed proper . . . or he made his mark. [*He reads.*] "If any single woman over fourteen years of age shall come to reside in our village, and if no one of this Confeder-acy shall of his own wish offer her his bed and board within a fortnit thereafter, then and in such case, our Board shall be called together, and shall appoint one to make her a visit, whose duty it shall be either to propose to her marriage, or, in default of performing the same, shall forfeit the approbation of the Company, and shall pay a fine sufficient to buy said lady thus neglected a new red dress." So you see our vote provides an equal chance for all of us.

PELEG. It ain't fair the deservin' shouldn't be them that gits.

LEVI. No, 'tain't!

PETER [*laughing*]. Peel can't think he's as good chances with the ladies as the rest of us?

PELEG [*glaring*]. I didn't say that! [*Looking at* LEVI, *who is gingerly smelling and shaping his bouquet.*] And I don't see why not!

Ross [*flexing his arms again; or perhaps standing on his head* as in a boyish display before the girls]. Prunella! Prunella! Prunella!

[PELEG *glares at him in turn.*]

[*Voices and sound of an arriving wagon are heard outside, with* OLD JOHN *"whoaing" the horses and so on, and* NELL *saying,* "You unhitch till we get help with them boxes, John," *and* JOHN *answering,* "Yes, ma'am, Mis' Tozer, I'll unhitch and feed, an' rub Bess down, yes'm."]

PELEG [*running to the door*]. There must be Old John bringin' Nell now! [*Looking out.*] Sure thing. An' there's th' gal with 'er!

[LEVI *crowds to the door to look out too.* ROSS *bounds up.* PETER *rises slowly.*]

PETER. Here, you two, don't forget you're gentlemen. You can't go pell-mell after the lady like you was going to eat her up. [*Commandingly.*] Come back here and line up front of the fireplace so's you can be introduced proper. [*He crosses to them and pushes them toward the left. All cross and line up expectantly before the fireplace, eyes fixed on the door in ardent anticipation.*]

ROSS [*downstage in the line, whispers expectantly*]. Prunella!

[*The voices of the women outside approach. Suddenly a smallish girl in long pigtails bounds through the door and stops in the middle of the room. She is dressed in a straight bag of a brown dress and stands awkwardly with her feet apart, toeing in. She wears little glasses and squints through them, wrinkling her forehead and nose in an attempt to see. Her voice is piping and harsh, and every now and then she giggles half-wittedly. She is painfully plain and acts as dumb as they make 'em. The men stare in amazement at her as she takes in the scene.*]

PRUNELLA [*giggling*]. Where 're the men? [*Giggles.*] Where 're they? Here's Prunella! [*She looks all around the room but is too nearsighted to see them.* NELL TOZER, *a husky, force-*

*ful, and rather handsome woman has entered behind her.*]

NELL [*pointing and taking* PRUNELLA'*s arm*]. There they are, Prunella, over by the fireplace . . . all four of them . . . 'n *all* bachelors! [*The men stare blankly.*]

PRUNELLA [*adjusting her glasses*]. Oh, I couldn't see them. [*Giggles and crosses.*] Let me get nearer so I can see.

NELL. The first is Mr. Peter Ten Broeck.

[PRUNELLA *squints very close into his face through her glasses.*]

PRUNELLA [*giggling*]. My, isn't he big though! And pretty!

NELL. The next is Mr. Peleg Robbins.

PRUNELLA [*peering closely at* PELEG *who is staring at her. She giggles.*] But Cousin Nelly! Is that his natural expression?

NELL [*with a trace of despair*]. The third is Mr. Levi Peet.

PRUNELLA [*coming very close to him to adjust her sight. Suddenly she screams and springs back a few steps and throws her arms around* NELL. *To* NELL.] My goodness . . . [*Advancing again but ready to spring back to* NELL.] . . . is he *safe?*

NELL. And the boy on the end is Ross Parish.

PRUNELLA [*approaching him, she adjusts her glasses and stares; then stands speechless for a moment; and finally says weakly in diminuendo*]. Oh! Oh! Oh! Hel-lo! [*She continues to stare at* ROSS.]

NELL [*severely*]. Prunella!

PRUNELLA [*giggling, she comes back center where she suddenly sits down on the floor—feet before her—and laughs*]. Oh, Cousin Nell, I never *saw* so many funny men. How can I ever decide which to marry? . . . Are there *more?*

NELL. There are more in the woods . . . but this is the best of the lot. [*Turning to* PETER *sharply and quickly.*] And where's Tozer, for Heaven's sake!

PETER [*dully, with eyes on* PRUNELLA, *but quickly*]. He ain't back from th' mill. He said he's sorry, but he had to go.

NELL [*mollified*]. Well, mebbe it's all for the best! [*She surveys* PRUNELLA *and the staring bachelors and quickly turns away.*] Land o' goodness! . . . Such a . . .

PRUNELLA [*giggling and pointing*]. Cousin Nell, don't they ever say anything?

PETER [*rousing himself, and gruffly*]. Well! Speak up for yourselves, men! Say something to the lady!

PELEG [*squirming*]. Hot day, ain't it, Miss?

PRUNELLA [*giggling*]. There ain't no denying it's practically hot as Tophet, Mister!

PETER. You brought the lady something, didn't you, Levi?

LEVI [*dumbly*]. Uh . . . uh . . . uh! What?

PETER [*pointing*]. Those.

LEVI [*who still holds the flowers, steps forward and thrusts them down at her*]. U-u-uh! Uh! Yeah! I brung these.

PRUNELLA [*giggling*]. Daisies! How thoughtful! Now I can . . . [*She begins to pick the petals with grotesquely romantic abandon.*] He loves me, he loves me not! [*Continuing the business till interrupted.*]

LEVI. I gotta b' goin'! [*He starts for the door.*]

PETER [*commandingly*]. No, you don't, Levi, not yet! Mebbe th' lady's some baggage to bring in or somethin'.

NELL. Yes, there's her trunk out in the wagon. You men can bring it.

PELEG. I'll go fer it!

LEVI [*starting out the door*]. I was first!

PETER [*coughing*]. If you'll excuse me, I guess I'll go help too! [*The men move gingerly toward the door,* Ross *last. At the door* Ross *turns and, with a sigh and shake of his head as though to relieve his hair of its slickness, rolls his eyes up and laments, "Prunella." They exit.*]

NELL [*as soon as they are gone*]. Landsakes, Prunella! I was never s' shamed in my life. You acted disgraceful! I'd my doubts what you'd be when first I laid eye on you, but this surpasses anything. No lady at all—worse 'n a little girl! I can't imagine what kind of a bringing up you had . . . 'n after I'd told all the men you'd be such a nice one too. Who do you think'll want to marry you now?

PRUNELLA [*sitting on the floor and picking the last of the petals. She pouts*]. Why, Cousin Nell, ain't I a nice young lady? [*She treasures the last petal.*]

NELL. You certainly *ain't*. A lady is quiet and dignified and not forward and brazen. You're a perfect little hoyden! 'N you need to be spanked!

PRUNELLA. And I suppose you don't like my glasses or little squeaky voice . . . like all the men at home didn't?

NELL. What the good Lord did to you can't be helped! But you no need to prance about like a nilly. [*She swishes back toward the door.*]

PRUNELLA [*suddenly taking off her glasses and dropping her voice to a natural, sweet tone and calling*]. Cousin Nell!

NELL [*turning, startled*]. Prunella!

PRUNELLA [*getting to her feet and beginning uncertainly*]. Cousin Nell, I hope you can take a joke. Even if it isn't a very ladylike joke.

NELL. Prunella Prescott, what does this mean?

PRUNELLA. Cousin Nell, when your letter told about the men all being so starved for the sight of any woman and so anxious to see me, I just couldn't resist. Did you see their faces? [*Laughing.*] Weren't they figures of fun, though! Oh, dear, oh, dear!

NELL. Prunella, whatever put it into your foolish head? Like 's not you've ruined your chances with all the men.

PRUNELLA. Oh, I don't think so. I wouldn't want to marry a man couldn't take a joke anyway.

NELL [*looking her over*]. Why, Prunella, you're really quite pretty, or would be with your hair done. But of all the crazy tricks . . . !

PRUNELLA. Maybe not so crazy. I'm dumb like a fox. Suppose I'd arrived all dressed fancy and looking kind of pretty, as

I *do* when my hair's up? Then all the men'd swarm round oily as silk. You couldn't tell beef steak from liver 'n lights for the honey there'd be on 'em! Not a man 'd show himself for the skunk he is, and how could a girl decide which male hypocrite to give her lily hand to?

NELL. Now, Prunella, my letter told you there's only one man for you to set your cap for. He's the best worker and provider in these woods. One day he'll be worth a pile in money and land.

PRUNELLA. Your Peter Ten Broeck. Honest, Nell, your letter made him sound so good he wasn't very attractive.

NELL. He's honest and a hard worker.

PRUNELLA. And would expect me to work just as hard!

NELL. Nonsense! Mark my word, silly, he's the catch here . . . if you ain't ruined everything already.

PRUNELLA [*moves dreamily left while* NELL *redds up around the table*]. If I'd known the choice'd be so easy, I'd not 've tried this prank.

NELL. You mean you'll really accept Peter?

PRUNELLA. Peter? Heavens, *no!* Look how he orders folks around.

NELL. There ain't a kinder heart in the Genesee Country.

PRUNELLA. No good, Nell! I made my mind up right away. The little blond fellow on the end is my fancy. [*She holds up the petal and laughs nervously.*] And "*he* loves me," . . . I hope! [*She kisses the petal and drops it down the neck of her dress.*]

NELL. Why, Ross's little more'n a boy!

PRUNELLA. And I'm little more than a girl.

NELL. He ain't half to offer you the rest has.

PRUNELLA. Then maybe he needs *me* to help him out!

NELL. If you ain't the craziest girl!

PRUNELLA. Maybe I'm crazy, but the minute I set eye on him . . . I *knew* just like *that!* [*She snaps her fingers.*]

[*They hear voices of the men approaching.*]

NELL. Here they come!

PRUNELLA. I can't drop my disguise just yet, Nell. Be good and don't give me away till the right time comes, please! [*She puts back her glasses and wrinkles her nose.*]

NELL. I'm ashamed to be party to such a hoax.

PRUNELLA. But don't tell yet! Pretty please? [*She gives the reluctant* NELL *an affectionate hug and kiss.*]

NELL. What can I do? After what I told your folks . . .

[*The men carry in the trunk, a light load for four men, and set it down.*]

PETER [*gravely*]. Here's your trunk, Miss.

PRUNELLA. Oh, thank you! Ain't you men strong! [*She giggles.*]

NELL [*keeping her silence with a struggle*]. You can put the trunk in the bedroom. [*The four men stoop to pick it up.*] But four men will never get in our little bedroom. [*They half straighten up.*] One of you had better pick it up and set it in. [*Each of the men starts to take the trunk alone; then each surrenders simultaneously to the other. The trunk crashes to the floor.*] Landsakes, can't four of you clumsies manage that little trunk? [*Four heads meet with a thump as each starts to pick it up again.*]

PRUNELLA [*giggling*]. Maybe I better carry it myself.

PETER [*sweeping the others back*]. I'll take the trunk into the bedroom, boys. [*He picks it up and moves deliberately and rather forbiddingly left.*]

NELL. Prunella, follow me and I'll show you your bed.

PRUNELLA [*crossing left and pausing at the door to giggle*]. You'll excuse me, won't you, boys? [*She exits.*]

[*The men stand looking after her, speechless.*]

ROSS [*turning away right and speaking mostly to himself*]. An' I been dreaming for two months what Prunella would be like! [*In disgust.*] Prunella! Abigail 'd be a better name!

[PETER *re-enters left. The men stand in a semi-circle looking at each other a moment and then speak low.*]

PETER. What do you think of her, boys?

LEVI. Kinda pe-culiar, ain't she?
PELEG [*shifting uneasily*]. Do you reckon she c'n see none too well?
PETER. And which one of us gets her?
PELEG. Well, 's I was sayin' afore she come, I don't aim t' be selfish 'bout it.
LEVI [*uneasily scratching his beard with both hands*]. Mebbe I'm a leetle too old to marry up with such a young critter.
PETER. Did I hear you say you was interested, Ross?
Ross [*bitterly*]. No!
PETER [*clearing his throat, and with a parliamentary touch*]. Then, boys, I hereby move that we raise that public community fund to buy said lady that new red dress.
PELEG [*hastily and firmly, before the rest can*]. I second th' motion.
PETER. All in favor . . .
ALL. Aye!
PETER. All oppo . . . [*They have all dug in their pockets and thrust coins on him simultaneously.*]
PETER [*receiving the money and planking his own on*]. The motion is carried!
 [PELEG *moves toward the outer door.*]
Ross [*turning to* PETER]. Peter, could y' see your way t' buying my fifty acres as you once said?
PETER. If you're thinking of selling, Ross!
Ross. Guess I'll pull out and head further west. They's mighty good land in Chatauquy. And not 's many trees to buck.
PETER. We'll all hate to lose you, Ross, but if you're sure . . .
Ross. Then I reckon I'll pack my things. Thanks.
PETER. Why leave so quick?
Ross. Summer's more'n half over now. [*He moves toward the door and stops.*] Goodbye, friends. . . . [*As he quickly goes.*] If I don't see you.
 [*They mumble rather startled goodbyes as behind them* PRUNELLA *enters giggling;* NELL *follows and looks out of*

*the window; the voices of* TOZER *and* OLD JOHN *are heard outside.*]

PRUNELLA. But I want to talk to the men!

[*The men have turned toward her, and back slinkingly toward the door.*]

PELEG. I reckon I'll have to go t' do my chores. [*Turns toward the door and pauses.*]

PRUNELLA. Oh, Mr. Robbins, I hardly seen you yet!

LEVI. M' cow needs milkin'. [*He heads for the door.*]

PETER [*tarrying a bit to lend some dignity to the escape*]. We gotta all be on our way, I reckon. Hope you'll like our village, Miss.

PRUNELLA. Where is the pretty young one?

PETER. Just sold out his farm to me, Miss. Ross's headin' west in the mornin'.

PRUNELLA [*startled*]. Heading west?

PETER. Yes, Miss. Got tired of these parts, I reckon. Good day, Miss.

[*The three men start simultaneously toward the door and collide, causing a general halt.*]

NELL. Before you go, boys, won't you bring in that other heavy box?

THE THREE MEN. Yes'm, glad to.

NELL. If you need help, get Tozer; I can hear he's back. [*With some sarcasm.*] But don't you men get drinkin' his russet cider t' celebrate!

[*They file out. The sound of their voices, chiefly* TOZER *and his hearty laughter, drifts back for a while and then dies away as the scene within proceeds.*]

PRUNELLA [*turning and dropping her disguise*]. Nell, don't tell me I've scared Ross away.

NELL. Serves you right 'f you have!

PRUNELLA [*crossing right in dismay*]. Oh! He couldn't just pull out like that.

NELL. Single men on the frontier ain't very permanent. It takes a woman to get 'em to plant their feet in the ground and stay there to fight it out.

PRUNELLA. That's what I came out here for, 'stead of staying in a dull little civilized town and marrying some tiresome little store-keeper. I want to be a part of something building and growing under my feet. That's what I want to do for Ross.

NELL. It'll be all for the best if Ross goes. Then you can marry Peter Ten Broeck and settle.

PRUNELLA. He doesn't need help. . . . He'll build and boss with no help from me or anyone.

NELL. Nonsense!

PRUNELLA. Nell, it's too late now. It's *got* to be Ross. I saw it in a flash: I'm in love at first sight! And he mustn't get away from me.

NELL [*dryly*]. 'Pears he *has!*

PRUNELLA. I've been stupid, very. But I've got to get him back. Nell, you've got to help me. How can I stop him?

NELL. Heaven knows! I'd be ashamed to admit to him what I'd done.

PRUNELLA. I've got to fix my hair and dress up a bit. Help me get that new dress out of the top of the trunk. [*Starting toward bedroom door.*]

NELL. Well . . . but I don't see what sense . . .

[Ross *suddenly appears in the doorway with an ax in his hand.*]

Ross [*coming in a few steps*]. I brought back Toze's ax I borrowed. I'm packin'.

NELL [*nervously*]. We heard you was leaving, Ross. We'll be sorry.

Ross. Figgerin' t' start at dawn.

PRUNELLA [*in a whisper, tugging* NELL'S *sleeve*]. Help me, Nell, get him to stay awhile.

NELL. You got yourself into this, now get yourself out. [*To* Ross.] I'll give the ax to Toze. Er prob'ly he's out to the shed if you want to see him. Er maybe he'll be in when the boys bring the box . . . if they ain't got talking and cider-drinking . . . as appears likely! [*She exits hurriedly into the bedroom.*]

[Ross *turns to go as though to take the ax to* TOZER.]

PRUNELLA [*nervously and having difficulty with her breathing; it is hard to tell which of her characters she is now.*] Wait a minute, Mister. Don't go. I want to talk to you about something most important.

ROSS [*only half turning*]. Well, Miss, I don't want to talk to you.

PRUNELLA [*weakly*]. Why not?

ROSS. If you want to know, I've decided to leave here because I don't want to see any more of you.

PRUNELLA [*utterly at a loss*]. Why?

ROSS. I been dreaming for months about what you'd be like; I been a-picturing you as a lady, with something about you'd make the whole place seem different because you was here. And look what you turned out to be!

PRUNELLA. I'm really not so bad.

ROSS [*earnestly*]. I know what's a lady, even 'f I do live out in this wilderness. My mother was a lady back East, and pretty, and you knew all the time she was a lady from the way she talked and walked. There was something gentle and kind about her, different t' anything out in these woods. Just being with her made you easy and rested . . . kept you from feeling you wasn't at home and had to push on some place else lookin'! My mother died, and I come out here with paw, and I ain't seen a lady since.

PRUNELLA [*really moved and her voice is gentle*]. You're just a lonely boy, aren't you?

ROSS [*looking at her in surprise*]. Your voice sounded different then.

[NELL *has appeared from the bedroom, holding behind her a red dress so* ROSS *cannot see it.*]

PRUNELLA [*in her own voice*]. Ross, turn around and don't you dare look. [*He does so.* PRUNELLA *grabs the dress from* NELL *and dashes into the bedroom.*]

NELL [*advancing and putting a hand on Ross's shoulder. She is both sympathetic with Ross and beginning to play* PRUNELLA'S *game for her*]. I'm sorry, Ross! Tell me. You've been dreaming what Prunella would be like when she came. Tell me what you were going to do when she came.

Ross. I don't rightly just know!

NELL. But what you'd dreamed of?

[PRUNELLA *peeks in, half-dressed, from the bedroom—to see how things are holding; she ducks hurriedly back, working all the while at her change.*]

Ross [*turning the ax around in his hands and fingering it*]. Maybe if Peleg hadn't raised too much fuss, and Pete'd been willin' and Prunella'd been nice, and picked me . . . maybe we'd been married and she'd lived in my house with me. [*Carried away with his fancy.*] And when I went into the house, it wouldn't seem still and small and empty. There'd be a voice was kind and warm, and she'd ask me how the work went, and I'd tell her I felled a tree shaded my field. And she'd ask how the corn was comin' an' I'd take her out and show her how much I'd hoed and we'd dream of how soon 'twould be ripe. And we'd both gather berries in the afternoon, an' 'f I saw a deer and shot it, she'd cook some of it in the evening. An' I'd farm 'cause she'd be waitin' to help me and encourage me and I'd want to do everything I could for her. Aw . . . what's the use talking like a fool. . . . [*He is acutely embarrassed.*] I'm sellin' th' farm to Pete an' goin' west t'night.

[PRUNELLA *appears at the bedroom door vividly transformed by a few quick changes. The new red dress and a quick hair-do make her seem years older. Her glasses and squint are gone, and a radiant smile has replaced them. Her deportment is quiet and graceful.*]

PRUNELLA. Here I am, Ross, look here.

[Ross *turns and looks at her with open mouth, doubt changing to irrationally radiant willingness to believe or hope; the ax slides through his hand until the head rests on the floor; then he drops the handle with a loud bang on the floor.*] Ross, I've been very bad. Can you forgive me?

ROSS. Prunella!

NELL. I'm surprised myself, Ross! But it's really her!

PRUNELLA. Ross, can you believe I want to be your lady to help you and cheer you?

ROSS [*dazed*]. I don't understand. You're not the same girl.

PRUNELLA. And never will be again, I promise you! [*She crosses her heart.*] 'Twas horrid of me.

ROSS. But you're *pretty*, and . . . and you're a *lady*!

PRUNELLA. Am I, Ross?

ROSS. But now Peleg'll want to marry you, or maybe Peter.

PRUNELLA. Do *you* want me, Ross?

ROSS. Well, I guess so . . . why, gosh, *yes* . . . *sure!* . . . but . . .

PRUNELLA. Then don't forget . . . it's always the lady's choice!

[*A babel of men's voices approaches from outside.*]

TOZER [*appearing in the door, cider-jug in hand, and calling back to the men carrying the box*]. Didn't I tell you 'at wuz th' best hard cider in the Genesee Country! [*A chorus of mellow-tongued approvals from the men.*] Now bring 'er in *easy*, boys! Nell's got some new chiny in there! An' we'll just have another gurgle offen the jug.

[*The men bring in the big box carefully, eyes bent on it; slowly they get it centerward, while scene proceeds.*]

TOZER [*as* NELL *approaches him, he advances with left arm outstretched to embrace her, jug in his right hand*]. Well, well, Nell, old gal, glad you're back! [*Gives her a resounding kiss.*] I sure missed you! [*Kisses her loudly again. His eyes fall with astonished delight on* PRUNELLA.] An' is this little Prunella? Well, well, well! Give yer ole cousin b' marriage a kiss. [*They kiss heartily.*] Ain't you a sight fer sore eyes though! Say, *boys,* I thought y' said . . . You must be blind. . . . Look here. . . . [*He holds her off and turns to present her to the men.*]

[*The men have reached center, carrying the chest; they look up at* Prunella; *and in their surprise, drop the box with a crash of broken china.*]

Nell [*cries out and starts toward the chest, wringing her hands; then stops and relaxes*]. Well, Prunella, there goes your wedding present kersmash! But you can blame yourself.

Tozer. Weddin'? Who's your lucky man? [Prunella *points at* Ross.]

Nell. Prunella 'n Ross is gettin' wed. Love at first sight!

Tozer. Well, kiss the bride! [*He does so resoundingly and swings the jug aloft.*] And drink her health! [*He drinks it and turns toward the men, holding out the jug in invitation. The men stand dumbfounded.*]

Peleg and Levi. But, gosh almighty! We didn't have a fair . . .

Ross. Remember it was what the lady was willin' to.

Prunella. And he's the lady's choice! [*She slips a firm arm through* Ross's.]

Peleg. An' she's got a purty red dress already! [Prunella *dips a half curtsy in it.*] Aw, hell, s'pose might as well . . . [*He takes hold of the jug, which* Tozer *hangs onto.*]

Levi. Does we git our money back, Pete?

Peter. We do not. . . . She gets it for a wedding present.

Peleg and Levi. Sure . . . good idea!!

Peleg [*tugging at the jug*]. An' here's to . . .

Tozer. Mind yer manners, Peleg! You kisses first!

[Peleg *wipes his hand across his mouth.* Levi *parts his whiskers and shifts from foot to foot; then dashes suddenly* out the door. PELEG *kisses* PRUNELLA; *then sucks the jug.* TOZER *pushes up* PETER *who kisses her gravely, then taking the jug, bows to her, and drinks rather formally and shortly.* LEVI *dashes in with a helter-skelter bouquet of wood-flowers; hee-heeing like a horse, he presents them to* PRUNELLA; *then he parts his whiskers and smacks her through his tickling brush; then hee-heeing, he turns to get the jug and drinks.*]

NELL [*takes the jug and pushes it on* Ross]. An' you drink your health too. . . . I surmise you'll need the best o' luck you can!

[Ross *takes the jug, waves it up to her, and drinks a swallow.*]

TOZER [*taking the jug*]. I'll finish 'er to the bride-to-be, and to my ole woman. An', young man, I hopes your luck's as good as I got in with Nell! [*He tips it up, shakes it for more, and sets it down empty.*]

PETER [*has been taking a bag of money out of his pocket, hefting the purse in his hands; he addresses* PRUNELLA *who with* Ross *advances to stand toward center*]. Ma'am! The bachelors of Farmersville, having, according to their vote and agreement, collected a fund to buy you a red dress, but seeing the which you has, and a right pretty one, the said bachelors present to you, and to Ross Parrish, your chosen man, this fund as a free wedding gift . . . and may you both live long and prosper in the Genesee Country. [*He presents it;* PRUNELLA *receives it and curtsies, wiping away a tear.*]

[PETER *shakes hands vigorously with* Ross *as* PELEG *and* LEVI *suddenly come to life and clap their hands awkwardly;* TOZER *and* NELL *join in;* NELL *kisses* PRUNELLA.]

LEVI. I gotta milk that cow! [*Dashes toward door.*]

PELEG. Yeah, it's ten past chore time! [*Stopping by the door, grinning, and taking off his cravat.*] Any time you want some help on that new house on your fifty acres, Ross . . .

LEVI [*with a grin*]. Yeah, glad to help . . . any time.
PETER [*moves close to the door*]. We'll all be glad to help you young folks any time.
PELEG and LEVI. Any time!
TOZER. Thanks, boys . . . and drop in any time t' drink t' th' bride . . . 'n groom!
PELEG and LEVI. Be round tomorrow. Goo-bye!

[*As they turn to go,* OLD JOHN *hobbles briskly through the door with another jug of cider.*]

OLD JOHN. Here's that other jug o' cider to finish the celebratin'! [*He hands it to* TOZER *as he steps quickly to the footlights, saying.*] An' ever'body line up to end th' play.

[OLD JOHN *then speaks the* EPILOG.]

### THE EPILOG

Well, folks, an' here I be agin
T' say "True love is great"—if you c'n get it—
An' t' jine in wishin' that th' lucky pair
Live happy ever after.
An' I guess with th' usual leetle difficulties
They will.

Don't be too sorry fer the other boys.
Good gals'll come along
Buxum an' strong
If not so neat
For Levi, Peleg, and fer Pete.

So take yer lady, Ross, young man,
Lead her down here by the han',
Promise to obey yer share,
Then kiss 'er—kiss 'er fair an' square—
So all th' folks here's sure t' know
We got a happy endin' to th' show.

That kiss c'n be long—as you want it t' be—
'Cause we're closin' th' curtain
So *them* folks can't see!
[*As they kiss*

### The Curtain Closes

[*Just as it is shutting out the scene,* OLD JOHN *sticks his head through and yells to the audience.*]
OLD JOHN. If you want t' see th' folks agin, you'll have to clap loud!

### The End

# MIXING UP THE RENT

## Hudson Valley Rent Wars
## Sunny Side Up

*by*

ROBERT GARD

# MIXING UP THE RENT

A DRAMATIC period of deep social concern to the people of New York was the century of intermittent but irrepressible Anti-rent outbreaks which kept sweeping over the State from the mid-Eighteenth Century down to the decent settlement of the land problem in the 1840's. James Fenimore Cooper's trilogy—*The Redskins, Satanstoe,* and *Chainbearers*—deals sympathetically with these struggles of tenant-farmers to earn the right to buy the land they worked from the great patent landholders. And the "wars" still provide materials for exciting stories as well as for scholarly research. *Rent Day,* by the popular English playwright, Douglas Jerrold, which dramatized similar English peasant uprisings against British landlords, played to excited audiences in America, especially along the Hudson River, where the land problem was most severe, and the agitation and violence most spectacular.

*Mixing Up the Rent* attempts to theatricalize Anti-rent materials in a vein of broad farce, a vein justified at this distance both by some of the superficial antics of the "wars," and by the healing passage of time over very real injustice and bitterness. The principal characters are sketched from types familiar to the Anti-rent struggles: the Sheriff, the Landlord, the Leader of the Anti-rent "Indians," and ladies who talk like Fenimore Cooper's stilted females. The ballad introduced at the end of the play is authentic: to the tune of "Old Dan Tucker" it was boisterously sung by the tenants in their meetings at the taverns, and as they marched in their numerous forays against the sheriffs and the landlords.

TIME: *Roughly 1845–50, any time of day.*
PLACE: *The* VAN RAN *Manor.*

## THE CHARACTERS OF THE PLAY

VAN RAN, *Lord of the Manor.*
JENNIE, *his daughter.*
LIZZIE, *a serving wench of Dutch descent.*
SHERIFF BOURCK.
JAMES MCGORK, *an Erie Canawl hero.*
MR. GROAT, *alias Wallace Perkins.*
A SERVING MAN, *from Saratoga.*
MRS. GROAT, *a plump lady who was once Miss Eloise Wilks, the Belle of New York State.*
ANTI-RENT BOYS.
*And perhaps some more ladies to dance with at the end.*

# MIXING UP THE RENT

THE SCENE *represents as simply as possible a room or stage in the middle 19th Century manner. Use painted scenery, or fancy wings and drop, or if these are not available, anything that comes handy. The only scenic essentials are a window up center through which a man can enter and window curtains fixed so that a man may hide behind them. An armchair is the only necessary piece of furniture. Entrances are right and left. The play should start with the curtain open.*

[*When it is time for the play to commence,* VAN RAN, *in a long black coat and boots, carrying his hat under his arm, appears at left of the stage and speaks to the audience.*]

VAN RAN. Folks, this is a rip-roarin' farce you're going to witness tonight. And along with the farce and sprinkled through it are some references to one of the most dramatic periods ever hit old New York State—I mean the period of the Anti-rent Wars of 1838 to 1845. 'Course there'd been considerable hollering done by the tenants on the big manors, like the Livingstones and others had, before that time, and before there was any considerable actual fightin' done.

Now, the plot of this farce is so mixed up and wild, that I don't know what it's about myself; so don't take this Antirent business too serious, and don't try to connect it up too much to the rest of the play. Only remember, when the play gets through, that there *were* plenty of tenants wanted to run the big landlords off the land, and that there were plenty of bold fellows in the country to spur the tenants along, too. And don't be too hard on me, as I'm supposed to be playing one of these landlord fellows; and am supposed, in the play, to be trying to hang onto my property, tooth and toenail—though seems to me, if I can criticize the author a little bit, that I got some mighty funny ways of doin' it! Well, folks, have a good time if you can, and if you really want to get educated on this Anti-rent business, read some of James Fenimore Cooper's works like . . . *The Redskins* or *Satanstoe* . . . or if you want to read something more modern, you might see the book by Carl Carmer called *The Hudson*. I *hear* it's pretty good. [JENNIE *and* LIZZIE *come on from right.* VAN RAN *points to them.*] That's my daughter, Jennie. And that gal followin' her's one of our Dutch servin' wenches we call Lizzie! [*As the girls take positions down stage,* VAN RAN *whips a big moustache out of his pocket and sticks it on.*] Let the play commence! [VAN RAN *crosses the stage and exits right.*]

JENNIE. Why can't girls marry whom they wish?

LIZZIE. 'Cause they don't wish the right ones, Miss.

JENNIE. Being forced to marry's an imposition against one's sovereign rights. It must be against the Constitution!

LIZZIE. The Constitution was written by *men*, Miss.

JENNIE. Well, I don't approve of being married against my will.

LIZZIE. It's not your will your pa's marryin' off, Miss Jennie, it's you!

JENNIE. Ah, la, la! And to an utter stranger!

LIZZIE. Oh, Mr. Wallace Perkins has been here near two weeks, Miss.

JENNIE. If it just wasn't for this Anti-rent trouble! The tenants don't want to pay the rent, and just because this Wallace Perkins told Father *he* would serve the writs, and collect every penny of the back rent, Father not only made him manager, but told him he could marry *me!*

LIZZIE [*aside to the audience*]. Her pa always loved the yellow gold!

JENNIE. Where does Pa think he is, in Turkey?

LIZZIE. Yes, Miss. And he'll do as the Turkies do, I expect.
JENNIE. Just because Mr. Perkins came from Saratoga Springs, and made a big show of collecting the rent! [*Stamping her foot.*] I won't marry him!
LIZZIE. He may marry you, Miss Jennie, but he won't collect the rent! Looks to me like your pa's estate is going to bust up, the way the farmers are carryin' on—dressin' up like wild Injuns, and blowin' on them tin dinner-horns! [*A tin dinner-horn is heard offstage. To audience.*] There's one now! [*To* JENNIE.] Dear, dear, though! I don't see why your pa's took such a fancy to that Mr. Perkins. He's not much to look at.
JENNIE. I'm sure I don't know! The fellow presented himself here two weeks ago, saying that he had been recommended for the vacant managership of Van Ran Manor, by a certain Miss Eloise Wilks, of Saratoga, who, it seems, is *some kind* of an old friend of Father's!
LIZZIE. And no sooner was he engaged to your father, than your father engaged him to you!
JENNIE. Oh, tra-la, tra-la, what to do! [*Resignedly.*] Well, maybe he'll take me back to Saratoga, to see the Southern Gentlemen, and the horses . . . and the Grand Union Hotel!
LIZZIE. Just between us, Miss Jennie, I believe your pa wants to get *your* little fortune into his hands before the break-up comes. Now, his manager . . .
JENNIE. I don't want the money! Like I said to Father yesterday, . . . "Pa, if it's the gold you want, keep it, and marry Mr. Perkins yourself!"
LIZZIE. If I was you I'd keep the money! You might need it for travelling expenses if you decide to run away!
JENNIE. Run away? [*Aside.*] And leave my dear father? He is cruel, but he must love me, his only daughter!
LIZZIE. I've heard there's a certain young man . . .
JENNIE. Hush! [*Runs to the window and peers out.*] Have you

seen him again? That certain strange young man, who has hidden in the bushes, and has followed me about the last few days, wherever I go?

Lizzie. The gardener said he's sure the man's in love with you, though he doesn't know who he is! [*Bending forward and speaking to the audience.*] The gardener says he's sure the man's a spy set by the tenants to find what the hell her father's up to!

Jennie. Tell the gardener to keep a close watch. If he can find out who it is, I'll give . . .

Van Ran [*calling from off right*]. Jennie!

Lizzie. It's your pa, Miss!

Jennie. Here, Father!

[Van Ran *and* Sheriff Bourck *enter running. The* Sheriff *has a big rifle and whiskers. He dashes about looking into all the corners, under the chairs, out the window.*]

Sheriff. I'll get 'im! I'll ketch 'im! I'll jail 'im! Where is he, the rascal?

Van Ran. Jennie, this is Sheriff Bourck, who has lately been tarred and feathered by the rascally tenants over in Schoharie County!

Sheriff [*coming down and speaking to the audience*]. Led by the smoothest ruffian you ever saw! They met me on a lonely road, and before I knew what they was about, they'd laid me stark and 'd fetched the tar-barrel! They made a goose outta me, but I'll make a *corpse* out of that leader, when I ketch 'im! [*Runs and looks out the window.*]

Van Ran. And the Sheriff says he's traced 'im here!

Sheriff [*coming back down*]. Where he's stirrin' *your* tenants to insurrection, or I'll eat my ramrod!

Van Ran [*loudly*]. You must get him, Sheriff! [*To* Jennie.] Have you seen any strangers about, Jennie?

Jennie [*turning away*]. No, no, Father!

Van Ran. Let's go, Sheriff! And I want all those eviction writs served today! I'll have my manager, Perkins, bring them

## MIXING UP THE RENT

right out! I'll show these dirty rebels! Come on! [*They rush out, the* SHERIFF *pointing his gun in front of him.*]

LIZZIE. Miss Jennie, do you suppose that strange young man is . . . [*She points after the* SHERIFF.]

JENNIE [*romantically*]. I don't know, but whoever he is, he's too nice-looking to rot in jail!

LIZZIE. And the gardener says the tenants are right, not to pay their rent! Well, goodbye, Miss Jennie!

JENNIE. I'll not marry Mr. Perkins, that I'm determined! I'll see the whole Hudson Valley in jail, first! [LIZZIE *exits.*] Whatever will I do?

[*As* JENNIE *poses downstage, the window opens, and* JAMES MCGORK *enters and poses in front of the window.* JAMES *is a good-looking "tough man" dressed in jerkin and boots.*]

JAMES. Alone at last!

JENNIE [*sees him and screams. Aside*]. It is he! [*Addressing* JAMES.] And who are you?

JAMES. Hush! Have you seen the Sheriff? [*Looks out the window.*]

JENNIE. Yes, and I am going to call him! [*As* JAMES *advances upon her.*] Keep away from me! I'll scream!

JAMES. Hear me first, *then* scream! First, let me apologize for coming in at the window, but the fact is, I'm a hunted man, and as I saw my old friend, the Sheriff, coming pellmell around the house with a gun as big as a birch tree, I found the upper air more pleasant!

JENNIE. Ah, then you are the one who tarred the Sheriff!

JAMES. A mere matter of sport, Miss.

JENNIE. You are a very bold and insolent person.

JAMES. Oh, don't say that, Ma'am! For my time here is short! In a word, the first time I beheld you in yonder woods a few days since, I knew that we were born for each other. Perhaps you felt the same?

JENNIE. No such a thing, Sir.

JAMES. Forgive me! It became essential to my plans for the future that you should come to know my feelings for you! Imagine then, my pure delight when I saw that window open. .... Fear bid me fear not, love gave me speed, an apple tree gave me wings . . . and here I am, [Advancing.] my heart upon my lips!

JENNIE. You, or it, cannot remain here! [As JAMES moves a foot or so.] Or there, Sir! My father's furious with you, and the Sheriff . . .

JAMES. Very well, Ma'am, if I cannot remain here, I will, with dignity, go out the same way I came in, and give myself to the Sheriff! [He goes to window, puts one leg across the sill, and waits.]

JENNIE. Wait!

JAMES. Wait? How sweet a word! [Climbing back into the room.] Certainly, Ma'am, anything to oblige! And as time passes ever so rapid when there's an agreeable topic of conversation, I'll talk about myself. My name is James McGork. My age? Well, I am still young. My fortune? It is here in my two hands. My past? I have been a captain on the Erie Canawl; hunted the buried treasure of Captain Kidd; ridden with the Loomis hoss thieves; done a bit of racing at Saratoga; held a ship's tiller on Lake Ontario; and have now bound up my fortunes with wresting the rights of tenants from grasping, idle landlords here in this Empire State of New York! God bless it! I roam the Helderbergs, have crossed the Hudson, and now, Ma'am, in the midst of my treasure hunting, I have found my treasure. [He takes her hand.] Let me clasp my treasure to my bosom!

JENNIE. Wait! Wait! And if I were to say "yes," perhaps you will tell me how we are to live?

JAMES. Together, of course!

JENNIE. You mean, starve together, for my father happens to be one of those grasping, idle landlords of yours!

JAMES. Quite so. But the father of a queen bee is a drone!
JENNIE. My father'd never accept you as a suitor. He'd . . . he'd . . . clap you in jail!
JAMES. Fortunately I have a slight access to—indeed I might say, hold on—your father . . . which I mean soon to exercise!
JENNIE. Through whom? The Sheriff?
JAMES. No. Through an ancient friend of your father's . . . Miss Eloise Wilks, of Saratoga. And when this pretty Sheriff goes away, I mean to introduce myself. You see, I am determined to make you happy!
JENNIE. You will practice no deception on my father! And as for being happy, would you be happy if you had to marry a man who can't be endured?
JAMES. Aha, I have a rival?
JENNIE. My father's manager.
JAMES [*facing audience*]. He *will die!*
JENNIE. No! No!
JAMES. Pardon me, I must kill him! [*The voice of* MR. WALLACE PERKINS *is now heard outside.*]
PERKINS. Yes, Mr. Van Ran. Yes, *Sir!* Yes, indeed, Sir! Yes, Sir!
JENNIE. It's Perkins, the manager. Quick! You must hide!
JAMES. A kiss?
JENNIE. Later . . . perchance! Hide, and quickly!
JAMES. I'll be back!
JENNIE. Go!
JAMES. Where? Ah, here!

[*He backs up, parts the window curtains without turning, and climbs out the window backwards as* PERKINS *enters.* PERKINS *is dressed in an old overcoat and hat and carries an armful of eviction-writ papers; papers stick out from under his hat; he carries a carpet-bag full of more papers.*]

PERKINS [*muttering to audience*]. All I can say is, if I am to do the work of twenty sheriffs, and am to serve all the eviction writs myself, and am to be loaded down like a wagon on the Catskill Turnpike, then I ought to have a horse to pull me about! [*To* JENNIE, *loudly.*] Ah, Miss Jennie!

JENNIE [*with sarcasm*]. You are well loaded, Mr. Perkins! I presume those are the famous writs of eviction which will expel the tenants from my father's land?

PERKINS. Certainly. They are of the utmost importance, or I should have dropped them long ago! [JENNIE *fans herself in disgust.*] Ah, you are faint! It's stifling here! I'll just open the window!

JENNIE. No, no!

PERKINS. Oh, but I insist, my dear! [*He drops all his papers in a heap and goes to open the curtains.* JAMES *has gone, and* JENNIE *sighs in relief.*]

JENNIE. Gone!

PERKINS. What's that?

JENNIE. I was afraid you might catch cold, that's all!

PERKINS. Be not alarmed on my account! I have on four suits of good woolens, and two or three . . .

JENNIE. Stop! Mr. Perkins, why have you determined to make me the most miserable of women?

PERKINS. Gracious! I make you an unfortunate woman? Madam, I am innocent!

JENNIE. Have you not promised to marry me?

PERKINS. Yes, Ma'am, so I have! Last Monday your father said to me, "Perkins, what do you think o' me daughter?" "She's a gorgeous rosebud," I says. "D'ye think she'd make a good wife?" he says. "Guess she'd do in a pinch," I says. "Then the girl's yours, Perkins.". . .

JENNIE. You fool! You should have asked for time to consider!

PERKINS. That I did, Miss Jennie. "Certainly," says he, "I'll give you a quarter hour, and if you say 'yes,' I'll make you my manager. If you say 'no,' I'll lambaste you all over forty acres!"

## MIXING UP THE RENT

JENNIE. You coward! You said "yes"!
PERKINS. Oh, I'll take a wife before a lickin' any day.
JENNIE. Now you listen to me! [*Advancing on him as he gives way before her.*] I don't like you! I never will like you! And if you insist on making me Mrs. Perkins, well, you know what the consequences will be, that's all!
PERKINS. Yes, Ma'am! By God, yes! The consequences will be *jail*! Because I happen to have a wife already! A woman I adore, but from whom I was forced to run away two weeks after our marital vows was spoke! This is the state of the case: Two weeks ago, as my wife was rather poorly, we went to Saratoga Springs so she could drink the water and take a few mud baths; and I went along to see the horses, take a fling at the Casino, and watch the nurse-maids. I was on my way through the grounds of the Casino, when it suddenly began to rain. I took shelter under the next tree, but as it began to rain harder and harder, I decided to run for it! I was clippin' through the bushes when I suddenly collided with an individual going *away* from the Casino as though the Devil were after 'im! When I recovered from the shock I discovered that my pocketbook was gone . . . whisked away! And since it contained all my money, I was afraid to return to my wife and was forced to become a detective to regain my cash. [*In a stage whisper.*] And I tracked the culprit to this manor! As soon as I learned who lived here I remembered that Eloise, my wife, had one time mentioned Mr. Van Ran as an old friend of hers. The rest you know. Now, as I believe the thief to be among your tenants, I will serve these writs until I find 'im. Then . . . [*He draws his finger across his throat.*]
JENNIE. Indeed! [*She exits.*]
   [PERKINS *shakes his head, stoops to pick up his writs as* JAMES MCGORK *enters.*]
JAMES. Now for a little *sport* with this sheriff-in-disguise. For I must keep these writs from being served on the tenants,

me friends! [*He slaps* PERKINS *on the back.*] How are you?

PERKINS [*falls forward, jumps up, comes very close to* JAMES, *and peers into his face*]. Aha!

JAMES [*drawing a big pistol*]. How are you?

PERKINS [*looking at the pistol*]. Why . . . er . . . very good! At first I thought you were an old friend of mine, someone I wanted to see . . . but now I can readily see you are not a bit like him. Not a bit!

JAMES. I have come to see the Lord of the Manor, Mr. Van Ran.

PERKINS [*backing off*]. Certainly! Er . . . what name shall I call you by?

JAMES. Groat, Sir. Lewis Groat.

PERKINS [*halting suddenly*]. Groat? Will you be good enough to say that again, Sir?

JAMES [*lifting his pistol*]. Lewis Groat. Dare you deny it?

PERKINS. Naturally not.

JAMES. I see the name is strange to you, but it was only recently that Eloise became my wife.

PERKINS. Eloise? *Your* wife?

JAMES. Yes, Sir, Miss Eloise Wilks, the flower of New York State, known from Lake Erie to Cohoes!

PERKINS [*coming to* JAMES]. Now let us understand each other. You say that Miss Eloise Wilks is now your wife?

JAMES. That she is.

PERKINS. And you say that you are Lewis Groat?

JAMES [*toying with his pistol*]. Do you doubt my word?

PERKINS. Oh no, no . . . I don't doubt your word . . . I . . . I . . . am simply confused.

JAMES. Ah, now I know you! You are that young fellow used to be sweet on my Elly before I married her. I call her Elly, for short.

PERKINS. Aha! A young fellow used to be sweet on Elly, did he?

JAMES. And they do say that your landlord, Van Ran, was also an admirer of hers . . . and that Millerite preacher from

# MIXING UP THE RENT

Ithaca, and that Mormon from Palmyra, and that soldier of fortune from Schoharie, and lots of others . . . but Groat cut 'em all out. Funny, eh? Ha, ha, ha, ha? [*He places his pistol against* PERKINS.]

PERKINS. Ha, ha, ha, ha!

VAN RAN [*entering*]. Oh ho! Here you are, Perkins! Have you tried to serve those writs? You and the Sheriff? [*Sees the pile of writs on the floor.*] What's this?

PERKINS. A stranger to see you, Mr. Van Ran.

VAN RAN. A stranger, here?

JAMES [*stepping forward*]. Mr. Lewis Groat, at your service.

PERKINS. But I say . . .

JAMES. The husband of our mutual friend, Miss Eloise Wilks.

VAN RAN. Oh! My sweet Miss Wilks!

PERKINS. But see here . . .

VAN RAN. And where is my sweet Miss . . . er, I mean Mrs. Groat?

JAMES. In Albany, at the Grand Union Hotel!

PERKINS. In Saratoga, at the race track!

VAN RAN [*to* PERKINS]. Hush! [*To* JAMES.] And how is she?

JAMES. Quite well!

PERKINS. Poorly.

JAMES [*to* VAN RAN]. So you think her charming, eh?

VAN RAN. Charming? [*To audience.*] I should know! [*To* JAMES.] Very odd if I didn't, eh? By the by, Mr. Groat, this is the young man she recommended to me. [*He slaps* PERKINS *on the shoulder.*] I engaged him immediately. He's going to marry my daughter, Jennie. [*Calling.*] Jennie!

JENNIE. Yes, Father? [*Entering and seeing* JAMES.] Oh!

VAN RAN. Why, what's the matter?

JENNIE. Nothing, only that stranger . . .

VAN RAN. Stranger? No such thing, my dear. This is Mr. Groat, the husband of my valued little friend, Miss Eloise Wilks, of whom I have so often spoke.

JENNIE. Groat?

JAMES [*to* JENNIE]. Hush! Not a word! [*To the audience.*] This will all come right!

JENNIE. But you . . . you . . .

VAN RAN [*shouting*]. Perkins!

PERKINS [*standing beside him, also shouting*]. What?

VAN RAN. Get Mr. Groat his supper.

PERKINS. And perchance clean the Saratoga mud off his boots? I'll get his supper, and it'll be dished up by the Sheriff, perhaps! [*He dashes out.*]

VAN RAN [*looking after him*]. Queer fellow, that.

JAMES. Definitely. [*He kneels and begins to pick up the writs.*]

VAN RAN. What are you going to do with those? Leave them be. Perkins will deliver them. Come with me for a stroll. We must talk about your little wife!

SHERIFF [*running in with gun*]. Where is he? I'll get 'im! [*Runs around the room peering into all the corners.*]

JENNIE. Where is who, Sheriff?

SHERIFF [*coming down*]. Just found out who he is. His name's Groat, that pesky Anti-renter I mean. I'll get 'im! [*Points his rifle and dashes out.*]

JENNIE. Oh dear, oh dear! I must do something! [*She runs out.*]

[LIZZIE *enters with a strange* SERVING MAN *dressed in straw hat and checked suit. He carries baggage of various kinds and has a very superior air.*]

LIZZIE. This way, this way! [*To audience.*] I declare, this fellow's not much to look at, but there's somethin' 'bout him makes my heart jar clean down to my toenails!

SERVING MAN. I am from Saratoga. [*Smirking.*] And I will have a bit of sport with this Dutch serving wench while my mistress settles her business.

LIZZIE. Who does your mistress want to see?

[*A strange* WOMAN *in travelling attire enters.*]

WOMAN. Mr. Van Ran, this instant!

LIZZIE. He's busy now, Ma'am. Perhaps his manager, Mr. Perkins, will do instead.

WOMAN. Send him to me!

## MIXING UP THE RENT

LIZZIE. Very well, Ma'am! [*Calling.*] Mr. Perkins!
PERKINS [*off, calling*]. Coming!
LIZZIE. Take a seat, Ma'am. [*To* SERVING MAN.] Come into the kitchen, my boy. Perhaps you and I could have a little talk, and *perhaps* a bit of clabber pie! [*They go out.*]
WOMAN [*sinking into the armchair*]. What a state I'm in! I returned to the hotel at Saratoga, and find that my husband, my Groat, has disappeared. No one knows where. A few lines on the dressing table, of which I could make nothing, only served to make matters worse; so I have come to my old friend, Mr. Van Ran, who I am sure will help me find him. Am I wife or widow? That is the question.
PERKINS [*enters with large pistol*]. This'll fix 'im. This'll lay 'im in the dust. This'll make 'im start for the California gold fields, I'll warrant. I'll give 'im this for his supper! [*Sees the* WOMAN.] Oh, my wife!
WOMAN [*aside*]. Run to earth at last! I am not widow at any rate, though there may be more here than meets the eye! [ *To* PERKINS.] Mr. Groat, Sir, explain your inexplicable behavior this instant, or . . . [*She waves her parasol.*]
PERKINS [*putting his finger to his lips*]. Hush!
WOMAN. I'll teach you to run away, the moment your wife's back is turned, leaving me with no money, and . . .
PERKINS. Hush! [*In a stage whisper.*] Things are not what they seem! There is an impostor here who says he is me, and that you are his wife!
WOMAN [*pleased*]. Ah, some old admirer, no doubt. But I'll soon set him right. I'll soon tell them that you are my husband, and I am Mrs. Groat!
 [*The* SHERIFF *runs in.*]
SHERIFF. Where is he? I'll get 'im! I'll get *Groat!* I'll teach these Anti-renters to tar Sheriff Bourck! [*To* MRS. GROAT.] Have you seen him, Ma'am? Have you seen *Groat*, the real leader of the Anti-rent Injuns? [*He dashes out without waiting for an answer.*]
MRS. GROAT. So! You are also a criminal!

PERKINS. No! On my honor, I am *after* a criminal! I am posing here as Wallace Perkins!
VAN RAN [*outside*]. Ah . . . a lady to see me? [*He enters.*]
PERKINS. I'll lay this impostor in the dust before there's a mix-up here! [*He dashes out.*]
MRS. GROAT. Oh!
VAN RAN. Why, my dear Miss Wilks, er . . . Mrs. Groat! I'm delighted. In fact, I . . .
MRS. GROAT. My husband . . . is . . .
VAN RAN. Er . . . yes! He's out talking with my daughter Jennie. I saw no harm in it, as Jennie is going soon to marry my manager, Perkins, who I hear, has been entertaining you.
MRS. GROAT. Marry her?
VAN RAN. Yes. I soon saw he was head-over-heels in love, so I proposed the match myself.
MRS. GROAT. And he?
VAN RAN. Said he'd be delighted . . . but that there was a slight obstacle which a little time would remove.
MRS. GROAT. Said a little time would remove?
VAN RAN. However, he jumped at the proposal, so it's all settled!
MRS. GROAT. So? Now for my revenge!
[JENNIE *and* JAMES *enter.*]
VAN RAN. Here they are now! My daughter, and your husband! [*To* JAMES.] Groat, here's a lady wants you!
MRS. GROAT [*aside*]. I will throw myself into this man's arms, and teach my husband a lesson! [*To* JAMES.] Well, dear?
JENNIE. Dear?
MRS. GROAT. You're not angry with me for coming? I only wanted to be with you, my husband!
JENNIE [*aside*]. Husband?
VAN RAN. Come, come, Groat! Kiss and be friends! I insist on it!
GROAT [*facing the audience*]. I play all of the cards, all of the time, for all they are worth! [*Seizes* MRS. GROAT.]

PERKINS [*entering, waving his pistol*]. Stand clear, Elly! I'll save you! Let me shoot 'im!
JENNIE. No! [*To* PERKINS.] Come to my arms, my affianced husband!
PERKINS. Well ... er ... [*Laying his pistol on the floor.*] Hell yes! What's there to lose? [PERKINS *and* JENNIE *embrace.*]
VAN RAN. Now, as it's bedtime, we will all go to bed! [*Both couples break their embraces, and the ladies whirl away from the men.*] Wallace, show Mr. and Mrs. Groat to their room!
JAMES [*to* JENNIE]. I'll explain, later.
JENNIE. You deceiver! [*She exits.*]
VAN RAN. Out with you, Wallace! Go see that our guests' room is prepared!
PERKINS. I'll go! [*He stalks out left, sticks his head back onstage.*] But I'll be back! [*Exits.*]
JAMES [*to* VAN RAN]. Sir, you and I must have a glass of grog before we retire.
MRS. GROAT. Yes indeed! And I'll go to bed! [*She runs out right.*]
VAN RAN. Of course! And I'll go and prepare it! [*Exits right.*]
JAMES. Good! [*As* VAN RAN *exits, he begins to pick up the writs.*]
PERKINS [*dashing back onstage*]. Hold on! Drop those eviction writs or you're a dead man! [*Raises his pistol.*]
JAMES [*putting his hand on his gun and rising*]. So! It has come to the show-down!
PERKINS [*pressing him with his pistol*]. I will lay you on the floor instantly, if you do not immediately take your hand from your gun. Sir, you not only have my money—ah, yes, I recognize you!—but you also want my wife!
JAMES [*raising his hands*]. I will not move from this room. I swear it.
PERKINS. I don't trust you. [*From off right someone flings a coil of rope into the room.* PERKINS *catches it.*] Here. Tie

an end of this rope to your leg. I will be waiting outside, and if you try to leave, you're a dead man!

JAMES. Anything to oblige! [*Ties the rope on his own leg.*] Satisfied?

PERKINS [*jerking* JAMES *off his feet*]. Yes, that will do. Now to tie you up! [VAN RAN's *voice is heard offstage.*]

VAN RAN. I'm coming!

PERKINS. Silence! [*He runs off left taking the coil of rope with him.* JAMES *now unties the rope from his leg and ties it to the leg of the armchair.*]

VAN RAN [*as he enters with two glasses of grog*]. This grog is strong! It's made from an old Palatine German receipt!

JAMES. Good! [*They drink, and as they drink there is a tug at the rope which moves the armchair.*]

VAN RAN [*seeing the chair move*]. Gad! This grog is strong. Stronger than I thought!

JAMES [*trying to keep the chair in place*]. Only the wind!

VAN RAN. Yes, I must be getting old! You are a pleasant fellow, Groat . . . a pleasant fellow. We could be great friends, but all my trouble with the rent has soured me! And all these writs! [*Points to the writs on the floor.*] No one can serve them! The tenants are too fierce!

JAMES. I will serve them!

VAN RAN. You?

JAMES. Certainly. I am a deputy sheriff!

VAN RAN. If you will, you will save my estate! Then let us discuss how to go about it! [VAN RAN *starts to sit in the armchair, which is violently jerked away by* PERKINS *from offstage.* VAN RAN *falls on floor.*] Help! Murder!

JAMES. Landlords of the Hudson, your time has come! Now to get the writs and destroy them!

PERKINS [*running in*]. None of that! [*Puts his pistol against* JAMES's *head.*]

VAN RAN. Here! Here!

[MRS. GROAT, JENNIE *and the* SHERIFF *run on.*]

SHERIFF. I'll get 'im! [*Looking from* JAMES *to* PERKINS.] Now! Which one of you's Groat! [JAMES *and* PERKINS *point at each other.*]

JAMES and PERKINS [*together*]. He's Groat!

SHERIFF. Come, come! I'll take you both to jail!

VAN RAN. There's a bit of a mix-up here!

JAMES [*coming down stage*]. A mix-up, my dear landlord, from which I shall soon extract you all! [*Puts his fingers to his lips and whistles. Offstage the chorus begins to sing "Big Bill Snyder" to the tune of "Old Dan Tucker."*]

CHORUS.
   The moon was shining silver bright.
   The Sheriff came at dead of night,
   High on a hill an Indian true,
   And on his horn this blast he blew—

      Get out of the way, Big Bill Snyder,
      We'll tar your coat and feather your hide, sir!

JAMES. My Anti-rent Boys! [*Eight to twelve* ANTI-RENTERS *march in, dressed in calico hoods, and carrying wooden guns and tin dinner-horns.*]

CHORUS [*singing as they march*].
   Bill ran and ran till he reached the wood,
   Then with horror still he stood—
   For he saw an Indian tall and grim,
   And heard a tin horn not a rod from him. . . .

      Get out of the way, Big Bill Snyder,
      We'll tar your coat and feather your hide, sir!

JAMES [*as the* ANTI-RENTERS *form a line center*]. Here, boys, are the writs. You know what to do with 'em! [*He scoops up some of the writs and tosses them to the* ANTI-RENTERS, *who tear them up while singing.*]

CHORUS [*as they tear the writs*].
Bill thought he heard the sound of a gun.
He cried in terror, "Oh my race is run!
Better that I had never been born,
Than come within sound of that big horn!"
Next day the body of Bill was found,
His writs were scattered over the ground;
And by his side a jug of rum
Told how Bill to his end had come!

JAMES [*to* VAN RAN]. Landlord, will you sell this land to your tenants, so that they may live in prosperity instead of starvation? So that feudal rents may be abolished in New York State? So that the ones who cleared the land can own it, like Americans should?

VAN RAN. Why . . . why . . . [ANTI-RENTERS *present guns at him.*] Yes! [ANTI-RENTERS *cheer.*]

JAMES. And to make it doubly sure, we may march on New York City and convince 'em there! And I *may* marry the girl! [*Puts his arm around* JENNIE, *while the* ANTI-RENTERS *cheer again.*]

[LIZZIE *now enters dragging the* SERVING MAN, *dishevelled and hanging back.*]

LIZZIE. We'll make it a double wedding! [*The* SERVING MAN *breaks away and starts for the exit, but the* SHERIFF *grabs him.*]

SHERIFF. Too late now, brother!

[*The three couples lines up center, arm in arm, with the group of* ANTI-RENTERS *on one side, and* VAN RAN *and the* SHERIFF *on the other.*]

VAN RAN [*stepping down and addressing the audience*]. Well, folks, looks like my manor's on the rocks! But as Nero fiddled while Rome burned, guess I can do the same! [*To the others.*] Let's end this off with a dance! [*To audience.*]

Any of you folks want to come up and join in, you kin! [*To* ANTI-RENTERS.] You boys strike up a tune?

[*The* ANTI-RENTERS *can strike up the tune, or a fiddler can appear and play. The couples join in a country dance with perhaps* VAN RAN *or another calling the figures.*]

[*And so on to the*

CURTAIN

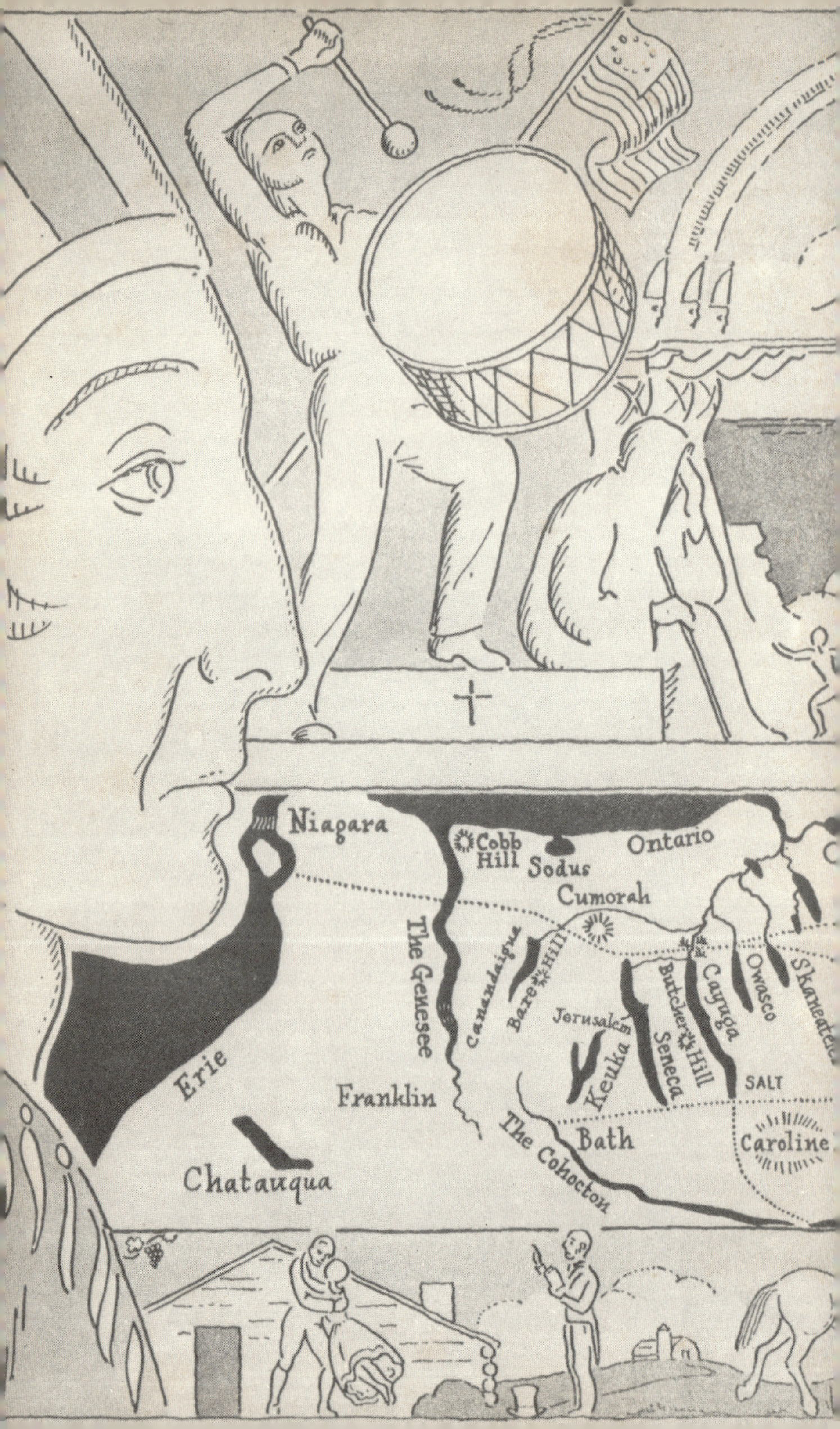
Niagara
Cobb Hill
Sodus
Ontario
Cumorah
The Genesee
Canandaigua
Bare Hill
Jerusalem
Keuka
Butcher Hill
Seneca
Cayuga
Owasco
Skaneateles
SALT
Erie
Franklin
Bath
Caroline
The Cohocton
Chatauqua